# Strategic Management:
# An Executive Perspective

# Strategic Management: An Executive Perspective

Cornelis A. de Kluyver and John A. Pearce II

BEP BUSINESS EXPERT PRESS

First published by
Business Expert Press, LLC
222 East 46th Street, New York, NY 10017
www.businessexpertpress.com

ISBN-13: 978-1-63157-073-5 (paperback)
ISBN-13: 978-1-63157-074-2 (e-book)

Business Expert Press Strategic Management Collection

Collection ISSN: 2150-9611 (print)
Collection ISSN: 2150-9646 (electronic)

Cover and interior design by S4Carlisle Publishing Services Private Ltd., Chennai, India

First edition: 2015

10 9 8 7 6 5 4 3 2 1

# Abstract

The principal objectives of this book are to assist practicing managers in preparing to assume executive responsibilities and to introduce MBA and Executive MBA students to an executive perspective on strategic management.

Organizational success crucially depends on having a superior strategy and effectively implementing it. Companies that outperform their rivals typically have a better grasp of what customers value, who their competitors are, and how they can create an enduring competitive advantage.

Successful strategies reflect a solid grasp of relevant forces in the external and competitive environment, a clear strategic intent, and a deep understanding of a company's core competencies and assets. Generic strategies rarely propel a firm to a leadership position. Knowing where to go and finding carefully considered, creative ways of getting there are the hallmarks of successful strategy.

Perhaps even more important to success is the ability to effectively implement a chosen strategy—marshaling the right resources and talent, creating a functional organizational structure, fostering a beneficial corporate culture and providing appropriate incentives.

# Keywords

Strategy formulation, corporate strategy, business unit strategy, competitive advantage, business model, innovation, value creation, value proposition, markets, segmentation, positioning, value disciplines, market participation, supply chain infrastructure, global management model, global industry, global branding, innovation, outsourcing, offshoring, board of directors

# Contents

# Acknowledgments

Writing a book is a mammoth undertaking. Fortunately, we had a lot of encouragement along the way from users of our other books, our publisher, our families, our colleagues, and our friends. We take this opportunity to thank them all for their constructive criticisms, time, and words of encouragement. We are grateful to all of them and hope the result meets their high expectations.

We are particularly indebted to our families: Louise de Kluyver and sons Peter and Jonathan, and Susie Pearce and sons David and Mark. We thank them for their unwavering support.

*Cornelis A. "Kees" de Kluyver*
*John A. "Jack" Pearce II*
*January 2015*

# Preface

Executive students at both our institutions inspired the writing of this book. Its content and structure reflect their probing questions, many constructive suggestions, and demand for practical examples. At the same time, we have worked hard to differentiate this book from rival entries by keeping it short, maintaining a conversational style, and adopting an executive orientation.

Every company claims to have a strategy although it may not always be explicitly articulated. In Chapter 1, **"What is Strategy?"**, we define strategy as the deliberate act of positioning a company for competitive advantage by focusing on unique ways to create value for customers. In doing so, we distinguish strategy from business models and tactics. We also differentiate between crafting a strategy and enhancing an organization's operational effectiveness, introduce the concept of a competitive advantage cycle, and define such commonly used terms as *mission, vision, strategic intent*, and *stretch*. We conclude with a discussion of the process by which strategy is formulated in most companies.

Distinguishing effective from poor strategies should ultimately be based on corporate performance. Chapter 2, **"Strategy and Performance,"** begins with a discussion of the importance of *economies of scale and scope* in today's competitive environment. Next, it argues that carefully defining a firm's *core* business is critical to sustained success as is a clear understanding of the *need and avenues for growth*. With this background, we introduce a conceptual framework that links strategy and performance. Finally, we discuss different approaches to evaluating strategy proposals. As part of this discussion, concepts such as shareholder value and the Balanced Scorecard are introduced.

Yearend strategy reviews are often devoted to "What has changed?" discussions. In Chapter 3, **"Analyzing the External Strategic Environment,"** we look at three environmental trends that continue to reshape the competitive environment. The first is globalization. We ask how global we have become, analyze the persistence of distance, and look at why companies and entire industries seek to become global. Next, we look at how the technology revolution is changing business with particular emphasis on the influence of the Internet, the impact of "Big Data" and the new business models it is spawning. Third, we look at how demands for corporate social responsibility (CSR) have created a new compact between business and society. We end with a description of different approaches to analyzing uncertainty in the competitive environment.

With Chapter 4, "**Analyzing an Industry,**" we begin the discussion of specific analytical concepts, tools and frameworks used in strategy formulation. We start by defining an industry along four principal dimensions: products, customer, geography, and stages in the production–distribution pipeline. Next, it introduces Porter's well-known five forces model, the so-called Rule of Three, and looks at patterns of industry evolution. It concludes with a discussion of segmentation, competitor analysis, and strategic groups.

In Chapter 5, "**Analyzing an Organization's Strategic Resource Base,**" we focus on analyzing a firm's strategic resources, including its physical assets, its relative financial position, the quality of its people, its market reputation and brand equity, and specific knowledge, competencies, processes, skills, or cultural aspects. As part of this discussion we consider the value of a company's global eco-system, look at internal change forces a company must deal with and present a model for assessing an organization's capacity to absorb change. We end with a section on the benefits associated with creating a green corporate strategy.

Two Chapters are devoted to the development of a competitive strategy at the business unit level. Business unit or competitive strategy is concerned with *how* to compete in a given competitive setting. In Chapter 6, "**Formulating Business Unit Strategy,**" we ask the question: What determines profitability at the business unit level? We look at how profitability is related to the nature of the industry in which a company competes and to the company's competitive position within that industry. Next, we discuss the concept of competitive advantage and introduce value chain analysis, Porter's generic strategy framework, and value disciplines.

Hyper-competition is becoming the norm in many industries. In Chapter 7, "**Business Unit Strategy: Contexts and Special Dimensions,**" we move beyond generic strategies to strategy formulation in specific different industry environments. Three contexts represent different stages in an industry's evolution—emerging, growth, and maturity. We also discus industry environments that pose unique strategic challenges such as fragmented, deregulating, hypercompetitive, and Internet-based industries. Because hyper-competition is increasingly characteristic of business-level competition in many industries, we conclude the chapter with a discussion of two critical attributes of successful firms in dynamic industries: speed and innovation.

Leveraging global opportunities is the subject of the next two Chapters. In Chapter 8, "**Global Strategy Formulation-Fundamentals,**" we introduce global strategy formulation as business model change— through principles of adaptation, aggregation and arbitrage. We also look at important changes companies have to make to their management model as they globalize such as creating a global mindset, and restructuring their operations for global competitive advantage.

Opening global markets, globalizing the value proposition and evaluating sourcing and supply chain options are the major topics covered in Chapter 9, "**Corporate Strategy Formulation: Specifics.**" The discussion includes a section on the strategic logic behind the use of alliances in pursuing global goals.

Visionary strategy development and implementation requires a diversity of perspectives and strong endorsement by a company's board of directors. In Chapter 10, "**The Board's Role in Strategic Management,**" we discuss what contributions directors can make to the strategy formulation process and when their involvement is essential. We conclude that a board's most important role is to monitor the strategy implementation process and provide feedback to stakeholders.

Entrepreneurial thinking is important to effective strategy development and implementation in any successful organization—at board level, for managers at all levels of the organization, and in strategic partnerships. Reflecting this thought, we end the book with a section on strategic metrics the board should consider and other actions the board can take to infuse an entrepreneurial spirit.

# CHAPTER 1

# What Is Strategy?

## Introduction

The question "What is strategy?" has stimulated lots of debates, countless articles, and serious disagreement among management thinkers. Perhaps this is why many executives also struggle with it. However, they deserve a pragmatic reply. Understanding how a strategy is crafted is important, because there is a proven link between a company's strategic choices and its long-term performance. Successful companies typically have a better grasp of customers' wants and needs, their competitors' strengths and weaknesses, and how they can create value for all stakeholders. Successful strategies reflect a company's clear strategic intent and a deep understanding of its core competencies and assets—generic strategies rarely propel a company to a leadership position.

Numerous attempts have been made at providing a simple, descriptive definition of *strategy* but its inherent complexity and subtlety preclude a one-sentence description. There is a substantial agreement about its principal dimensions, however. Strategy is about *positioning* an organization for *competitive advantage*. It involves making *choices* about *which markets to participate in, what products and services to offer,* and *how to allocate corporate resources.* And its primary goal is to *create long-term value for shareholders and other stakeholders* by providing *customer value.* Strategy therefore is different from vision, mission, goals, priorities, and plans. It is *the result of choices executives make, about what to offer, where to play and how to win, to maximize long-term value.*

*What to offer* refers to a company's value proposition and comprises the core of its business model; it includes everything it offers its customers in a specific market or segment. This comprises not only the company's bundles of products and services but also how it differentiates itself from its competitors. A value proposition therefore consists of the full range of tangible and intangible benefits a company provides to its customers and other stakeholders.

*Where to play* specifies the target markets in terms of the customers and the needs to be served. The best way to define a target market is highly situational. It can be defined in any number of ways, such as by where the target customers are (for example, in certain parts of the world or in particular parts of town), how they buy (perhaps through specific channels), who they are (their particular demographics and other innate characteristics), when they buy (for example, on particular occasions), what they buy (for instance, are they price buyers or do they place more value on service?), and for whom they buy (themselves, friends, family, their company, or their customers?).

*How to win* spells out the capabilities and policies that will give a company an essential advantage over key competitors in delivering the value proposition. As such, it has two dimensions. The first is the *value chain infrastructure* dimension. It deals with questions such as: What key internal resources and capabilities has the company created to support the chosen value proposition and target markets? What partner network has it assembled to support the business model? and How are these activities organized into an overall, coherent value creation and delivery model? The second is the *management* dimension. It summarizes a company's choices about its organizational structure, financial structure, and management policies. Organization and management style are closely linked. In companies that are organized primarily around product divisions management is often highly centralized. In contrast, companies operating with a more geographic organizational structure usually are managed on a more decentralized basis.

Choices must be made because there is usually more than one way to win in every market, but not everyone can win in any given market. With good choices, a business gains the right to win in its target markets. The target market, value proposition, capabilities and management regime must hang together in a coherent way.

Most companies face innumerable options for what value proposition to choose, where to play and how to win. As well, they have to sort out seemingly conflicting objectives such as the need for both long-term growth and short-term profitability. To "maximize long-term value" means—when there are mutually exclusive options—to select options that will give the greatest sustained increase to the company's economic value. It is worth emphasizing that "maximizing long-term value" is not the same thing as "maximizing share price" or "maximizing shareholder value." Those objectives typically represent the more short-term demands of current shareholders or their advisers, and they do not always align with what is best for all stakeholders, On the other hand, "maximizing long-term value" does not mean forgetting about the short term. Economic value takes into account growth and profitability, the short term and long term, and risk as well as reward.

Strategic thinking has evolved substantially in the past 25 years. We have learned much about how to analyze the competitive environment, define a sustainable position, develop competitive and corporate advantages, and how to sustain advantage in the face of competitive challenges and threats. Different approaches—including industrial organization theory, the resource-based view, dynamic capabilities and game theory—have helped academicians and practitioners understand the dynamics of competition and develop recommendations about how firms should define their competitive and corporate strategies. But drivers such as globalization and technological change continue to profoundly change the competitive game. The fastest growing firms in this new environment appear to be those that have taken advantage of these structural changes to innovate in their business models so they can compete differently.

In addition to the business model innovation drivers noted above, much recent interest has come from three other environmental shifts. Advances in *information technology* have been a major force behind the recent interest in business model innovation. Many e-businesses are based on new business models. New strategies for the *'bottom of the pyramid'* in emerging markets have also steered researchers and practitioners toward the systematic study of business approaches. Third, the quest for *sustainability* and commitment to *corporate social responsibility* in all aspects of a business have become an imperative: A company that creates profit for its shareholders while protecting the environment and improving the lives of those with whom it interacts is likely to enjoy a significant competitive advantage over its rivals. These companies operate in such a way that their business interests and the interests of the environment and society intersect.

The evolution of strategic thinking reflects these changes and is characterized by a gradual shift in focus from an *industrial economics* to a *resource-based* perspective to a *human and intellectual* capital perspective. It is important to understand the reasons underlying this evolution, because they reflect a changing view of what strategy is and how it is crafted.

The early *industrial economics* perspective held that environmental influences—particularly those that shape industry structure—were the primary determinants of a company's success. The competitive environment was thought to impose pressures and constraints, which made certain strategies more attractive than others. Carefully choosing where to compete—selecting the most attractive industries or industry segments—and control strategically important resources, such as financial capital, became the dominant themes of strategy development at both the business unit and corporate levels. The focus, therefore, was on *capturing economic value* through adept positioning. Thus, industry analysis, competitor analysis, segmentation, positioning, and strategic planning became the most important tools for analyzing strategic opportunity.[1]

As globalization, the technology revolution, and other major environmental forces picked up speed and radically changed the competitive landscape, key assumptions underlying the industrial economics model came under scrutiny. Should the competitive environment be treated as a constraint on strategy formulation, or was strategy really about shaping competitive conditions? Was the assumption that businesses should control most of the relevant strategic resources needed to compete still applicable? Were strategic resources really as mobile as the traditional model assumed, and was the advantage associated with owning particular resources and competencies therefore necessarily short lived?

In response to these questions, a *resource-based* perspective of strategy development emerged. Rather than focusing on positioning a company within environment-dictated constraints, this new school of thought defined strategic thinking in terms of building core capabilities that transcend the boundaries of traditional business units. It focused on creating corporate portfolios around *core businesses* and on adopting goals and processes aimed at enhancing *core competencies*.[2] This new paradigm reflected a shift in emphasis from capturing economic value to creating value through the development and nurturing of key resources and capabilities.

The current focus on knowledge and *human and intellectual capital* as a company's key strategic resource is a natural extension of the resource-based view of strategy and fits with the transition of global commerce to a knowledge-based economy. For a majority of companies, access to physical or financial resources no longer is an impediment to growth or opportunity; not having the right people or knowledge has become the limiting factor. Microsoft, Google, and Yahoo scan the entire pool of U.S. computer science graduates every year to identify and attract the few they want to attract. Today it is recognized that competency-based strategies are dependent on people, that scarce knowledge and expertise drive product development, and that personal relationships with clients are critical to market responsiveness.[3]

## Strategy Formulation: Concepts and Dimensions

### Strategy, Business Models, and Tactics

Every company has a *business model*—a blueprint of how it does business—defined by its core strategy although it may not always be explicitly articulated. This model most likely evolved over time as the company rose to prominence in its primary markets and reflects key choices about what value it provides to whom, how, and at what price and cost. As shown in Figure 1.1, it describes who its customers are, how it reaches them and relates to them (*market participation*); what a company offers its customers (*the value proposition*); with what resources, activities, and partners it creates its offerings (*value chain infrastructure*); and finally, how it organizes, finances, and manages its operations (*management model*).

A company's *value proposition* comprises the core of its business model; it includes everything it offers to its customers in a specific market or segment. This comprises not only the company's bundles of products and services, but also how it differentiates itself from its competitors. A value proposition therefore consists of the full range of tangible and intangible benefits a company provides to its customers and other stakeholders.

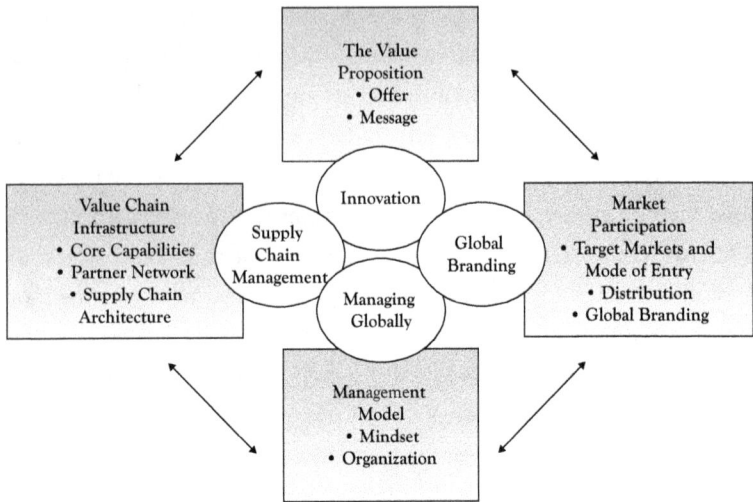

*Figure 1.1  Four components of a business model*

The *market participation* dimension of a business model has three components. It describes what specific *markets or segments* a company chooses to serve, domestically or abroad; what methods of distribution it uses to reach its customers; and how it promotes and advertises its value proposition to its target customers.

The *value chain infrastructure* dimension of the business model deals with such questions as: What key *internal resources and capabilities* has the company created to support the chosen value proposition and target markets? What *partner network* has it assembled to support the business model? and How are these activities organized into an overall, coherent value creation and delivery model?

The *management* submodel summarizes a company's choices about a suitable organizational structure, financial structure, and management policies. Typically, organization and management are closely linked. In companies that are organized primarily around product divisions management is often highly centralized. In contrast, companies operating with a more geographic organizational structure usually are managed on a more decentralized basis.

Business models can take many forms. The well-known "razor–razor blade model" involves pricing razors inexpensively, but aggressively marking-up the consumables (razor blades). Jet engines for commercial aircraft are priced the same way—manufacturers know that engines are long lived, and maintenance and parts are where Rolls Royce, General Electric (GE), Pratt & Whitney and others make their money. In the sports apparel business, sponsorship is a key component of today's business models. Nike, Adidas, Reebok, and others sponsor football and soccer clubs and teams, providing kit and sponsorship dollars as well as royalty streams from the sale of replica products.

In industries characterized by a single dominant business model competitive advantage is won mainly through better execution, more efficient processes, lean organizations, and product innovation. Increasingly, however, industries feature multiple- and co-existing business models. In this environment, competitive advantage is achieved by creating focused and innovative business models. Consider the airline, music, telecom or banking industries. In each one there are different business models competing against each other. For example, in the airline industry there are the traditional flag carriers, the low-cost airlines, the business class only airlines, and the fractional private jet ownership companies. Each business model embodies a different approach to achieving a competitive advantage.

Describing a company's strategy in terms of its business model allows explicit consideration of the logic or architecture of each component and its relationship to others as a set of designed *choices* that can be changed. Thus, thinking holistically about every component of the business model—and systematically challenging orthodoxies within these components—significantly extends the scope for innovation and improves the chances of building a sustainable competitive advantage.

The term "strategy", however, has a broader meaning. It extends beyond the design of business models—and redesigning them as competitive positions change—for long-term economic value: *Strategy formulation embodies a "contingency" notion—a good strategy anticipates a wide range of changes in the competitive environment and contains provisions to deal effectively with those changes.* A business model therefore is more generic than a specific business strategy. Coupling strategic analysis with business model evaluation is necessary in order to protect whatever competitive advantage results from the design and implementation of new business models. Selecting a business strategy is a more granular exercise than designing a business model. Linking competitive strategy analysis to business model design requires segmenting the market, creating a value proposition for each segment, setting up the apparatus to deliver that value, and then figuring out how to prevent the business model/strategy from being undermined through imitation by competitors or disintermediation by customers.[4]

We also need to distinguish between the terms "*strategy*" and "*tactics*". New business concepts, technologies, and ideas are born every day. The Internet, innovation, outsourcing, offshoring, total quality, flexibility, and speed, for example, all have come to be recognized as essential to a company's competitive strength and agility. But although enhancing operational effectiveness is crucial in today's cut throat competitive environment, it is no substitute for sound strategic thinking. There is a difference between *strategy* and *tactics*—the application of operational tools and managerial philosophies focused on *operational effectiveness*. Both are essential to competitiveness. But whereas *tactics* are aimed at doing things *better* than competitors, *strategy* focuses on doing things *differently*. Understanding this distinction is critical, as recent history has shown. Companies that embraced the Internet as "the strategic answer" to their business rather than just another, if important, new tool were in for a rude awakening. By focusing too much on e-business options at the expense of broader strategic concerns, many found themselves chasing customers indiscriminately, trading quality and service for price, and, with it, losing their competitive advantage and profitability.[5]

### Good Strategy Takes a Long-term Perspective and Forces Trade-offs

Strategic thinking, instead, focuses on the longer term and on taking *different* approaches to deliver customer value; on choosing *different* sets of activities that cannot easily be imitated, thereby providing a basis for an enduring competitive advantage. Amazon is a good example.

Today, Amazon offers 230 million items for sale in America—some 30 times the number sold by Wal-Mart, the world's biggest retailer, which has its own fast-growing online business. Its total 2013 revenues were $74.5 billion, but when one takes into account the merchandise that other companies sell through its "marketplace" service the sales volume is nearly double that. Though by far the biggest online retailer in America,

Amazon is still growing faster than the 17 percent pace of e-commerce as a whole. It is the top online seller in Europe and Japan, too, and has designs on China's vast market. Last year Amazon was the world's ninth-biggest retailer ranked by sales; by 2018 it may well be in the top two.

On top of its online-retail success, Amazon has produced two other transformative businesses. The Kindle e-reader pioneered the shift from paper books to electronic ones, creating a market that now accounts for more than a 10th of spending on books in America and which Amazon dominates. Less visible but just as transformative is Amazon's invention in 2006 of cloud-computing as a pay-as-you-go service, now a $9 billion market. That venture, called Amazon Web Services (AWS), has slashed the technology costs of starting an enterprise or running an existing one.

And Amazon enjoys an advantage most competitors envy: Remarkably patient shareholders. The company made a net profit of just $274 million last year, a minuscule amount in relation to its revenues and its $154 billion value on the stock exchange; its shares are valued at more than 500 times last year's earnings, 34 times the multiple for Wal-Mart. Ités core retail business is thought to do little better than break-even; most of its profits come from the independent vendors who sell through Amazon's marketplace.

Such long-termism takes investment. In its early days Amazon avoided direct competition with retailers because its lack of stores made it "capital-light". Today its empire of warehouses and data centers has changed that. Now its pitch to merchants and technologists is that it will build physical assets so that they do not have to. By doing so, it keeps its competitors close and makes them depend on Amazon for key parts of their business models.[6]

ING DIRECT (the trading name of ING Bank [Australia] Limited) is the world's leading direct savings bank and provides another example of a company with a potentially (industry-) transformative strategy that forces competitors to reexamine their entire business model. ING Direct operates a *branchless direct bank* with operations in Australia, Austria (branded *ING-DiBa*), Canada, France, Germany (branded *ING-DiBa*), Italy, Spain, the United Kingdom, and the United States. It offers services over the Internet and by phone, ATM, or mail and focuses on simple, high-interest savings accounts. Customers do business exclusively online, over the phone, or by mail. The bank's value proposition is simple and direct—great rates, 24 × 7 convenience, and superior customer service. In the United States alone, ING DIRECT has already attracted more than two million customers.

Whereas operational effectiveness tools can improve competitiveness, they do not by themselves force companies to choose between entirely different, internally consistent *sets* of activities. Other banks could copy ING DIRECT and other competitors by also offering banking services directly to end users, but they would have to dismantle their traditional distribution structures—branch offices primarily—to reap the benefits ING realizes from its strategy. Thus, choosing a *unique competitive positioning*—the essence of strategy—forces trade-offs in terms of what to do and, equally important, what *not* to do and creates *barriers to imitation*.

### Value Erodes Over Time

Good strategy formulation focuses on creating *value*—for customers, shareholders, partners, suppliers, employees, and the community—by satisfying the needs and wants of the market place better than anyone else. If a company can deliver value to its customers better than its rivals can over a sustained period of time, that company likely has a superior strategy. This is not a simple task. Customers' wants, needs, and preferences change, often rapidly, as they become more knowledgeable about a product or service, as new competitors enter the market, and as new entrants redefine what value means. As a result, what is valuable today might not be valuable tomorrow. The moral of this logic is simple but powerful: *The value of a particular product or service offering, unless constantly maintained, nourished, and improved, erodes with time.*

Consider the U.S. market for coffee. Thirty years ago, coffee was more or less a commodity. Traditional coffee shops and "office" coffee defined consumer behavior, and Nescafé, Folgers, and Hills Brothers accounted for approximately 90 percent of the retail market. Then Starbucks came along. The company redefined "drinking a cup of coffee" into a new value proposition consisting of three elements: (1) "great" coffee—Starbuck's relentless search for the highest quality coffee in the world was the cornerstone of a differentiated market positioning; (2) a unique physical environment—Starbucks created a "second" living room for customers to enjoy their coffee, relax, and meet people; and (3) a new service philosophy—"baristas" were expected to be experts in coffee and provide a high level of customized service. The new value proposition took off and redefined the competitive playing field for traditional coffeemakers and grocery stores, chains such as Dunkin' Donuts and McDonald's and many others. To this day, major companies such as General Foods and Procter & Gamble are having trouble launching a major counteroffensive for marketing gourmet coffee through traditional (grocery) channels, a clear indication of how radically customer perceptions of value about coffee have changed.

The Starbucks example illustrates the principle of "value migration" and its consequences for creating competitive advantage. At any given point in time a company competes with a particular mix of resources. Some of the company's assets and capabilities are better than those of its rivals; others are inferior; the superior assets and capabilities are the source of positional advantages. Whatever competitive advantage the firm possesses, it must expect that ongoing change in the strategic environment and competitive moves by rival firms continuously work to erode it. Competitive strategy thus has a dual purpose: (1) slowing down the erosion process by protecting current sources of advantage against the actions of competitors and (2) investing in new capabilities that form the basis for the next position of competitive advantage. The creation and maintenance of advantage is therefore a continuous process.

### Strategy Is About Creating Options

At the time a strategy is crafted some outcomes are more predictable than others. When Motorola invests in a new technology, for example, it might know that this technology holds promise in several markets. Its precise returns in different applications, however, might not be known with any degree of certainty until much later.[7] Therefore, strategy formulation is about crafting a long-term *vision* for an organization while maintaining a degree of flexibility about how to get there and creating a portfolio of options for adapting to change. Strategy formulation therefore includes considering a host of environmental and organizational contingencies.

This implies *learning* is an essential component of the process. As soon as a company begins to implement a chosen direction, it starts to learn—about how well attuned the chosen direction is to the competitive environment, how rivals are likely to respond, and how well prepared the organization is to carry out its competitive intentions.

### Strategy: An Ecosystem Perspective

In today's increasingly interconnected world, a single company focus often is not strategically viable. Most companies rely heavily on networks of partners, suppliers, and customers to achieve market success and sustain performance. These networks function like a biological ecosystem, in which companies succeed and fail as a collective whole.

Business ecosystems have become a widespread phenomenon within industries such as banking, biotechnology, insurance, and software. As with biological systems, the boundaries of a business ecosystem are fluid and sometimes difficult to define. Business ecosystems cross entire industries and can encompass the full range of organizations that influence the value of a product or service.

Technology increasingly is the connective tissue that lets the ecosystem function, grow, and develop in widely diverse ways. Corporations planning to craft an effective ecosystem strategy must have a technical infrastructure in place that allows them to share information and encourage collaboration, as well as integrate systems within the ecosystem. Wal-Mart's success as the world's largest retailer, for example, is based, in part, on information technology decisions that are closely tied to its understanding of the ecosystem on which it depends. Wal-Mart maintains a vast supply-chain ecosystem that stretches from manufacturer to consumer. This centralized supply chain brings efficiencies to Wal-Mart and also creates value for its suppliers, both large and small, by providing a massive new channel for them to reach consumers worldwide.

An ecosystem-based strategy perspective makes clear the importance of interdependency in today's business environment. Stand-alone strategies often no longer suffice, because a company's performance is increasingly dependent on its ability to influence assets outside its direct control.

## Strategy as Alignment

Strategy is concerned with analyzing and making decisions about numerous activities ranging from acquiring and allocating resources to building capabilities to shaping corporate culture to installing appropriate support systems. All these decisions are aimed at *aligning* an organization's resources and capabilities with the goals of a chosen strategic direction. Strategic alignment can be directed at *closing strategic capability gaps* or at *maintaining strategic focus.*

*Strategic capability gaps* are substantive disparities in competences, skills, and resources between what customers demand or are likely to demand in the future and what the organization currently can deliver. This strategic alignment dimension, therefore, focuses on closing the gap between *what it takes* to succeed in the marketplace and *what the company currently can do.* Examples of activities in this category are developing better technologies, creating faster delivery mechanisms, adopting a stronger branding, and building a stronger distribution network.

A second dimension of alignment is concerned with *maintaining strategic focus.* Strategy formulation and implementation are human activities and thus are subject to error, obstruction, or even abuse. Therefore, to successfully execute a chosen strategy an organization must find ways to ensure that *what is said*—by groups and individuals at all levels of the organization—*is in fact done.* Making sure strategic objectives are effectively communicated, allocating the necessary resources, and creating proper incentives for effective alignment are examples of activities in this category.

## Is All Strategy Planned?

Even the best-laid plans do not always result in the intended outcomes. Between the time a strategy is crafted—that is, when *intended* outcomes are specified—and the time it is implemented, a host of things can change. For example, a competitor might introduce a new product or new regulations might have been passed. Thus, the *realized* strategy can be somewhat different from the *intended* strategy.[8]

## Multiple Levels of Strategy

Strategy formulation occurs at the *corporate, business unit,* and *functional* levels. In a multibusiness, diversified corporation, *corporate* strategy is concerned with what kinds of businesses a firm should compete in and how the overall portfolio of businesses should be managed. In a single-product or single-service business or in a division of a multibusiness corporation, *business unit* strategy is concerned with deciding what product or service to offer, how to manufacture or create it, and how to take it to the marketplace. *Functional* strategies typically involve a more limited domain, such as marketing, human resources, or technology. All three are parts of strategic management—the totality of managerial processes used to guide the long-term future of an organization.

## The Role of Stakeholders

Most companies rely, to a great extent, on a network of external *stakeholders*—suppliers, partners, and even competitors—in creating value for customers. The motivation of internal stakeholders—directors, top executives, middle managers, and employees—also is critical to success. A misstep in managing suppliers, a major error in employee relations, or a lack of communication with principal shareholders can set back a company's progress by years. The importance of different stakeholders to a company's competitive position depends on the *stake* they have in the organization and the kind of *influence* they can exert. Stakeholders can have an *ownership stake* (shareholders and directors, among others), an *economic stake* (creditors, employees, customers, and suppliers), or a *social stake* (regulatory agencies, charities, the local community, and activist groups).[9] Some have *formal power*, others *economic* or *political power.* Formal power is usually associated with legal obligations or rights; economic power is derived from an ability to withhold products, services, or capital; and political power is rooted in an ability to persuade other stakeholders to influence the behavior of an organization.

## Vision and Mission

A *vision* statement represents senior management's long-range goals for the organization—a description of what competitive position it wants to attain over a given period of time and what core competencies it must acquire to get there. As such, it summarizes a company's broad strategic focus for the future. A *mission* statement documents the purpose for an organization's existence. Mission statements often contain a code of corporate conduct to guide management in implementing the mission.

In crafting a *vision* statement, two important lessons are worth heeding. First, most successful companies focus on relatively few activities and do them extremely well. Domino's is successful precisely because it sticks to pizza; H&R Block because it concentrates on tax preparation; and Microsoft because it focuses on software. This suggests that effective strategy development is as much about deciding *what not to do as it is about choosing what activities to focus on.*

The second lesson is that most successful companies achieved their leadership position by adopting a vision far greater than their resource base and competencies would allow. To become the market leader, a focus on the drivers of competition is not enough; a vision that paints "a new future" is required. With such a mindset, gaps between capabilities and goals become challenges rather than constraints, and the goal of winning can sustain a sense of urgency over a long period of time.[10] Consider Amazon's vision statement: "Our vision is to be the earth's most consumer centric company; to build a place where people can come to find and discover anything they might want to buy online".

A vision statement should provide both strategic guidance and motivational focus. A good vision "is clear, but not so constraining that it inhibits initiative, meets the legitimate interests and values of all stakeholders, and is feasible; that is, it can be implemented."[11]

Increasingly, companies are adopting formal statements of corporate *values*, the core of a *mission* statement, and senior executives now routinely identify ethical behavior, honesty, integrity, and social concerns as top issues on their companies' agendas. Whole Foods Market is an example of a company with a well-defined mission statement. It lists eight core values that guide all of its strategic thinking:

- Selling the highest quality natural and organic products available.
- Satisfying, delighting, and nourishing our customers.

- Supporting Team Member happiness and excellence.
- Creating wealth through profits and growth.
- Serving and supporting our local and global communities.
- Practicing and advancing our environmental stewardship.
- Creating ongoing win–win partnerships with our suppliers.
- Promoting the health of our stakeholders through healthy eating education.

### Strategic Intent and Stretch

A statement of *strategic intent* is both an executive summary of the strategic goals a company has adopted and a motivational message. Properly articulated, a statement of strategic intent does more than paint a vision for the future; it signals the desire to win and recognizes that successful strategies are built as much around what can be as around what is. It focuses the organization on key competitive targets and provides goals about which competencies to develop, what kinds of resources to harness, and what segments to concentrate on. Instead of worrying about the degree of fit between current resources and opportunities, it shifts the focus to how to close the capability gap. Current resources and capabilities become starting points for strategy development, not constraints on strategy formulation or its implementation.[12]

A related idea is the concept of *stretch*. Stretch reflects the recognition that successful strategies are built as much around *what can be* as around *what is*. Ultimately, every company must create a fit between its resources and its opportunities. The question is over what time frame? Too short a time frame encourages a focus on *fit* rather than *stretch*, on resource *allocation* rather than on getting more value from existing resources. The use of too long a time horizon, however, creates an unacceptable degree of uncertainty and threatens to turn stretch objectives into unrealistic goals.

## The Strategy Formulation Process

### Steps

The process of crafting a strategy can be organized around three key questions: *Where are we now? Where do we go? How do we get there?* Each question defines a part of the process and suggests different types of analyses and evaluations. It also shows that the components of a strategic analysis overlap, and that feedback loops are an integral part of the process.

1. The *Where are we now?* part of the process is concerned with assessing the current state of the business or the company as a whole. It begins with revisiting such fundamental issues as what the organization's mission is, what management's long-term vision for the company is, and who its principal stakeholders are. Other key components include a detailed evaluation of the company's current performance; of pertinent trends in the broader sociopolitical, economic, legal, and technological environment in which the company operates; of opportunities and threats in the industry environment; and of internal strengths and weaknesses.

2. The *Where do we go?* questions are designed to generate and explore strategic alternatives based on the answers obtained to the first question. At the business unit level, for example, are optional decisions, such as whether to concentrate on growth in a few market segments or adopt a wider market focus, go it alone or partner with another company, or focus on value-added or low-cost solutions for customers. At the corporate level, this part of the process is focused on shaping the portfolio of businesses the company participates in and on making adjustments in parenting philosophies and processes. At both levels, the output is a statement of *strategic intent,* which identifies the guiding business concept or driving force that will propel the company forward.

3. The *How do we get there?* component of the process is focused on how to achieve the desired objectives. One of the most important issues addressed at this stage is how to bridge the *capability gap* that separates current organizational skills and capabilities from those that are needed to achieve the stated strategic intent. It deals with the "strategic alignment" of *core competences* with *emerging market needs* and with identifying *key success factors* associated with successfully implementing the chosen strategy. The end product is a detailed set of initiatives for implementing the chosen strategy and exercising strategic discipline and control.

## Strategy and Planning

A strategy review can be triggered by a host of factors—new leadership, disappointing performance, changes in ownership, and the emergence of new competitors or technologies—or be part of a scheduled, typically annual, review process.

Most companies employ some form of strategic planning. The impetus for imposing structure to the process comes from two main pressures: (1) the need to cope with an increasingly complex range of issues—economic, political, social, and legal on a global scale—and (2) the increasing speed with which the competitive environment is changing. A formal system ensures that the required amount of time and resources are allocated to the process, that priorities are set, that activities are integrated and coordinated, and that the right feedback is obtained.

This planning process is usually organized in terms of a *planning cycle.* This cycle often begins with a review at the corporate level of the overall competitive environment and of the corporate guidelines to the various divisions and businesses. Next, divisions and business units are asked to update their long-term strategies and indicate how these strategies fit with the company's major priorities and goals. Third, divisional and business unit plans are reviewed, evaluated, adjusted, coordinated, and integrated in meetings between corporate and divisional/business unit managers. Finally, detailed operating plans are developed at the divisional/business unit level, and final approvals are obtained from corporate headquarters.

A formal strategic planning system or planning cycle, by definition, attempts to structure strategy development and implementation as a primarily linear, sequential process. Environmental and competitive changes do not respect a calendar-driven process, however. When a significant new competitive opportunity or challenge emerges, a company cannot afford to wait to respond. This does not mean that formal processes should be abandoned altogether. Rather, it underscores that even though strategy is about crafting a long-term *vision* for an organization, it should maintain a degree of flexibility about how to get there and preserve options for adapting to change.

# CHAPTER 2

# Strategy and Performance

## Introduction

Carefully crafted strategies often deliver only a fraction of their promised financial value. Why should this be so? Is it because CEOs press for better execution when they really need a sounder strategy? Or is it because they focus on crafting a new strategy when execution is the organization's true weakness? Are there other reasons? And how can such errors be avoided? A good starting point is a better understanding of how strategy and performance are linked.

A plethora of research on this issue exists. Much of what we know about the determinants of industry, firm, and business (financial) performance is in the form of measures of individual relationships in models linking various hypothesized causal variables to various measures of performance. The causal variables usually describe some combination of elements of environment, firm strategy, and organizational characteristics. This type of research is conducted in disciplines such as economics, management, business policy, finance, accounting, management science, international business, sociology, and marketing. Comparing the results from these studies is difficult, principally because research methodologies, model specifications, and the definition and measurement of explanatory and dependent variables differ widely. Estimation techniques, ranging from simple cross tables to complex "causal" models, also differ substantially.

It is not surprising then that more has been learned about the impact of specific environmental, organizational, and strategic variables on (financial) performance than about the efficacy of entire (multidimensional) strategies in different settings. We know, for example, that all else being equal, the following hold true:

(1) High growth situations are desirable; growth is consistently related to profits under a wide variety of circumstances.

(2) Having a high market share is helpful, but we do not know exactly when trying to gain market share is a good idea or not.

(3) Bigness per se does not confer profitability but can have significant other strategic advantages.

(4) In many industries dollars spent on R&D have a strong relationship to increased profitability; investment in advertising is also worthwhile, especially in producer goods industries.

(5) High-quality products and services enhance performance, excessive debt can hurt performance, and capital investment decisions should be made with caution.

But knowing these relationships exist is a far cry from understanding how strategy and performance are linked, because no simple prescription involving one or just a few factors is likely to be helpful in crafting comprehensive effective strategies.

Two, widely cited studies shed a different light on how companies achieve superior, sustained performance. The first, by Jim Collins, entitled *Good to Great: Why Some Companies Make the Leap... and Others Don't*, originally published in 2001, focused on what good companies can do to become truly great. Its findings have inspired many CEOs to change their views about what drives success. It shows, among other findings, that factors such as CEO compensation, technology, mergers and acquisitions, and change management initiatives played relatively minor roles in fostering the *Good to Great* process. Instead, successes in three main areas—*disciplined people, disciplined thought, and disciplined action*—were likely the most significant factors in determining a company's ability to achieve greatness. The second, *What Really Works: The 4+2 Formula for Sustained Business Success*, by Joyce, Nohria, and Roberson, in association with McKinsey & Co., was aimed at identifying the must-have management practices that truly produce superior results. As part of this so-called Evergreen Project, more than 200 well-established management practices were evaluated as they were employed over a 10-year period by 160 companies. It concluded that eight management practices—four primary and four secondary—are directly correlated with superior corporate performance as measured by total return to shareholders. Winning companies achieved excellence in all four of the primary practices, plus any two of the secondary practices, suggesting the *4+2 Formula* title. Losing companies failed to do so.

Although the two studies differ significantly in terms of their methodology, there is substantial agreement in the findings. As it turns out, a company's strategy, execution, leadership and talent pool, organization, process, and corporate culture *all* are critical to sustained success. What is more, they *all* are inextricably linked and *together* determine performance.

### Leverage: Economies of Scale and Scope

Business historian Alfred D. Chandler argued that "to compete globally, you have to be big."[1] Looking back over a century of corporate history, he noted that the "logic of managerial enterprise" begins with economics—and the cost advantages that come with scale and scope in technologically advanced capital-intensive industries. Large plants frequently produce products at a much lower cost than can small ones because the cost per unit decreases as volume goes up (*economies of scale*). In addition, larger plants can use many of the same raw- and semi-finished materials and production processes to make a variety of different products (*economies of scope*). What is more, these principles are not limited to the manufacturing sector. Procter & Gamble, through its multibrand strategies, benefits from economies of scope because of its considerable influence at the retail level. In the service sector, the scale and scope economies of the major accounting firms have enabled them to dominate the auditing services market for large companies by displacing a number of respectable local and regional accounting firms.

### Economies of Scale

More formally, *economies of scale* occur when the unit cost of performing an activity decreases as the scale of the activity increases. Unit cost can fall as scale is increased for reasons such as the use of better technologies in production processes or greater buyer power in large-scale purchasing situations. A different form of scale economics occurs when cost can be reduced as a result of finding better ways to perform a given task. In this scenario, the cumulative number of units processed or tasks performed drives the cost reduction. This is referred to as the *economics of learning*. The graphical representation of this phenomenon is called the *learning or experience curve*.

## Economies of Scope

*Economies of scope* occur when the unit cost of an activity falls because the asset used is shared with some other activity. When Frito-Lay Corporation, for example, uses its trucks to deliver not only Frito corn chips and Lay's potato chips but also salsa and other dips to be used with the chips, it creates economies of scope. Decision opportunities for creating economies of scope fall into three broad classes: (1) *horizontal scope*, (2) *geographical scope*, and (3) *vertical scope*.

*Horizontal scope decisions* mainly concern choices of product scope. General Electric (GE) is a highly diversified company with interests in appliances, medical systems, aircraft engines, financing, and many other areas. Intangible assets such as knowledge—Sony's expertise in miniaturizing products, for example—or brands—think of the Virgin brand—can also be sources of horizontal economies of scope when they are used in the development, production, and marketing of more than one product.

*Geographical scope decisions* involve choices about geographical coverage. McDonald's has operations in almost 100 countries, Whirlpool has production facilities in a few countries but markets its products in a large number of countries, and Internet-based companies such as eBay and Amazon have achieved geographical scope on a virtual basis.

*Vertical scope decisions* are concerned with how a company links its value chain activities vertically. In the computer industry, IBM has traditionally been highly vertically integrated. Dell, in contrast, does not manufacture anything. Rather, it relies on an extensive network of third-party suppliers in its value creation process.

Size alone, of course, is not enough to guarantee competitive success. To capitalize on the advantages that scale and scope can bring, companies must make related investments to create marketing and distribution organizations. They must also create the right management infrastructure to effectively coordinate the myriad activities that make up the modern multinational corporation.

### *Defining the "Core" Business— Key to Sustained Performance*

A useful starting point for crafting a strategy is to define the *core* business. For most companies, the *core* is defined in terms of their most valuable customers, most valuable products, most important channels, and distinctive capabilities. The challenge is to define the company as different from others in a way that builds on real strengths and capabilities—that avoids "strategy by wishful thinking"—in a manner that is relevant to all stakeholders, with room for growth.[2] Here is where the art and science of strategy formulation meet and where CEOs have a unique opportunity to position their companies with customers, suppliers, alliance partners, and financial markets.

Not choosing what is core by default also is a choice. Not making a deliberate choice risks confusion about a company's positioning in its served markets, however, and might make it more difficult to create value on a sustained basis.

The story of Colgate-Palmolive illustrates what is possible when a company chooses to focus on building its core business and driving it to its full potential. Since 1984, Colgate's share price has outperformed its peers and delivered a return three times that of S&P 500. These results are remarkable, because Colgate operates in low-to medium-growth segments. The company's long history of strong performance stems from an absolute focus on its core businesses: oral care, personal care, home care, and pet nutrition. This has been combined with a successful global financial strategy. Around the world, Colgate has consistently increased gross margins while at the same time reducing costs in order to fund growth initiatives, including new product development and increases in marketing spending. These, in turn, have generated greater profitability.

### *The Need for Growth*

Achieving consistent revenue and profit growth is hard—especially for large companies. To put this challenge in perspective, for a $30 billion company, about average for a *Fortune* 100 company, to grow 6 percent, it must spawn a new $2 billion company every year. What is more, a growth strategy that works for one company might not be appropriate for another. It might even be disastrous. A high percentage of mergers and acquisitions, for example, fail to meet expectations. Making the right acquisition, successfully integrating an acquired company into the acquirer's operations, and realizing promised synergies is difficult even for experienced players such as GE. Companies that only occasionally make an acquisition have a dismal track record. Relying on internal growth alone to meet revenue targets can be equally risky, especially in years of slow economic growth. Few companies consistently achieve higher-than-GDP growth from internal sources alone.

To formulate a successful growth strategy, a company must carefully analyze its strengths and weaknesses, how it delivers value to customers, and what growth strategies its culture can effectively support. For price-value leaders like Wal-Mart, a growth strategy focused on entering adjacent markets is highly suitable. For performance-value players such as Intel or Genentech, on the other hand, continuous innovation might be a more effective platform for revenue growth. Selecting the right growth strategy, therefore, requires a careful analysis of opportunities, strategic resources, and cultural fit.[3]

Whether a company chooses to pursue growth through further investments in its core business or by expanding beyond its current core, it has only three avenues by which to grow its revenue base: (1) organic or internal growth, (2) growth through acquisition, and (3) growth through alliance-based initiatives. This is often referred to as the "Build, Buy, or Bond" paradigm. Wal-Mart primarily relies on organic growth. GE regularly makes strategic acquisitions in markets it deems attractive in order to achieve its growth objectives. Amazon and eBay have numerous alliances and supplier relationships that fuel their revenue growth.

We characterize growth strategies using product–market choice as the primary criterion into three categories: (1) concentrated growth (2) vertical and horizontal integration, and (3) diversification.

### Concentrated Growth Strategies

Existing product markets often are attractive avenues for growth. A corporation that continues to direct its resources to the profitable growth of a single product category, in a well-defined market and possibly with a dominant technology, is said to pursue a *concentrated growth* strategy.[4] The most direct way of pursuing concentrated growth is to target increases in market share. This can be done in three ways: (1) increasing the number of users of the product, (2) increasing product usage by stimulating higher quantities of use or by developing new applications, and/or (3) increasing the frequency of the product's use.

Concentrated growth can be a powerful competitive weapon. A tight product–market focus allows a company to finely assess market needs, develop a detailed knowledge of customer behavior and price sensitivity, and improve the effectiveness of marketing and promotion efforts. High success rates of new products are also tied to avoiding situations that require undeveloped skills, such as serving new customers and markets, acquiring new technologies, building new channels, developing new promotional abilities, and facing new competition. Corporations that successfully use concentrated growth strategies include Allstate, Amoco, Avon, Caterpillar, Chemlawn, KFC, John Deere, and Goodyear.

### Vertical and Horizontal Integration

If a corporation's current lines of business show strong growth potential, two additional avenues for growth—*vertical* and *horizontal integration*—are available.

*Vertical integration* describes a strategy of increasing a corporation's vertical participation in an industry's value chain. *Backward integration* entails acquiring resource suppliers or raw materials or manufacturing components that used to be sourced elsewhere. *Forward integration* refers to a strategy of moving closer to the ultimate customer, for example, by acquiring a distribution channel or offering after-sale services. Vertical integration can be valuable if the corporation possesses a business unit that has a strong competitive position in a highly attractive industry—especially when the industry's technology is predictable and markets are growing rapidly. However, it can reduce a corporation's strategic flexibility by creating an exit barrier that prevents the company from leaving the industry if its fortunes decline.

Decisions about vertical scope are of key strategic importance at both the business unit and corporate levels because they involve the decision to redefine the domains in which the firm will operate. Vertical integration, therefore, also affects industry structure and competitive intensity. In the oil industry, for example, some companies are fully integrated from exploration to refining and marketing, whereas others specialize in one or more "upstream" or "downstream" stages of the value chain.

How profitable is vertical integration? The evidence is not clear cut but suggests that *backward* integration has a greater potential for raising Return on Investment (ROI) than *forward* integration, whereas partial integration generally hurts ROI. Studies also show that the impact of vertical integration on profitability varies with the size of the business. Larger businesses tend to benefit to a greater extent than smaller ones. This suggests that vertical integration might be a particularly attractive option for businesses with a substantial market share in which further backward integration has the potential for enhancing competitive advantage and increasing barriers to entry. Finally, with respect to the question of what other factors should be considered, the results suggest that (1) alternatives to ownership, such as long-term contracts and alliances, should actively be considered; (2) vertical integration almost always requires substantial increases in investment; (3) projected cost reductions do not always materialize; and (4) vertical integration sometimes results in increased product innovation.

*Horizontal integration* involves increasing the range of products and services offered to current markets or expanding the firm's presence into a wider number of geographic locations. Horizontal integration strategies are often designed to leverage brand potential. In recent years, *strategic alliances* have become an increasingly popular way to implement horizontal growth strategies.

### Diversification

The term *diversification* has a wide range of meanings in connection with many aspects of business activity. We talk about diversifying into new industries, technologies, supplier bases, customer segments, geographical regions, or sources of funds. In a strategic context, however, *diversification* is defined as a strategy of entering product markets different from those in which a company is currently engaged. Berkshire Hathaway is a good example of a company engaged in diversification; it operates insurance, food, furniture, footwear, and a host of other businesses.

Diversification strategies pose a great challenge to corporate executives. In the 1970s, many U.S. companies, facing stronger competition from abroad and diminished growth prospects in a number of traditional industries, moved into industries in which they had no particular competitive advantage. Believing that general management skill could offset knowledge gained from experience in an industry, executives thought that because they were successful in their own industries, they could be just as successful in others. A depressing number of their subsequent experiences showed that these executives overestimated their relevant competence and, under these circumstances, bigger was worse, not better.

Diversification strategies can be motivated by a variety of factors, including a desire to create revenue growth, increase profitability through shared resources and synergies, and reduce the company's overall exposure to risk by balancing the business portfolio, or an opportunity to exploit underutilized resources. A company might see an opportunity to capitalize on its current competitive position—leveraging a strong brand name, for example—by moving into a related business or market. Entering a new business may also counterbalance cyclical performance or use excess capacity.

*Relatedness* or the potential for *synergy* is a major consideration in formulating diversification strategies. Related diversification strategies target new business opportunities, which have meaningful commonalities with the rest of the company's portfolio. Unrelated diversification lacks such commonalities. *Relatedness* or *synergy* can be defined in a number of ways. The most common interpretation defines relatedness in terms of *tangible links* between business units. Such links typically arise from opportunities to share activities in the value chain among related business units, made possible by the presence of common buyers, channels, technologies, or other commonalities. A second form of relatedness among business units is based on common *intangible resources,* such as knowledge or capabilities. Sony's expertise in "miniaturizing" products is a good example. A third form of relatedness concerns the ability of business units to jointly *gain* or *exercise market power.* Examples of this form of relatedness include a company's ability to cross-subsidize competitive battles across product markets or geographies; take advantage of reciprocal buying opportunities; provide complementary products or "total solutions," rather than individual products; and confront challenges from societal stakeholder groups or regulatory bodies. *Strategic relatedness* is a fourth type of relatedness. It is defined in terms of the similarity of the strategic challenges faced by different business units. For example, a company might have developed a special expertise in operating businesses in mature, low-tech, slow-growing markets. All these scenarios offer companies an opportunity to exploit the different types of relatedness—which are not available to single-business competitors—for competitive advantage.

A well-known study links a company's performance to the degree of *relatedness* among its various businesses. It identifies three categories of relatedness based on a firm's *specialization ratio*, defined as the proportion of revenues derived from the largest single group of related businesses: *dominant business companies, related business companies,* and *unrelated business companies.*[5] Dominant business companies, such as Microsoft and IBM, derive a majority of their revenues from a single line of business. Related business companies, such as General Foods, Eastman Kodak, and DuPont, diversify beyond a single type of business but maintain a common thread of relatedness throughout the portfolio. The components of the portfolios of unrelated business companies, or diversified conglomerates, have little in common. Rockwell International and Textron are examples of conglomerates that lack synergistic possibilities in products, markets, or technologies. The study concluded that companies with closely related portfolios tend to outperform widely diversified corporations.

Porter suggests three tests for deciding whether a particular diversification move is likely to enhance shareholder value:

(1) *The attractiveness test.* Is the industry the company is about to enter fundamentally attractive from a growth, competitive, and profitability perspective, or can the company create such favorable conditions?
(2) *The cost of entry test.* Are the costs of entry reasonable? Is the time horizon until the venture becomes profitable acceptable? Are risk levels within accepted tolerances?
(3) *The better-off test.* Does the overall portfolio's competitive position and performance improve as a result of the diversification move?[6]

Diversification is a powerful weapon in a corporation's strategic arsenal. It is not a panacea for rescuing corporations with mediocre performance, however. If done carefully, diversification can improve shareholder value, but it needs to be planned carefully in the context of an overall corporate strategy.

*Mergers and Acquisitions.*  Companies can implement diversification strategies through internal development; joint ventures or alliances; or *mergers and acquisitions.* Internal development can be slow and expensive. Alliances involve all of the complications and compromises of a renegotiable relationship, including debates over investments and profits. As a result, permanently bonding with another company is sometimes seen as the easiest way to diversify. Two terms describe such relationships: *mergers* and *acquisitions.* A *merger* signifies that two companies have joined to form one company. An *acquisition* occurs when one firm buys another. To outsiders, the difference might seem small and related less to ownership control than to financing. However, the critical difference is often in management control. In acquisitions, the management team of the buyer tends to dominate decision making in the combined company.

The advantages of buying an existing player can be compelling. An acquisition can quickly position a firm in a new business or market. It also eliminates a potential competitor and therefore does not contribute to the development of excess capacity.

Acquisitions, however, are generally expensive. Premiums of 30 percent or more over the current value of the stock are not uncommon. This means that, although sellers often pocket handsome profits, acquiring companies frequently lose shareholder value. The process by which merger and acquisition decisions are made contributes to this problem. In theory, acquisitions are part of a corporate diversification strategy based on the explicit identification of the most suitable players in the most attractive industries as targets to be purchased. Acquisition strategies should also specify a comprehensive framework for the due diligence assessments of targets, plans for integrating acquired companies into the corporate portfolio, and a careful determination of "how much is too much" to pay.

In practice, the acquisition process is far more complex. Once the board has approved plans to expand into new businesses or markets, or once a potential target company has been identified, the time to act is typically short. The ensuing pressures to "do a deal" are intense. These pressures emanate from senior executives, directors, and investment bankers, who stand to gain from *any* deal; shareholder groups; and competitors bidding against the firm. The environment can become frenzied. Valuations tend to rise as corporations become overconfident in their ability to add value to the target company and expectations regarding synergies reach new heights. Due diligence is conducted more quickly than is desirable and tends to be confined to financial considerations. Integration planning takes a back seat. Differences in corporate cultures are discounted. In this climate, even the best-designed strategies can fail to produce a successful outcome, as many companies and their shareholders have learned.

What can be done to increase the effectiveness of the merger and acquisition process? Although there are no formulas for success, six themes have emerged:

(1) Successful acquisitions are usually part of a well-developed corporate strategy.

(2) Diversification through acquisition is an ongoing, long-term process that requires patience.

(3) Successful acquisitions usually result from disciplined strategic analysis, which looks at industries first before it targets companies, while recognizing that good deals are firm specific.

(4) An acquirer can add value in only a few ways and before proceeding with an acquisition the buying company should be able to specify how synergies will be achieved and value created.

(5) Objectivity is essential, even though it is hard to maintain once the acquisition chase ensues.

(6) Most acquisitions flounder on implementation—strategies for implementation should be formulated before the acquisition is completed and executed quickly after the acquisition deal is closed.

*Cooperative Strategies.*    Cooperative strategies—*joint ventures, strategic alliances,* and *other partnering* arrangements—have become increasingly popular in recent years. For many corporations, cooperative strategies capture the benefits of internal development and acquisition while avoiding the drawbacks of both.

Globalization is an important factor in the rise of cooperative ventures. In a global competitive environment, going it alone often means taking extraordinary risks. Escalating fixed costs associated with achieving global market coverage, keeping up with the latest technology, and increased exposure to currency and political risk all make risk sharing a necessity in many industries. For many companies, a global strategic posture without alliances would be untenable.

Cooperative strategies take many forms and are considered for many different reasons. However, the fundamental motivation in every case is the corporation's ability to spread its investments over a range of options, each with a different risk profile. Essentially, the corporation is trading off the likelihood of a major pay off against the ability to optimize its investments by betting on multiple options. The key drivers that attract executives to cooperative strategies include the need for risk sharing, the corporation's funding limitations, and the desire to gain market and technology access.[7]

*Risk Sharing.* Most companies cannot afford "bet the company" moves to participate in all product markets of strategic interest. Whether a corporation is considering entry into a global market or investments in new technologies, the dominant logic dictates that companies prioritize their strategic interests and balance them according to risk.

*Funding Limitations.* Historically, many companies focused on building sustainable advantage by establishing dominance in *all* of the business' value-creating activities. Through cumulative investment and vertical integration, they attempted to build barriers to entry that were hard to penetrate. However, as the globalization of the business environment accelerated and the technology race intensified, such a strategic posture became increasingly difficult to sustain. Going it alone is no longer practical in many industries. To compete in the global arena, companies must incur immense fixed costs with a shorter payback period and at a higher level of risk.

*Market Access.* Companies usually recognize their lack of prerequisite knowledge, infrastructure, or critical relationships necessary for the distribution of their products to new customers. Cooperative strategies can help them fill the gaps. For example, to further its growth strategy in Latin America, GE Money, the consumer lending unit of GE Company, acquired a minority position in Banco Colpatria–Red Multibanca Colpatria S.A., a consumer and commercial bank based in Bogota, Colombia. Banco Colpatria, a member of the Mercantil Colpatria S.A. group, has over $2.4 billion in assets and is the second largest credit card issuer in Colombia. With 139 branches, the bank serves more than one million customers. The new partnership positions the two companies to deliver enhanced consumer credit products to the growing Colombian financial services market.

*Technology Access.* A large number of products rely on so many different technologies that few companies can afford to remain at the forefront of all of them. Automakers increasingly rely on advances in electronics; application software developers depend on new features delivered by Microsoft in its next-generation operating platform, and advertising agencies need more and more sophisticated tracking data to formulate schedules for clients. At the same time, the pace at which technology is spreading globally is increasing, making time an even more critical variable in developing and sustaining competitive advantage. It is usually beyond the capabilities, resources, and good luck in R&D of any corporation to garner the technological advantage needed to independently create disruption in the marketplace. Therefore, partnering with technologically compatible companies to achieve the prerequisite level of excellence is often essential. The implementation of such strategies, in turn, increases the speed at which technology diffuses around the world.

Other reasons to pursue a cooperative strategy are a lack of particular *management skills;* an *inability to add* value in-house; and a *lack of acquisition opportunities* because of size or geographical or ownership restrictions.

Cooperative strategies cover a wide spectrum of nonequity, cross-equity, and shared-equity arrangements. Selecting the most appropriate arrangement involves analyzing the nature of the opportunity, the mutual strategic interests in the cooperative venture, and prior experience with joint ventures of both partners. The essential question is: How can we structure this opportunity to maximize the benefit(s) to both parties?

The airline industry provides a good example of some of the drivers and issues involved in forging strategic alliances. Although the U.S. industry has been deregulated for some time, international aviation remains controlled by a host of bilateral agreements that smack of protectionism. Outdated limits on foreign ownership further distort natural market forces toward a more global industry posture. As a consequence, airline companies have been forced to confront the challenges of global competition in other ways. With takeovers and mergers blocked, they have formed all kinds of alliances—from code sharing to aircraft maintenance to frequent-flier plans.

### Disinvestments: Sell-Offs, Spin-Offs, and Liquidations

At times, companies are faced with the prospect of having to retrench in one or more of their lines of business. A sell-off of a business unit to a competitor or its spin-off into a separate company makes sense when analysis confirms the corporation is the wrong corporate parent for the business. In such circumstances, value can be realized by giving the markets the opportunity to decide the fate of the business. If there are no potential buyers, liquidation might have to be considered.

## Strategy and Performance: A Conceptual Framework

Although some of the conclusions of the studies cited differ in emphasis or detail, there is a remarkable consistency to these findings. They clearly show that in today's complex business environment, no single individual—or even the top two or three people—can do all that is required to make a company successful. Corporate success increasingly depends on the willingness and ability of every manager to not just meet their own functional or divisional responsibilities but to think about how their actions influence the performance of the company as a whole. Viewed this way, organizational performance is ultimately the result of thousands of decisions and trade-offs made every day by individuals at all levels of an organization. The choices that these individuals make reflect their aspirations, knowledge, and incentives, and usually are sensible in the context of what each knows, sees, and understands.[8]

When strategies are not effective, it is therefore not very useful to question peoples' rationality. Merely restating the organization's aspirations or exhorting employees to do better is equally unproductive. Instead, the focus should be on changing the organizational environment to encourage decision making that is aligned with the overall objectives of the company. This means reexamining who makes what decisions and what information, constraints, tools, and incentives affect the way they evaluate those decisions. Understanding why and where suboptimal decisions are made is the first step to realigning the organizational environment with the chosen strategy.

Success requires that the right people—armed with the right information and motivated by the right incentives—have clear authority to make critical decisions. Developing the right organizational model thus, requires identifying which activities are critical to achieving a chosen strategy and then defining the organizational attributes that must be present to encourage the right behaviors. Therefore, companies must focus on three critical dimensions: people, knowledge, and incentives.

Figure 2.1 shows a conceptual framework for understanding the complex links between strategy and a company's performance. It has three interrelated components. The first links corporate purpose to strategy and leadership. The second describes the organizational environment in terms of five interacting components: structure, systems, processes, people, and culture. The third links a company's definition of performance with two distinct philosophies of exercising control. This framework is helpful in identifying actual or potential challenges and obstacles to successfully implementing a chosen strategic direction. It can also be used to analyze the process of strategic change.

### Strategy, Purpose, and Leadership

The so-called *strategy–structure–systems* paradigm dominated thinking about the role of corporate leaders for many years. Developed in the 1920s, when companies such as General Electric began to experiment

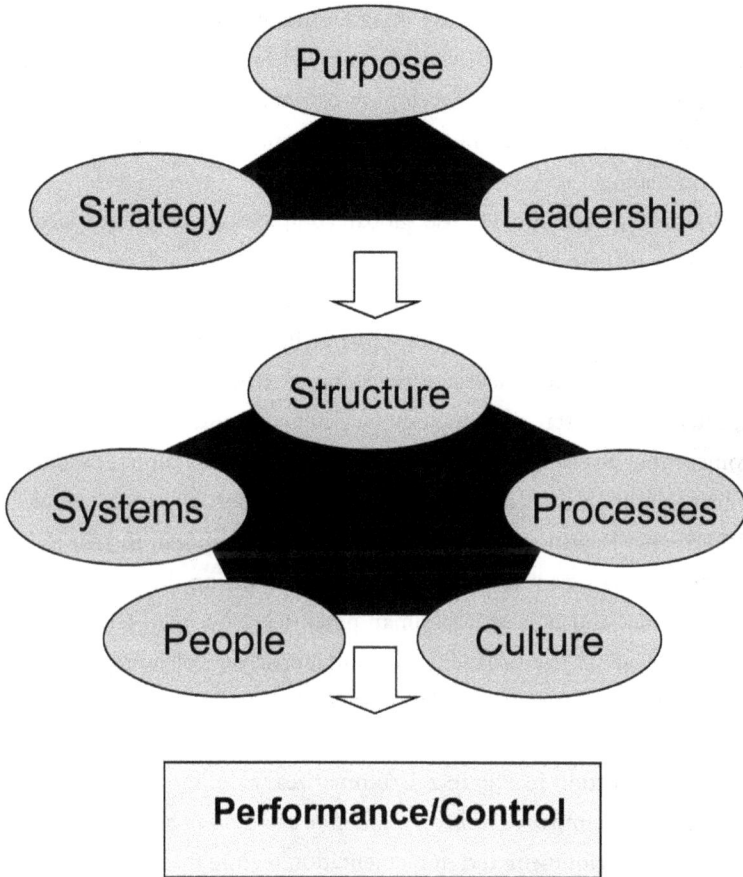

*Figure 2.1 Strategy and performance: A conceptual framework*

with diversification strategies, it held that the key to successfully executing a complex strategy was to create the right organizational structure
and disciplined planning and control support systems. Doing so, it was
thought, would systematize behavior and minimize ineffective and coun-
ter-effective actions, thereby helping managers cope with the increased
complexity associated with a multibusiness enterprise.

This doctrine remained dominant for most of the twentieth century.
It helped companies cope with high growth, integrate their operations
horizontally, manage their diversified business portfolios, and expand
internationally. The advent of global competition and the technology
revolution greatly reduced its effectiveness, however. What had been its

principal strength—minimizing human initiative—became its major weakness; the new competitive realities called for a different managerial thrust that was focused on developing corporate competencies such as innovation, entrepreneurship, horizontal coordination, and decentralized decision making.[9]

To deal with more intense global competition, corporate leaders began to articulate a broader, long-term strategic intent rooted in a clear sense of corporate purpose. In effect, they redefined their task from being the "chief strategist" to being the "chief facilitator" and sought ways to involve employees at all levels in the strategic management process. Top executive agendas started to include such items as creating organizational momentum, instilling core values, developing human capital, and recognizing individual accomplishment. In the process, the preoccupation with structural solutions was replaced by a focus on process, and the rationale behind systems was redirected toward supporting the development of capabilities and unleashing human potential rather than guiding employee behavior.[10] This broader, more humanistic view of strategic leadership recognizes that strategic discipline and control are secured through commitment, not compliance.

The top portion in Figure 2.1 summarizes these important relationships among a company's *strategy, leadership, and sense of purpose*. Successful strategy development and implementation require that these elements mutually reinforce each other as a basis for obtaining commitment, focus, and control at all levels of the organization.

## Strategy and Organizational Change

A host of factors—from structural and cultural rigidities to a lack of adequate resources to an adherence to dysfunctional processes—can reduce a company's capacity for absorbing change. It is important, therefore, for executives charged with developing and implementing new strategic directions to understand the dynamics of the various organizational forces at work.

The middle portion of Figure 2.1 shows five organizational variables— *structure, systems, processes, people,* and *culture*—that are key to creating effective organizational change. As shown, they are interrelated, which explains why the successful implementation of a new strategy often requires change in all variables. In other words, an implementation effort or corporate reorganization that is focused on just one of these variables is doomed to fail. Style, skills, and superordinate goals—values around which a business is built—are as important as strategy or structure in bringing about fundamental change in an organization.

*Structure.* To become more competitive, many companies have shed layers of management and adopted flatter organizational structures. As organizations became leaner, the problem of "how to organize" changed from one of dividing up tasks to one focused on issues of coordination. The issue of *structure,* therefore, is not just one of deciding whether to centralize or decentralize decision making. Rather, it involves identifying dimensions that are crucial to an organization's ability to adapt and evolve strategically and then adopting a structure that allows it to refocus as and when necessary.

Choosing the right organizational model is difficult. Most organizations were not created to support a specific strategy, but evolved over time in response to a host of known, as well as unknown, market forces. Finding the right model becomes more difficult as companies become larger, because growth increases complexity. As complexity increases, aligning the interests of an individual with the interests of the company becomes much more difficult. Nevertheless, the goal should be to create an organizational environment that allocates resources effectively and is naturally self-correcting as strategic changes need to be made.[11]

In considering structural options, it is important to realize that there is no "one right form of organization"; each structural solution has specific advantages and drawbacks. What is more, organizations are not homogeneous entities; what is right for one part of an organization or set of tasks might not be the preferred solution for another. No matter what form of organization is used, however, *transparency* is critical; effective strategy implementation cannot occur if lines of authority are blurred or responsibility is ill defined.

Corporate structures typically reflect one of five dominant approaches to organization: (1) *Functional* organizational structures make sense when a particular task requires the efforts of a substantial number of specialists. (2) *Geographically* based structures are useful when a company operates in a diverse set of geographical regions. (3) *Decentralized* (divisional) structures have been found to reduce complexity in a multibusiness environment. (4) *Strategic business units* help define groupings of businesses that share key strategic elements. (5) *Matrix structures* allow multiple channels of authority and are favored when coordination among different interests is key.

The growing importance of human and intellectual capital as a source of competitive advantage has encouraged companies to experiment with new organizational forms. Some companies are creating organizational structures centered on knowledge creation and dissemination. Others, in a drive to become leaner and more agile, are restricting ownership or control to only those intellectual and physical assets that are critical to their value-creation process. In doing so, they are becoming increasingly virtual and more dependent on an external network of suppliers, manufacturers, and distributors.

*Systems and Processes.*    Having the right *systems* and *processes* enhances organizational effectiveness and facilitates coping with change. Misaligned systems and processes can be a powerful drag on an organization's ability to adapt. Checking what effect, if any, current systems and processes are likely to have on a company's ability to implement a particular strategy is therefore well advised.

Support *systems,* such as a company's planning, budgeting, accounting, information, and reward and incentive systems, can be critical to successful strategy implementation. Although they do not by themselves define a sustainable competitive advantage, superior support systems help a company adapt more quickly and effectively to changing requirements. A well-designed *planning* system ensures that planning is an orderly process, gets the right amount of attention by the right executives, and has a balanced external and internal focus. *Budgeting and accounting* systems are valuable in providing accurate historical data, setting benchmarks and targets, and defining measures of performance. A state-of-the-art *information* system supports all other corporate systems and facilitates analysis as well as internal and external communication. Finally, a properly designed *reward and incentive* system is key to creating energy through motivation and commitment.

A *process* is a systematic way of doing things. Processes can be formal or informal; they define organizational roles and relationships and can facilitate or obstruct change. Some processes look beyond immediate issues of implementation to an explicit focus on developing a stronger capacity for adapting to change. Processes aimed at creating a learning organization and fostering continuous improvement are good examples.

*People.* Attracting, motivating, and retaining the right *people* have become important strategic objectives. After several episodes of mindless downsizing and rightsizing, many companies have recognized how expensive it is to replace knowledge and talent. As a result, much greater emphasis is being placed on attracting, rewarding, and retaining talent at all levels of the organization. A focus on continuous improvement through skill development is an important element of this strategy. Many companies have come to realize that developing tomorrow's skills—individually and collectively—is key to strategic flexibility. Leadership skills, in particular, are in increasing demand. Increased competitive intensity has created a greater need for leadership at all levels of the organization. The rapid pace of change and greater uncertainty in the strategic environment also have increased the difficulty of providing effective leadership.[12]

*Culture.* Performance is linked to the strength of a company's corporate culture. Common elements of strong culture include leaders who demonstrate strong values that align with the competitive conditions; a company commitment to operating under pervasive principles that are not easily abandoned; and a concern for employees, customers, and shareholders. Conversely, below-average profit performance is associated with weak corporate cultures. Employees in these cultures report experiencing separateness from the organization, development of fiefdoms, prevalence of political maneuvering, and hostility toward change.

A company's corporate culture is a shared system of values, assumptions, and beliefs among a firm's employees that provides guidance on how to think, perceive, and act. It is manifested through artifacts, shared values, and basic assumptions. *Artifacts* are visible or audible processes, policies, and procedures that support an important cultural belief. *Shared values* explain why things should be as they are. Shared values often reinforce areas of competitive advantage and can be found in internal corporate language. The words can be well defined within mission statements and codes of ethics or ambiguously embedded within company lingo. Either way, these words and phrases are used to define the image a firm wants to portray. Microsoft, for example, supports a culture of high energy, drive, intellect, and entrepreneurship. The day-to-day company language is filled with "nerdisms" such as "supercool" and "totally random." Employees touted as having "high bandwidth" (energetic and creative thinkers) are the most respected.[13] Finally, *basic assumptions* are invisible reasons why group members perceive, think, and feel the way they do about operational issues. They are sometimes demonstrated in corporate myths and stories that highlight corporate values. These legends are of considerable value because employees can identify with them and easily share them with others.

Because of its pronounced effect on employee behavior and effectiveness, companies increasingly recognize that corporate culture can set them apart from competitors. At United Parcel Service (UPS), for instance, culture is considered a strategic asset, ever growing in importance: "Managing that culture to competitive advantage involves three key priorities: recruiting and retaining the right people, nurturing innovation, and building a customer mindset."[14] UPS executives believe that the firm's culture is so important that the company spends millions of dollars annually on employee training and education programs, with a great deal of the expenditures involving the introduction of the company's culture to new employees.

A pronounced corporate culture can be an advantage or an impediment in times of rapid change. On the one hand, the continuance of core values can help employees become comfortable with or adjust to new challenges or practices. On the other hand, a company's prevailing organizational culture can inhibit or defeat a change effort when the consequences of the change are feared. For example, in a company in which consensus decision making is the norm, a change to more top–down decision making is likely to be resisted. Similarly, an organization focused on quarterly results will culturally resist a shift to a longer-term time horizon. These reactions do not constitute overt resistance to change. Rather, they represent expected responses fostered by the cultural elements ingrained over a long period of time in the organization. The failure to recognize and work within the prevailing cultural elements can doom a change agenda. For example, a large global pharmaceutical company discovered that R&D professionals resisted their promotions to management. An examination revealed that the resistance stemmed from an organizational culture bias that prevented them from competing with their peers for career rewards.[15]

## Evaluating Strategic Options

### Criteria

Estimating the likely specific impact of different broad strategy options on the long-term value or profitability of a corporation is extremely difficult. Quantifying such judgments is difficult because the impact of strategic intent and proposals aimed at realizing such intent cannot always be reduced to a cash-flow forecast. Clearly, the financial effect on the corporation of specific strategy options, such as acquisitions at the corporate level or specific new product or market entries at the business unit level, can and should be quantified. A good argument can be made, however, that broader strategic thinking does not lend itself to purely quantitative assessments. Think, for example of making a commitment to a long-term R&D program or adopting a new positioning/branding platform for the company. An alternative is to focus on a firm's future competitiveness and ask whether the long-term objectives that have been set are appropriate; whether the strategies chosen to attain such objectives are consistent, bold enough, and achievable; and whether these strategies are likely to produce a sustainable competitive advantage with above-average returns.

Nevertheless, executives face enormous pressure from within the organization and from external sources such as the financial community to forecast business unit and corporate performance and, implicitly, to quantify anticipated strategic outcomes. Traditionally, *Return on Investment* (ROI) was the most common measure for evaluating a strategy's efficacy. Today, *shareholder value* is one of the most widely accepted yardsticks.

### Shareholder Value

The *shareholder value approach* (SVA) to strategy evaluation holds that the value of the corporation is determined by the discounted future cash flows it is likely to generate. In economic terms, value is created when companies invest capital at returns that exceed the cost of that capital. Under this model, new strategic initiatives are treated as any other investment the company makes and evaluated on the basis of shareholder value. A whole new managerial framework—*value-based management* (VBM)—has been created around it.[16]

The use of shareholder value or related measures, such as *economic value added* (EVA), defined as after-tax operating profit minus the cost of capital, as the principal yardstick for evaluating alternative strategy proposals is somewhat contentious. Besides implementation problems, there are issues of transparency in the relationship between shareholder value on the one hand and positioning for sustained competitive advantage on the other. Even though shareholder value and strategy formulation are ultimately about the same thing—generating long-term sustained value—they use different conceptions of value and view the purpose of strategy from a fundamentally different point of view.

Strategists focus on creating a sustainable competitive advantage through *value delivered to customers*. But SVA measures *value to shareholders*. Though in the long run the two should be highly correlated, individual strategy proposals can force short-term trade-offs between the two. This explains why shareholder value has not been universally embraced as the preferred method for measuring a strategy's potential and has encouraged the development of new less restrictive, but also possibly less rigorous, evaluation schemes, such as the Balanced Scorecard, discussed next, in the last few years.[17]

### The Balanced Scorecard

The Balanced Scorecard is a set of measures designed to provide strategists with a quick, yet comprehensive, view of the business.[18] Developed by Robert Kaplan and David Norton, the Scorecard asks managers to look at their business from customer, company capability, innovation and learning, and financial perspectives. It provides answers to four basic questions:

(1)  How do customers see us?

(2)  At what must we excel?

(3)  Can we continue to improve and create value?

(4)  How do we look to our company's shareholders?

The Balanced Scorecard approach requires managers to translate a broad *customer-driven* mission statement into factors that directly relate to customer concerns such as product quality, on-time delivery, product performance, service, and cost. Measures are defined for each factor based on customers' perspectives and expectations, and objectives for each measure are articulated and translated into specific performance metrics. Apple Computer Corporation uses the Balanced Scorecard to introduce customer satisfaction metrics. Historically, Apple was a technology and product-focused company that competed by designing better products. Getting employees to focus on customer satisfaction metrics enabled Apple to function more as a customer-driven company.

Customer-based measures are important, but they must be translated into measures of what the company must do *internally* to meet customer expectations. Once these measures are translated into operational objectives such as cycle time, product quality, productivity, and cost, managers must focus on the internal business processes that enable the organization to meet the customers' needs.

Customer-based and internal business process measures directly relate to competitive success. The ability to create new products, provide value to customers, and improve operating efficiencies provides the basis for entering new markets that drive incremental revenue, margins, and share-holder value. Financial performance measures signal whether the company's strategy and its implementation are achieving the company objectives that relate to profitability, growth, and shareholder value. Measures such as cash flow, sales growth, operating income, market share, return on assets, ROI, return on equity, and stock price quantify the financial effects of strategies and link them to other elements of the Balanced Scorecard. A failure to convert improved operational performance, as measured in the scorecard, into improved financial performance should spur executives to rethink the company's strategy.

The application of the Balanced Scorecard has evolved into an overall management system. In essence, the scorecard encompasses four management processes: translating a vision, communicating goals and linking rewards to performance, improving business planning, and gathering feedback and learning. Separately, and in combination, the processes contribute to linking long-term strategic objectives with short-term actions.[19]

The objective of *translating a vision* is to clarify and gain employee support for that vision. For people to be able to act effectively on a vision statement, that statement must be expressed in terms of an integrated set of objectives and measures that are based on recognized long-term drivers of success. The application of the scorecard also is useful in highlighting gaps in employee skill sets, information technology, and processes that can hamper an organization's ability to execute a given strategy.

Thorough and broad-based *communication* is essential to ensure that employees understand the firm's objectives and the strategies that are designed to achieve them. Business unit and individual goals must then be aligned with those of the company to create ownership and accountability. *Linking rewards* to the Balanced Scorecard is a direct means of measuring and rewarding contributions to strategic performance. Clearly defined, objective performance measures and incentives are key to creating the right motivational environment.

Creating a Balanced Scorecard forces companies to *integrate* their strategic planning and budgeting processes. The output of the business-planning process consists of a set of long-term targets in all four areas of the scorecard (customer, internal, innovation/learning, and financial), a set of clearly defined initiatives to meet the targets, an agreed-upon allocation of resources to support these initiatives, and a set of appropriate measures to monitor progress. In this process, financial budgeting remains important but does not drive or overshadow the other elements. Finally, managers must constantly gather *feedback* on the Balanced Scorecard's short-term measurements to monitor progress in achieving the long-term strategy and to *learn* how performance can be improved. Deviations from expected outcomes indicate that assumptions regarding market conditions, competitive pressures, and internal capabilities need to be revisited. As such, this feedback assists in assessing whether a chosen strategy needs to be revised in light of updated information about competitive conditions.

# CHAPTER 3

# Analyzing the External Strategic Environment

## Introduction

Changes in the broader economic, technological, political, and sociocultural environment, which often are beyond the control of any single company, can have a profound effect on a company's success. *Environmental* forces of change arise from the interactions between people and their environment, such as the growth in the world's population or the phenomenon of urbanization. They impact resource management, health, and the quality of life for people around the world. *Technological* forces of change—advances in biotechnology, nanotechnology, and information systems—power economic growth and development, global integration, and the speed by which the global economy is becoming a "knowledge" economy. *Societal* forces of change represent shifts in international governance and in political and cultural values, such as the current wave of democratization, deregulation, and governance reform.

We focus on three forces that perhaps have had the greatest impact on strategic thinking.

*Globalization* has increased the interdependence between the world's major economies and intensified competition in many industries. In the process, entire industries have been restructured based on deconstructed value chains, new forms of competition have emerged, and "virtual corporations" have become a reality. The *technology* revolution has changed the way we live, work, and unwind, spawning entirely new industries. And a growing concern for the environment has prompted many companies to research their "footprint," restructure supply chains, or even radically change their business models, all because they recognize that a commitment to *corporate social responsibility* (CSR) has virtually become a business imperative.

## Globalization

Globalization as a political, economic, and social force appears all but unstoppable. The ever-faster flow of information across the globe has made people aware of the tastes, preferences, and life styles of citizens in other countries. Through this information flow, we are all becoming—at varying speeds and at least in economic terms—global citizens. This convergence is controversial, even offensive, to some who consider globalization a threat to their identity and way of life. It is therefore not surprising that globalization has evoked counterforces aimed at preserving differences and deepening a sense of local identity.

At the same time, we increasingly take advantage of what a global economy has to offer—we drive BMWs and Toyotas, work with an Apple or IBM notebook, communicate with a Samsung phone, wear Zara clothes or Nike sneakers, and drink Coca-Cola and Heineken beer. This is equally true for the buying habits of businesses. The market boundaries for IBM global services, GE aircraft engines, or PricewaterhouseCoopers are no longer defined in political or geographic terms. Rather, it is the intrinsic value of the products and services that defines their appeal. Like it or not, we are living in a global economy.

Globalization is not new. For thousands of years, people—and, later, corporations—have been buying from and selling to each other in lands at great distances, such as through the famed Silk Road across Central Asia that connected China and Europe during the Middle Ages. Likewise, for centuries, people and corporations have invested in enterprises in other countries. In fact, many of the features of the current wave of globalization are similar to those prevailing before the outbreak of the First World War in 1914.

The current wave of globalization is driven by policies that have opened economies domestically and internationally. In the years since the Second World War, a growing number of countries have adopted free-market economic systems, vastly increasing their own productive potential and creating myriad new opportunities for international trade and investment. Governments have also negotiated dramatic reductions in barriers to commerce and have established international agreements to promote trade in goods, services, and investment. Taking advantage of new opportunities in foreign markets, corporations have built foreign factories and established production and marketing arrangements with foreign partners. A defining feature of globalization, therefore, is an international industrial and financial business structure.

Technology has been the other principal driver of globalization. Advances in information technology, in particular, have dramatically transformed economic life. Information technologies have given all sorts of individual economic actors—consumers, investors, and businesses—valuable new tools for identifying and pursuing economic opportunities, including faster and more informed analyses of economic trends around the world, easy transfers of assets, and collaboration with far-flung partners.

### How Global Are We?

Nevertheless, it would be wrong to conclude that we are inevitably moving toward a fully globalized, integrated, and homogenized future. There are regions and markets that resist globalization—especially Western globalization—evidence that differences between countries and cultures remain substantial, perhaps larger than is generally acknowledged and that *"semiglobalization"* is the real state of the world today and likely to remain so for the foreseeable future.[1]

Research by Moore and Rugman supports the notion of a semiglobalized world and suggest a more regional perspective. They note that while companies source goods, technology, information, and capital from around the world, business activity tends to be centered in certain cities or regions around the world and suggest that regions rather than global opportunity should be the focus of strategy analysis and organization. As examples, they cite recent decisions by DuPont and Procter & Gamble to roll their three separate country subsidiaries for the United States, Canada, and Mexico into one regional organization.[2]

The histories of Toyota, Wal-Mart, and Coca-Cola corroborate the diagnosis of a semiglobalized /regionally divided world. Toyota's globalization has always had a distinct regional flavor. Its starting point was *not* a grand, long-term vision of a fully integrated world in which autos and auto parts can flow freely from anywhere to anywhere. Rather, the company anticipated expanded free-trade agreements within the Americas, Europe, and East Asia, but not across them.[3]

The globalization of Wal-Mart also illustrates the complex realities of a more nuanced global competitive landscape. It has been successful in markets that are culturally and economically closest to the United States: Canada, Mexico, and the United Kingdom. In others, it has failed to meet its profitability targets. The point is not that Wal-Mart should not have ventured into culturally more distant markets, but rather that such opportunities require a different competitive approach. For example, in India, which restricts foreign direct investment in retailing, Wal-Mart was forced to enter a joint venture with an Indian partner Bharti that operates the stores while Wal-Mart deals with the back-end of the business.

Finally, consider the history of Coca-Cola which, in the late 1990s under CEO Roberto Goizueta, fully bought into the notion that a fully globalized, homogeneous future was imminent. Goizueta embarked on a strategy that involved focusing resources on Coke's megabrands, an unprecedented amount of standardization, and the official dissolution of the boundaries between Coke's U.S. and international organization. Years later and under new leadership, Coke's strategy looks very different and is no longer always the same in different parts of the world: In big emerging markets, such as China and India, Coke has lowered price points, reduced costs by localizing inputs and modernizing bottling operations, and upgraded logistics and distribution, especially in rural areas. The boundaries between the U.S. and international organizations have been restored recognizing the fact that Coke faces very different challenges in the United States than it does in most of the rest of the world since per capita consumption is an order of magnitude higher in the United States.

### The Persistence of Distance[4]

The notion of a semiglobalized world exemplifies the persistence of distance. Ghemawat analyzes distance between countries or regions in terms of four dimensions: *cultural, administrative, geographic, and economic,* each of which influences business in different ways.

*Cultural Distance.*    A country's culture shapes how people interact with each other and with organizations. Differences in religious beliefs, race, social norms, and language can quickly become barriers; that is, "create distance." The influence of some of these attributes is obvious. A common language, for example, makes trade much easier and therefore more likely. The impact of others is much more subtle, however. Social norms, the set of unspoken principles that strongly guides everyday behavior, are mostly invisible. Japanese and European consumers, for example, prefer smaller automobiles and household appliances than Americans, reflecting a social norm that highly values space. The food industry must concern itself with religious attributes; Hindus do not eat beef because it is expressly forbidden by their religion. Thus, cultural distance shapes preference and ultimately choice.

*Administrative or Political Distance.*    Administrative or political distance is created by differences in governmental laws, policies, and institutions, including international relationships between countries, treaties, and membership in international organizations. The greater the distance, the less likely it is that extensive trade relations develop. This explains the advantage shared historical colonial ties, membership in the same regional trading bloc, and the use of a common currency can confer. The integration of the European Union over the last half-century is probably the best example of deliberate efforts to reduce administrative distance among trading partners. Bad relationships can increase administrative distance, however. Although India and Pakistan share a colonial past, a land border, and linguistic ties, their long-standing mutual hostility has reduced official trade to almost nothing.

*Geographic Distance.*    Geographic distance is about more than how far away a country is in miles. Other geographic attributes include the physical size of the country, average within-country distances to borders, access to waterways and the ocean, and topography, and such man-made as a country's transportation and communication infrastructure. Geographic attributes most directly influence transportation costs and therefore are particularly relevant to businesses with low value-to-weight or bulk ratios, such as steel and cement. Likewise, costs for transporting fragile or perishable products become significant across large distances. Intangible goods and services are affected by geographic distance as well; cross-border equity flows between two countries fall off significantly as the geographic distance between them rises. This is a direct result of differences in information infrastructure—telephone, Internet, and banking.

*Economic Distance.*    Disposable income is the most important economic attribute that creates distance between countries. Rich countries engage in proportionately higher levels of cross-border economic activity than poorer ones. The greater the economic distance is between a company's home country and the host country, the greater the likelihood that it must make significant adaptations to its business model. Wal-Mart in India, for instance, would be a very different business from Wal-Mart in the United States. But Wal-Mart in Canada is virtually a carbon copy.

### Industry Globalization Drivers

Four sets of "industry globalization drivers"—underlying conditions in each industry that create the potential for that industry to become global—affect the viability of a global approach to strategy formulation.[5] *Market drivers*—the degree to which customer needs converge around the world, customers procure on a global basis, worldwide channels of distribution develop, marketing platforms are transferable, and "lead" countries can be identified in which most innovation takes place—define how customer behavior distribution patterns evolve. *Cost globalization* drivers—the opportunity for global scale or scope economics, experience effects, sourcing efficiencies reflecting differentials in costs between countries or regions, and technology advantages—shape the economics of the industry. *Competitive* drivers are defined by the actions of competing firms—the extent to which competitors from different continents enter the fray, globalize their strategies and corporate capabilities, and the degree to which they create interdependence between geographical markets. *Government* drivers include such factors as favorable trade policies, a benign regulatory climate, and common product and technology standards.

## Globalization Has Changed Competition's Center of Gravity

The rapid emergence of the developing economies—led by the so-called BRIC countries (Brazil, Russia, India, and China)—has shifted the global competitive center of gravity. For the last 50 years, the globalization of business has primarily been interpreted as the expansion of trade from developed to emerging economies. Today this view is no longer tenable—business now flows in both directions, and increasingly also from one developing economy to another. Or, as the authors of "Globality," consultants at the Boston Consulting Group (BCG), put it: Business these days is all about "competing with everyone from everywhere for everything."[6]

The evidence that this shift in the global competitive landscape will have seismic proportions is already formidable. Consider, for example, the growing number of companies from emerging markets that appear in the *Fortune* 500 rankings of the world's biggest firms. It now approaches 100, mostly from the BRIC economies, and is set to rise further. If current trends persist, emerging-market companies may well account for one-third of the *Fortune* list within 10 years.

Look also at the recent sharp increase in the number of emerging-market companies acquiring established rich-world businesses and brands, proof that "globalization" is no longer just another word for "Americanization." For instance, Budweiser, the maker of United States' favorite beer, was bought by a Belgian–Brazilian conglomerate. And several of United States' leading financial institutions avoided bankruptcy only by being bailed out by the sovereign-wealth funds (state-owned investment funds) of various Arab kingdoms and the Chinese government. As these examples suggest, "Globality" is creating huge opportunities—as well as threats—for developed-world multinationals and new champions from developing countries alike.

## Globalization Pressures on Companies

Gupta, Govindarajan, and Wang identify five "imperatives" that drive companies to become more global: *to pursue growth, efficiency, or knowledge, to better meet customer needs, and to preempt or counter competition.*[7]

*Growth.*   In many industries, markets in the developed countries are maturing at a rapid rate limiting the rate of growth. Consider household appliances. In the developed part of the world, most households have or have access to appliances, such as stoves, ovens, washing machines, dryers, and refrigerators. Industry growth is therefore largely determined by population growth and product replacement. In developing markets, in contrast, household penetration rates for major appliances are still low compared to Western standards thereby offering significant growth opportunities for manufacturers.

*Efficiency.*   A global presence automatically expands a company's scale of operations giving it larger revenues and larger asset base. A larger scale can help create a competitive advantage if a company undertakes the tough actions needed to convert scale into *economies of scale* by (1) spreading fixed costs, (2) reducing capital and operating costs, (3) pooling purchasing power, and (4) creating critical mass in a significant portion of the value chain. On the demands side, increasing or decreasing the scope of marketing and distribution by entering new markets or regions, or by increasing the range of products and services offered offers opportunities to realize *economies of scope.* The economic value of global scope can be substantial when serving global customers through providing coordinated services and the ability to leveraging a company's expanded market power.

*Knowledge.*   Foreign operations can be a reservoir of knowledge. Some locally created knowledge is relevant across multiple countries and, if leveraged effectively, can yield significant strategic benefits to a global enterprise, such as (1) faster product and process innovation, (2) lower cost of innovation, and (3) reduced risk of competitive preemption. For example, Fiat developed Palio—its global car—in Brazil; Texas Instruments uses a collaborative process between Indian and U.S. engineers to design its most advanced chips; and Procter & Gamble's liquid Tide was developed as a joint effort by U.S. employees (technology to suspend dirt in water), the Japanese subsidiary (cleaning agents), and the Brussels operations (agents that fight mineral salts found in hard water). Most companies tap only a fraction of the full potential in realizing the economic value inherent in transferring and leveraging knowledge across borders. Significant geographic, cultural, linguistic distances often separate subsidiaries. The challenge is to create systematic and routine mechanisms to uncover opportunities for knowledge transfer.

*Globalization of Customer Needs and Preferences.* When customers start to globalize their behavior, a firm has little choice but to follow and adapt its business model to accommodate them. Multinationals such as Coca-Cola, GE, and DuPont increasingly insist that their suppliers—from raw material suppliers to advertising agencies to personnel recruitment companies—become more global in their approach and be prepared to serve them whenever and wherever required. Individuals are no different; global travelers insist on consistent worldwide service from airlines, hotel chains, credit card companies, television news, and others.

*Globalization of Competitors.* Just as the globalization of customers compels companies to consider globalizing their business model, so does the globalization of one or more major competitors. A competitor who globalizes early may have a first-mover advantage in emerging markets, greater opportunity to create economies of scale and scope, and an ability to cross-subsidize competitive battles thereby posing a greater threat in the home market. A good example of these forces at work is provided by the global beer market. Over the past decade, the beer industry has seen significant consolidation and this trend continues. On a pro forma basis, beer sales by the top 10 players now total approximately 65 percent of total global sales compared to less than 40 percent at the start of the century.

### Global Strategy and Risk[8]

Even with the best planning, globalization carries substantial risks. Many globalization strategies represent a considerable stretch of the company's experience base, resources, and capabilities. The firm might target new markets, often in new—for the company—cultural settings. It might seek new technologies, initiate new partnerships, or adopt market-share objectives that require earlier or greater commitments than current returns can justify. In the process, new and different forms of competition can be encountered, and it could turn out that the economic model that got the company to its current position is no longer applicable. Often, a more global posture implies exposure to different cyclical patterns, currency, and political risk. In addition, there are substantial costs associated with coordinating global operations. As a consequence, before deciding to enter a foreign country or a continent, companies should carefully analyze the risks involved. In addition, companies should recognize that the management style that proved successful on a domestic scale might turn out to be ineffective in a global setting.

## The Technology Revolution[9]

Technological advances continue to challenge and surprise us in all dimensions of life—from social to economic to political and personal. Advances in biotechnology will enable us to identify, understand, manipulate, improve, and control living organisms (including ourselves). The information revolution continues to profoundly change how we work, interact, and relax. And smart materials, agile manufacturing, and nanotechnology are altering the way we create products and processes. Soon, all these may be joined by "wild cards" such as molecular manufacturing—the idea of assembling objects atom-by-atom (or molecule-by-molecule) from the bottom-up (rather than from the top-down using conventional fabrication techniques)—if barriers to their development are resolved in time.

The results will likely be astonishing. Effects may include longer life spans, a redistribution of wealth, shifts in power from nation states to nongovernmental organizations and individuals, mixed environmental effects, improvements in quality of life, and the possibility of human eugenics and cloning.

The actual realization of these possibilities will depend on a host of factors, including local acceptance of technological change, levels of technology and infrastructure investments, market drivers and limitations, and technology breakthroughs and advancements. Since these factors vary across the globe, the implementation and effects of technology will also vary, especially in developing countries. Nevertheless, the overall revolution and trends will continue through much of the developed world.

### The Internet Has Changed Business

The Internet has revolutionized the way business is conducted. Some of the major changes brought about by the Internet relate to the way we purchase products and services, obtain information, and conduct our banking. Customers can quickly find product and price information and obtain advice from a wide variety of sellers. Online visitors can check product availability, place an order, check the status of an order, or pay electronically. This so-called "e-tailing" has increased competition by pitting local against national and international competitors.

Internet-based technologies have significantly reduced the marginal cost of producing and distributing digital goods such as software, news stories, music, photographs, stock quotes, horoscopes, sports scores, and health tips. Some firms such as America Online are selling large aggregations of such digital goods for a low flat monthly fee. Such aggregation of so many products would be extremely expensive using traditional distribution media. Such bundling offers economies of scale and scope that favor large distributors and make it difficult for smaller companies that sell unbundled products to compete effectively.[10] The Internet also enables customization of products. Online customers can purchase personal computers on the Internet in a variety of combinations by choosing the appropriate features. Music retailers can create CDs containing songs ordered by customers. And search engines such as Google and Yahoo recommend relevant products or services on the basis of keywords supplied by users.

Online companies have successfully created strong e-brands and highly satisfied customers by providing them with a positive experience and with the use of traditional advertising and promotional efforts. Many of the factors that lead to higher customer satisfaction and loyalty in traditional businesses also work in e-businesses. Delivering excellent service and value is equally important for customer satisfaction, customer loyalty, and retention in offline and online businesses. Companies hoping to attract and most importantly retain visitors to their website need to offer online customers superior value and satisfaction. Branding is becoming important in Internet-based businesses because online consumers prefer to buy from well-known and reputable e-companies. Companies such as

Amazon.com and Schwab are widely known, recognized, and trusted by online consumers. Gaining people's trust is a major challenge for Internet companies as many online visitors are reluctant to provide credit-card information because they do not trust the sites they visit. Traditional retailers with established names usually have an advantage over certain Internet-only companies because they have been known for years and enjoy a higher degree of trust by consumers. The reputation and image of the website may have an impact on the offline business.

### The Impact of "Big Data"

We have entered the era of "big data." Today companies collect and process an exponentially growing volume of transactional data about their customers, suppliers, and operations. To capture these data, millions of networked sensors are being embedded in devices such as mobile phones, smart energy meters, automobiles, and industrial machines that sense, create, and communicate. Social media sites, smartphones, and other consumer devices including PCs and laptops have allowed billions of individuals around the world to contribute to the amount of big data available. Many citizens regard this collection of information with deep suspicion, fearing a growing potential for invasion of their privacy. But there is another side to this coin—big data has the potential to create significant value and enhance competitiveness.[11]

ShopAlerts, developed by PlaceCast of San Francisco and New York, is a location-based "push SMS" product that companies including Starbucks, North Face, Sonic, REI, and American Eagle Outfitters are using to drive traffic to their stores. Advertisers define a geographic boundary in which to send opted-in users a push SMS typically in the form of a promotion or advertisement to visit a particular store; in general, a user would receive no more than three such alerts a week. ShopAlerts claims 1 million users worldwide. In the United States, the company says it can locate more than 90 percent of the mobile phones in use nationwide. The company reports that 79 percent of consumers surveyed say that they are more likely to visit a store when they receive a relevant SMS; 65 percent of respondents said they made a purchase because of the message; and 73 percent said they would probably or definitely use the service in the future.[12]

Tesco—a major grocery chain in the United Kingdom—credits its use of big data for capturing market share from its local competitors. Its loyalty program generates a tremendous amount of customer data that the company mines to inform decisions from promotions to strategic segmentation of customers. Similarly, Amazon uses customer data to power its recommendation engine "you may also like..." based on a type of predictive modeling technique called collaborative filtering. By making supply and demand signals visible between retail stores and suppliers, Wal-Mart was an early adopter of vendor-managed inventory to optimize the supply chain. Harrah's, the U.S. hotels and casinos group, compiles detailed holistic profiles of its customers and uses them to tailor marketing in a way that has increased customer loyalty. Progressive Insurance and Capital One are both known for conducting experiments to segment their customers systematically and effectively and to tailor product offers accordingly.

### New Business Models

The arrival of big data, coupled with other advances in business, is enabling the emergence of innovative business models that threaten traditional ones. In the retail sector, for example, two new business models with the most traction today are price-comparison services and web-based markets.

*Price-Comparison Services.* It is common today for third parties to offer real-time or near-real-time pricing and related price transparency on products across multiple retailers. Consumers can instantly compare the price of a specific product at multiple retail outlets. Where these comparisons are possible, prices tend to be lower. Studies show that consumers are saving an average of 10 percent when they can shop using such services. Retailers need to carefully think about how to respond to such price-comparison services. Those that can compete on price will want to ensure that they are the most visible on such services. Retailers that cannot compete on price will need to determine how to differentiate themselves from competitors in a price-transparent world, whether it is in the quality of the shopping experience, differentiated products, or the provision of other value-added services.

*Web-Based Markets.*   Web-based marketplaces, such as those provided by Amazon and eBay, provide searchable product listings from a large number of vendors. In addition to price transparency, they offer access to a large number of niche retailers that otherwise would not have the marketing or sales horsepower to reach consumers. They also provide a tremendous amount of useful product information, including consumer-generated reviews that provide further transparency to consumers.

Beyond increasing productivity, big data is spawning innovative services and entirely new business models in manufacturing as well. For example, sensor data have made possible innovative after-sale services. BMW's ConnectedDrive offers drivers directions based on real-time traffic information, automatically calls for help when sensors indicate trouble, alerts drivers of maintenance needs based on the actual condition of the car, and feeds operation data directly to service centers. The ability to exchange data across the extended enterprise has also enabled production to be unbundled radically into highly distributed networks. For example, Li and Fung, a supplier to apparel retailers, manages a network of more than 7,500 suppliers, each of which focuses on delivering a very specific part of the supply chain.

## Corporate Social Responsibility— A New Business Imperative

CSR, concerned with better aligning a company's activities with the social, economic, and environmental expectations of its stakeholders, has become an important strategic issue for most companies. Also sometimes referred to with terms such as *corporate responsibility, corporate citizenship, responsible business, sustainability, eco-friendliness,* or *corporate social performance,* CSR promotes the integration of a form of corporate self-regulation into a whole range of corporate business practices. Ideally, a focus on CSR would function as a built-in, self-regulating mechanism whereby companies would monitor and ensure their adherence to law, ethical standards, environmental standards, and international norms, and take full responsibility for the impact of their activities on the environment, consumers, employees, communities, stakeholders, and other citizens. CSR-focused businesses proactively promote the public interest by encouraging community growth and development, and voluntarily eliminate practices that are viewed as harmful, regardless of legality. CSR therefore reflects the deliberate inclusion of public interest into corporate decision making and the honoring of a triple bottom line: people, planet, and profit.

## A New Compact Between Business and Society?

Given its recent origin and complexity, it is not surprising that CSR is often misunderstood. Is it a moral and ethical issue? Is it a new approach to compliance and risk management? Or is it a strategic issue—an opportunity to differentiate a company and build customer loyalty based on distinctive ethical values? The simple answer is that it can be all of the above.

Societal considerations increasingly force companies to rethink their approach to core strategy and business model design. Dealing more effectively with a company's full range of stakeholders therefore has become a strategic imperative. Historically, the amount of attention paid to stakeholders, other than directly affected parties, such as employees or major investors, in crafting strategy has been limited. Issues pertaining to communities, the environment, the health and happiness of employees, human rights violations of global supply chains, and activist NGOs, among numerous other issues, were dealt with by the company's public relations department or its lawyers.

Today, "business as usual" is no longer an option, and traditional strategies for companies to grow, cut costs, innovate, differentiate, and globalize are now subject to a set of new laws of doing business in relationship to society[13]:

1. *Size means scrutiny.* The bigger a company is, and the more market dominance it achieves, the more attention and demand it faces for exemplary performance in ethical behavior, good governance, environmental management, employee practices, product development that improves quality of life, support for communities, honest marketing, and so on.

2. *Cutting costs raises compliance risk.* The more companies use traditional means to cut costs—finding low-wage producers in less

developed countries, pressuring suppliers, downsizing, cutting corners, and so on—the more potential there is for crises related to noncompliant ethical practices. The risks involved in successfully complying with society's expectations for ethical behavior, safety, product liability, environmental practices, and good treatment of all stakeholders might well outweigh the benefits accrued from these kinds of cost savings.

3. *Strategy must involve society.* For forward-thinking companies, social and environmental problems represent the growth opportunities of the future. For example, GE is looking to solve challenges related to the scarcity of global natural resources and changing demographics, while IBM has made social innovation a priority alongside business product and process innovation.

4. *Reducing risks means building trust.* Classic risk management strategies must expand beyond financial and currency analysis to include destabilizing trends and events arising from society. Smart leaders realize that no company can manage these risks if it does not earn the trust of society's leaders and of its communities.

5. *Satisfying shareholders means satisfying stakeholders.* In the long run, the company that pays attention to the business–society relationship ultimately serves its investors' interests because (a) its antennae are better tuned to identifying risk, (b) it is able to build trust with its stakeholders, and (c) it is well positioned to develop goods and services that society values.

6. *Global growth requires global gains.* Increasingly, growth requires a global perspective that recognizes the importance of strong local communities that supply infrastructure; maintain stable business climates; attract investment capital; supply healthy, educated workers; and support growth that generates consumers with greater purchasing power. But long-term growth also requires development.

7. *Productivity requires sustainability.* Companies have seen that commitment to environmental management and safety in the workplace has been a driver of lower costs and greater productivity. In addition, companies that take on the challenge of constraining their behavior through commitments to corporate citizenship find new incentive

to innovate to compete. The more companies innovate, the more productive and sustainable they become.

8. *Differentiation relies on reputation.* In the United States, an estimated 50 million people, representing over $225 billion a year in purchasing power, comprise the emerging "lifestyles of health and sustainability" consumer base. As the influence of these activist consumers grows, they will demand companies to demonstrate sterling reputations and commitment to society.

9. *Good governance needs good representation.* A spate of corporate scandals has generated stricter controls and comprehensive governance reforms. These changes reflect an underlying revolution calling for companies to include stakeholders in formal governance.

These "laws" are likely to play a key role in strategy formulation in the years ahead. Companies that accept, understand, and embrace them will find that being a "good citizen" has significant strategic value and does not detract from but actually enhances business success.

## How "Going Green" Can Pay Off[14]

One area where a concern for society and strategic opportunity can be seen to be firmly aligned is the environment. Thanks to aggressive leadership by some of the world's biggest companies—Wal-Mart, GE, and DuPont among them—green growth has risen to the top of the agenda for many businesses. From 2007 to 2009, eco-friendly product launches increased by more than 500 percent. A recent IBM survey found that two-thirds of executives see sustainability as a revenue driver, and half of them expect green initiatives to confer competitive advantage. This dramatic shift in corporate mind-set and practices over the past decade reflects a growing awareness that environmental responsibility can be a platform for both growth and differentiation.[15]

Reducing energy use, for example, is one environmental tenet that is a virtual no-brainer. United Parcel Service (UPS), one of the world's largest package delivery companies, began adding hybrid vehicles to its fleet in 2006 to test whether the introduction of these vehicles might reduce their fuel costs (about 5 percent of their operating expenditures in 2006). UPS has demonstrated that a shift in consumer sentiment toward environmental preservation can be good for the company's bottom line. For almost a decade, it has managed fuel consumption and greenhouse gas emissions as a business opportunity—one that can improve the bottom line, reduce the company's impact and on the environment, and increase the long-term viability of the company.

In addition, with pressure increasing for the government to make regulations to curb corporate pollution, many companies are moving toward adopting some environmental practices before such regulations are put in place. Companies like Alcoa and Dupont, for example, have established systems to reduce carbon emission and other harmful chemicals, the most likely targets for government intervention. Leading the way, these companies, while reducing their impact on the environment, are also mitigating the future risks of regulatory shocks in the future.

Today, manufacturers, service sector companies, professional service firms, retailers, and Internet and telecommunication companies are all focused on finding smart ways to make sustainability work in their businesses. For example:

- General Mills redesigned the packaging of Hamburger Helper to conserve paperboard without reducing the product content. Thanks to increased shipping efficiency, product distribution now requires 500 fewer trucks per year.
- Interface, one of the world's leading interior furnishing companies, formed an "Eco Dream Team" to design a safer and healthier way to run the business. The team helped the company cut the use of fossil fuels by 45 percent and landfill use by 80 percent.
- Hubbard Hall, a leading chemical distributor, has developed a series of green services to help customers track their chemical inventories, handle regulatory paperwork, and properly dispose of hazardous containers. These services make a valuable contribution to the environment. They also help Hubbard Hall compete effectively with Internet direct marketers.

- 3M's Pollution Prevention Pays (3P) program has helped eliminate more than 2 billion pounds of pollutants from the environment. When it was launched in 1970, it achieved $1 billion in savings the very first year.[16]

Improved public relations and positive public perception can also have a major impact on a company's bottom line. Nike Inc., which set targets to reduce waste and packaging and become "climate neutral," and Hewlett-Packard (HP), which is working toward reducing waste and setting up recycling services for electronic waste, made the Global 100 Most Sustainable Corporations in the World list based on how well they managed environmental risks and opportunities compared to their competitors. The Global 100 compares companies to peers in their sectors and selects companies on a "best-in-class" basis. Global 100 analysts believe these sustainable corporations will create long-term value for shareholders through cost reduction, innovation, and other competitive advantages that result from sustainable practices. This suggests that, if constructively approached, getting ahead of the curve by being green actually represents an opportunity for companies to create a competitive advantage over their rivals.

## Risk and Uncertainty

Many strategic choices involve future events that are difficult to predict. The success of a new product introduction, for example, can depend on such factors as how current and potential competitors will react, the quality of components procured from outside suppliers, and the state of the economy. To capture the lack of predictability, decision-making situations are often described along a continuum of states ranging from *certainty* to *risk* to *uncertainty*. Under conditions of certainty, accurate, measurable information is available about the outcome of each alternative considered. When an event is risky, we cannot predict its outcome with certainty but have enough information to assess its probability. Under conditions of uncertainty, little is known about the alternatives or their outcomes.

To make analysis of the strategic environment actionable, we must be able to assess the degree of *uncertainty* associated with relevant events, the *speed* with which changes are likely to occur, and the possible *outcomes* they foreshadow. Conditions of certainty and risk lend themselves to formal analysis; uncertainty presents unique problems. Some changes take place gradually, and are knowable, if not predictable. We might not be able to determine exactly when and how they affect a specific industry or issue, but their broad effect is relatively well understood. The globalization of the competitive climate and most demographic and social trends fall into this category. The prospect of new industry regulations creates a more immediate kind of uncertainty—the new regulatory structure will either be adopted or it will not. The collapse of boundaries between industries constitutes yet another scenario: The change forces themselves may be identifiable, but their outcomes might not be totally predictable. Finally, there are change forces such as the sudden collapse of foreign governments, outbreaks of war, or major technological discoveries that are inherently random in nature and cannot be easily foreseen.

### Analyzing Uncertainty[17]

Courtney, Kirkland, and Viguerie argue that a binary approach to dealing with uncertainty in which the future is either thought to be known or unknown can be dangerous and that forcing precise predictions in inherently uncertain situations can lead to seriously deficient strategic thinking. Instead, they suggest we focus on the degree of *residual* uncertainty present in the strategic environment—the uncertainty that remains after all knowable change forces have been analyzed and distinguished between four levels of residual uncertainty:

> *Level 1: A clear-enough future*: Some strategic environments are sufficiently transparent and stable that a single forecast of the future can be made with a reasonable degree of confidence. A number of mature, low-technology industries fall into this category. It also applies to more narrowly defined strategic challenges such as countering a specific competitor in a specific market or region.
>
> *Level 2: Alternate futures*: At times, the future can be envisioned in terms of a small number of *discrete* scenarios. In such cases, we may not be able to forecast with any precision which outcome will

occur, but the set of possible outcomes is fully understood. Businesses that are affected by major legislative or regulatory changes fall into this category.

*Level 3: A range of futures*: This level defines a higher level of uncertainty in which we can identify the key variables that are likely to shape the future, but we cannot reduce this knowledge to a few discrete, plausible outcomes. Instead, a range of almost *continuous* outcomes is possible. Courtney et al. cite the example of a European consumer goods company trying to decide whether to introduce its products to the Indian market. The best available market research might identify only a broad range of potential market shares.

*Level 4: True ambiguity*: At this level, even the driving forces that are likely to shape the future are hard to identify. As a consequence, no discrete scenarios or even ranges of outcomes can be predicted. While level four situations are rare, they do exist. Take, for example, the challenges faced by companies doing business in the Middle East: Every aspect of the strategic environment is fraught with uncertainty. There is uncertainty about the legal aspects of doing business, about the availability of raw materials and components, about the likely demand for various products and services, and about the political stability of the region. In such situations, traditional analysis techniques and forecasting tools are of little assistance.

Situations characterized by *level one* uncertainty lend themselves to conventional analysis. Simple trend extrapolation may be sufficient to identify what is happening in the broader sociopolitical, economic, and technological environment; standard techniques of competitor analysis can also be used to clarify the picture at the industry level. At *level two*, standard techniques can be used for analyzing each discrete set of outcomes, but a different analysis may be needed for different scenarios. This can make it difficult to compare them. In addition, we must then assess the likelihood that each scenario will occur with the use of decision-analysis techniques. *Level three* situations are prime candidates for techniques such as scenario planning, described earlier. *Level four* environments are most difficult to analyze. At best a partial, mostly qualitative analysis can be performed. In these situations, it may be useful to analyze comparable, past environments and extract strategic lessons learned.

### Implications for Strategy

Courtney et al. use the terms *strategic posture*—a company's strategic intent—and *strategic moves* to construct a generic framework for formulating strategy in uncertain environments. In characterizing how firms deal with uncertainty, they distinguish between *shapers, adapters, and companies reserving the right to play.*

*Shapers* drive the industry toward a structure that is to their benefit. They are out to change the rules of the competitive game and try to control the direction of the market. An example is Amazon's goal to fundamentally change the way people shop for broad classes of products.

*Adapters* are companies that exhibit a more reactive posture. They take the current industry structure as given and often bet on gradual, evolutionary change. In strategic environments characterized by relatively low levels of uncertainty, adapters position themselves for competitive advantage within the current structure. At higher levels of uncertainty, they may behave more cautiously and fine-tune their abilities to react quickly to new developments. The airline industry provides examples of this type of strategic behavior.

The third posture, also reactive in nature, *reserves the right to play.* Companies pursuing this posture often make incremental investments to preserve their options until the strategic environment becomes easier to read or less uncertain. Making partial investments in competing technologies, taking a small equity position in different start-up companies, and experimenting with different distribution options are examples of reserving the right to play. Universities hedging their bets about the future of higher education and investing in online course delivery exemplify this strategic posture.

*Strategic moves* are action patterns aimed at realizing strategic intent. *Big bets* are large commitments mostly used by companies with shaping postures such as Tesla in the automotive industry. They often carry a high degree of risk: Potential payoffs are large but so are potential losses. *Options* target high payoffs in best-case scenarios while minimizing losses in worst-case situations. Licensing an alternative technology in case it proves superior to current technology is a good example. Finally, a *no-regret* move has a positive or neutral outcome under all scenarios and is often associated with a reserve-the-right-to-play posture.

In *level one* strategic environments—a clear-enough future—most companies are *adapters*. The industry structure is fairly stable and its evolution is relatively predictable. In this environment, conventional analysis techniques can assist with positioning the company for sustained competitive advantage. Because of the relatively high degree of predictability, such strategies by definition consist of a sequence of *no-regret* moves. This state of relative tranquility typically is maintained until a *shaper* upsets the apple cart, usually with a *big bet* move. Consider, for example, the actions of Wayne Huizinga's Republic Industries in the movie rental and waste management industries, and now with automobile dealerships.

Whereas *shapers* in level one environments raise the level of uncertainty by challenging the existing order, at levels two, three, and four their objective is to reduce uncertainty through determined action. At *level two*—alternate futures—a shaping strategy is designed to tilt the probabilities toward a specific outcome. Making a big commitment to building new capacity as a way of deterring a potential rival from entering the industry is illustrative of a shaping strategy. A heavy lobbying effort for or against a piece of legislation is an example of a non–market shaping posture. At level two, *adapting* or *reserving the right to play* is easier than at higher levels of uncertainty because the forces of change are known and only a few discrete scenarios are thought to occur.

Whereas at level two *shaping* was about forcing a particular outcome, at *level three* no discrete outcomes can be identified. As a result, at this level of uncertainty shaping strategies focus on limiting the range of possible outcomes to a smaller set of more desirable futures. Consider the earlier example of a European manufacturer wishing to enter the Indian market. A shaping strategy might involve a local partnerships or tie-ins with already-established products. *Adapter* and *reserving the right to play* strategic postures are more common at this level. Both are aimed at keeping the company's options open: *Adapters* are generally more aggressive and will craft strategy in real time as opportunities emerge; companies adopting a *reserve-the-right-to-play* posture often wait until a more definitive strategy can be adopted. At this level, options and no-regret moves are more common than big bets.

*Level four* environments are the most uncertain. Extreme uncertainty, however, may represent enormous opportunities to *shapers* who can exploit it. When true ambiguity prevails, the situation invites new rules and a sense of order. As a consequence, shaping strategies may not require big bets and in fact can be less risky at this level than at level two or three. Alternatively, adaptive strategies or a reserve-the-right-to-play posture may represent opportunities lost. Battles for technological standards, discussed earlier, come to mind.

### Scenario Analysis

Originally developed at Royal Dutch/Shell in London, *scenario analysis* is one of the most widely used techniques for constructing alternative plausible futures of a business's external environment. Its purpose is to analyze the effects of various uncontrollable change forces on the strategic playing field and to test the resiliency of specific strategy alternatives. It is most heavily used by businesses that are highly sensitive to external forces such as energy companies.

Scenario analysis is a disciplined method for imagining and examining possible futures.[18] It divides knowledge into two categories: (1) things we believe we know something about and (2) elements we consider uncertain or unknowable. The first category mainly focuses on the forward projection of knowable change forces. For example, we can safely make assumptions about demographic shifts or the substitution effects of new technologies. Obvious examples of uncertain aspects—the second category—are future interest rates, oil prices, results of political elections, and rates of innovation. Because scenarios depict possible futures but not specific strategies to deal with them, it makes sense to invite into the process outsiders, such as major customers, key suppliers, regulators, consultants, and academics. The objective is to see the future broadly in terms of fundamental trends and uncertainties and to build a shared framework for strategic thinking that encourages diversity and sharper perceptions about external changes and opportunities.

The scenario-building process involves four steps:

1. Deciding what possible future developments to probe, which trends—technological change, demographic change, or resource issues—to include, and what time horizon to consider.
2. Identifying what forces or developments are likely to have the greatest ability to shape the future.
3. Constructing a comprehensive set of future scenarios based on different combinations of possible outcomes. Some combinations will be of greater interest than others, either because they have a greater effect on the strategic issue at hand or because they are more or less likely to occur. As a result, a few scenarios usually emerge that become the focus of a more-detailed analysis.
4. Generating scenario-specific forecasts that allow an assessment of the implications of the alternative futures for strategic postures and choices.

### Limitations of Scenario Planning

Although scenario planning has gained much adherence in industry, its subjective and heuristic nature leaves many executives uncomfortable. How do we know if we have the right scenarios? And how do we go from scenarios to decisions?

Apart from some inherent subjectivity in scenario design, the technique can suffer from various process and content traps. These traps mostly relate to how the process is conducted in organizations (such as team composition and role of facilitators) as well as the substantive focus of the scenarios (long term vs. short term, global vs. regional, incremental vs. paradigm shifting, etc.). One might think of these as merely challenges of implementation, but since the process component is integral to the scenario experience, they can also be viewed as weaknesses of the methodology itself. Limited safeguards exist against political derailing, agenda control, myopia, and limited imagination when conducting scenario planning exercises within real organizations.

A third limitation of scenario planning in organizational settings is its weak integration into other planning and forecasting techniques. Most companies have plenty of trouble dealing with just one future, let alone multiple ones. Typically, budgeting and planning systems are predicated on single views of the future, with adjustments made as necessary through variance analysis, contingency planning, rolling budgets, and periodic re-negotiations. The reality is that most companies do not handle uncertainty well and that researchers have not provided adequate answers about how to plan under conditions of high uncertainty and complexity.

# CHAPTER 4

# Analyzing an Industry

## Industry Influences a Company's Options and Outcomes

The Affordable Care Act (ACA) thrust the healthcare industry into decades of upheaval and uncertainty. The ACA is designed to increase insurance coverage by expanding Medicaid eligibility in 2014 to include individuals within 138 percent of the federal poverty level, and by creating state-based insurance exchanges where individuals and small business can buy health insurance, with federal subsidies available for individuals with incomes less than 400 percent of the federal poverty level.

Accommodating 30 million new consumers, most of whom are low-income patients with little medical care histories, challenges the industry's established delivery systems. The industry, which was regularly castigated for his escalating costs and low levels of productivity, faces challenges in every facet of its operations. No business, in any segment of the healthcare industry, is immune from meaningful change because of the ACA.

Consequently, McKinsey & Company concluded that healthcare executives have entered an era of an increased number of new competitors, harsher scrutiny of their pricing structures, unprecedented focus on their operational efficiency, heightened customer sophistication, numerous changes in profitable industry segments, and an upsurge in corporate mergers in the industry.[1] Thus, healthcare is a prime example of power of industry to impact the strategic planning of individual competitors and, as we will discuss in this chapter, to influence the likelihood of their economic success.

This example highlights the importance that an industry plays in the strategic success of its corporate competitors. People tend to think of an industry as a group of companies that compete directly with each other in the marketplace. Although intuitive, the simplicity of this definition masks complex issues. Is competition primarily between products, companies, or networks of alliance partners? Should we analyze rivalry at the business unit level or at the functional level? Should we distinguish between regional competition and global rivalry?

As these questions suggest, deciding on industry boundaries is difficult and misspecification of an industry can be extremely costly. The use of too narrow a definition can lead to strategic myopia and cause executives to overlook important opportunities or threats, such as would occur by judging railroads as competing only with other railroads. The use of too broad a definition, such as identifying a firm's industry simply as "high technology," can prevent a meaningful assessment of the competitive environment.

## What Is an Industry?

An industry is a collection of firms that offer similar products or services. It can be assessed on four dimensions the *products* its competitors provide, the *customers* they serve, the *geography* in which the customers are located, and the *stage* in the *production–distribution pipeline* that is represented by its member companies. The product dimension can be further broken down into its function and technology.

Function refers to what the product or service does. Some cooking appliances bake. Others bake and roast. Still others fry or boil. Functionality can be actual or perceived. Some over-the-counter remedies for nasal congestion, for example, are positioned as cold relievers, whereas others with similar chemical formulations are promoted as allergy medicines. The difference is as much a matter of positioning and perception as of actual functionality. Technology is a second distinguishing factor: Some cooking appliances use gas, whereas others are electric; some cold remedies are available in liquid form, whereas others are sold in gel capsules.

Defining an industry's boundaries requires the simultaneous consideration of all of these dimensions. In addition, it is important to distinguish between the *industry* in which a company competes and the *market(s) it serves*. For example, a company might compete in the large kitchen appliance *industry* but choose refrigerators as its *served market*. This can be depicted as a collection of (adjacent) three-dimensional cells, each characterized by a particular combination of functions/uses, technologies/materials, and types of customers. The task of defining an industry, therefore, consists of identifying the group of market cells that are most relevant to the firm's strategic analysis.

In the process of generating strategic alternatives, it is often helpful to use multiple industry definitions. Assessing a company's growth potential, for example, might require the use of a different industry/market definition than assessing its current relative cost position.

## Industry Structure and Porter's Five Forces Model

The *five forces* model developed by Michael Porter is a useful tool for industry and competitive analysis.[2] It holds that an industry's profit potential is largely determined by the intensity of the *competitive rivalry* within that industry, and that rivalry, in turn, is explained in terms of five forces: (1) the *threat of new entrants*, (2) the *bargaining power of customers*, (3) the *bargaining power of suppliers*, (4) the *threat of substitute products or services*, and (5) the *jockeying among current rivals*.

*The Threat of Entry.*    When it is relatively easy to enter a market, an industry can be expected to be highly competitive. Potential new entrants threaten to increase the industry's capacity, to intensify the fight for market share, and to upset the balance between demand and supply. The likelihood of new entrants depends on (1) what barriers to entry exist and (2) how entrenched competitors are likely to react.

There are six major barriers to market entry: (1) economies of scale, (2) product differentiation (brand equity), (3) capital requirements, (4) cost disadvantages that are independent of size, (5) access to distribution channels, and (6) government regulations. Consider, for example, the difficulty of entering the soft drink industry and competing with advertising giants such as Coca-Cola and Pepsi Cola or the plight of microbrewers trying to gain distribution for their brands of beer against major companies such as Anheuser-Busch. In high-technology industries, capital requirements and accumulated experience serve as major barriers. Industry conditions can change, however, and cause strategic windows of opportunity to open.

*Powerful Suppliers and Buyers.*    Buyers and suppliers influence competition in an industry by exerting pressure over prices, quality, or the quantity demanded or sold.

Generally, suppliers are more powerful when (1) there are a few dominant companies and they are more concentrated than the industry they serve; (2) the component supplied is differentiated, making switching among suppliers difficult; (3) there are few substitutes; (4) suppliers can integrate forward; and (5) the industry generates but a small portion of the suppliers' revenue base.

Buyers have substantial power when (1) there are few of them and/ or they buy in large volume; (2) the product is relatively undifferentiated, making it easy to switch to other suppliers; (3) the buyers' purchases represent a sizable portion of the sellers' total revenues; and (4) buyers can integrate backward.

*Substitute Products and Services.*    Substitute products and services continually threaten most industries and, in effect, place a lid on prices and profitability. HBO and pay-per-view are substitutes to the movie rental business and effectively limit what the industry can charge for its services. Moreover, when cost structures can be changed, for example, by employing new technology, substitutes can take substantial market share from existing businesses.

The increased availability of pay-per-view entertainment over cable networks, for example, erodes the competitive position of movie rental companies. From a strategic perspective, therefore, substitute products or services that deserve scrutiny are those that (1) show improvements in price performance relative to the industry average and (2) are produced by companies with deep pockets.

*Rivalry Among Participants.*    The intensity of competition in an industry also depends on the number, relative size, and competitive prowess of its participants; the industry's growth rate; and related characteristics. Intense rivalry can be expected when (1) competitors are numerous and relatively equal in size and power; (2) industry growth is slow and the competitive battle is more about existing customers than about creating new customers; (3) fixed costs are high or the product or service is perishable; (4) capacity increases are secured in large increments; and (5) exit barriers are high, making it prohibitively expensive to discontinue operations.

Andrew Grove, founder of Intel, has suggested adding a sixth force to Porter's model: the influence of *complementary products*. Computers need software, and software needs hardware; cars need gasoline, and gasoline needs cars. When the interests of the industry are aligned with those of complementors, the status quo is preserved. However, new technologies or approaches can upset the existing order and cause complementors' paths to diverge.[3] An example is a change in technological standards, which renders *previously* compatible products and services incompatible.

The influence of these forces continues to shift as industry structures and business models change. For example, companies are increasingly using the Internet to streamline their procurement of raw materials, components, and ancillary services. To the extent this enhances access to information about products and services and facilitates the valuation of alternate sources of supply, it increases the bargaining power of manufacturers over suppliers. However, the same technology might reduce barriers to entry for new suppliers and provide them with a direct channel to end users, thereby reducing the leverage of intermediaries.

The effect of the Internet on the possible threat of substitute products and services is equally ambiguous. On the one hand, by increasing efficiency, it can expand markets. On the other hand, as new uses of the Internet are pioneered, the threat of substitutes increases. At the same time, the Internet's rapid spread has reduced barriers to entry and increased rivalry among existing competitors in many industries. This has occurred because Internet-based business models are generally hard to protect from imitation and, because they are often focused on reducing variable costs, they create an unwanted focus on price. Thus, although the Internet does not fundamentally alter the nature of the forces affecting industry rivalry, it changes their relative influence on industry profitability and attractiveness.[4]

# Industry Evolution

Industry structures change over time. Entry barriers can fall, as in the case of deregulation, or rise considerably, as has happened in a number of industries where brand identity became an important competitive weapon. Sometimes industries become more concentrated as real or perceived benefits of scale and scope cause businesses to consolidate. Models of industry evolution can help us understand how and why industries change over time. Perhaps the word evolution is somewhat deceptive; it suggests a process of slow, gradual change. Structural change can occur with remarkable rapidity, as in the case when a major technological innovation enhances the prospects of some companies at the expense of others.

## Four Trajectories of Change

Industries evolve according to one of the four distinct trajectories of change: radical, progressive, creative, and intermediating.[5] Two types of obsolescence define these paths of change: (1) a threat to an industry's *core activities*, which account for a significant portion of an industry's profits; and (2) a threat to the industry's *core assets*, which are valued as differentiators. The steady decrease in importance of a dealer's traditional sales activities as online shopping has increased is a good example of the first type of obsolescence. The eroding brand value of many prescription drugs in the face of generic competition illustrates the second.

   *Radical* change occurs when an industry is threatened with obsolescence of both its core activities and core assets at the same time. Professor Anita McGahan cites the major changes in the travel business as an example. As airlines modernized and began to compete more directly with enhanced reservation systems, and corporate travel clients turned to Internet-based service providers such as Expedia and Travelocity, many traditional travel agents had to reinvent themselves as a matter of survival.

   *Progressive* change can be expected when neither form of obsolescence is imminent. This is the most common form of industry change. The long-haul trucking industry has seen changes, but its fundamental value proposition has remained the same. In such environments, competitive strategies and innovation are often targeted at increased efficiencies through scale and cost reduction.

*Creative and intermediating* change paths are defined by the dominance of one of the two forms of obsolescence. Under creative change, the core assets are threatened, but the core activities retain their value. Strategically, this scenario calls for the renewal of asset values; think of a movie studio having to produce another blockbuster. Under intermediating change, the core assets remain valuable, but the core activities are threatened. Museums are highly valuable as repositories of art, for example, but modern communication methods have reduced their power as educators.

### Industry Structure, Concentration, and Product Differentiation

It is useful to analyze changes in industry structure in terms of the movement from a primarily *vertical* to a more *horizontal* structure, or vice versa; increases or decreases in the degree of *product differentiation*; and changes in the degree of industry *concentration*.

These dimensions are illustrated by the convergence of three industries that originated some 50 years apart: telecommunications, computers, and television. This convergence has spawned an integrated multimedia industry in which traditional industry boundaries have all but disappeared. Instead of consisting of three distinct businesses in which being vertically integrated was key to success, the industry has evolved into five primarily horizontal segments in which businesses can successfully compete: content (products and services), packaging (bundling of content and additional functionality), the network (physical infrastructure), transmission (distribution), and display devices. In this new structure, strategic advantage for many companies is determined primarily by their relative positions on one of the five segments. However, vertical integration is likely to become an important business strategy once again when economics of scale and scope become more critical to competitive success.

In *fragmented* industries, which characterized by a relatively *low* degree of *concentration*, no single player has a major market share. Such industries are found in many areas of the economy. Some are highly *differentiated*, such as application software; others tend to *commodity* status, as in the case of lumber. In the absence of major forces for change, fragmented industries can remain fragmented for a long time.

### Industry Concentration

When economies of scale are important and market share and total unit costs are inversely related, industry structures are often *concentrated*. In such industries, the size distribution of business firms is often highly skewed. In stable markets, there may be very few significant competitors and they will share a high total percentage of industry sales.

Research into approximately 200 industries has revealed that markets evolve in a highly predictable fashion, supporting a "Rule of Three."[6] When market forces are free to operate, unrestricted by regulatory constraints and artificial entry barriers, two kinds of competitors emerge, called full-line generalists and product/market specialists:

- Generalists offer a broad range of products to multiple markets. They are volume-driven competitors that depend on market share to improve their financial performance.
- Specialists restrict themselves to limited products or to limited markets. They are margin-driven competitors that can suffer serious declines if they attempt to increase their market share too rapidly.

Researchers Jagdish Sheth and Rajendra Sisodia found that in competitive, mature markets, there is only room for three full-line generalists, plus several product or market specialists. In some combination, the three generalists typically control between 70 and 90 percent of the total sales in the industry. The smallest of these generalists must control no less than a 10 percent market share to remain competitively profitable.

The financial performance of specialists drops rapidly as their market share increases. In contrast, the three market-driven generalists enjoy profit improvement with gains in market share. These relationships are shown in Figure 4.1 to illustrate the central paradigm of the Rule of Three. The figure plots financial performance against market share, for generalists and specialists separately.

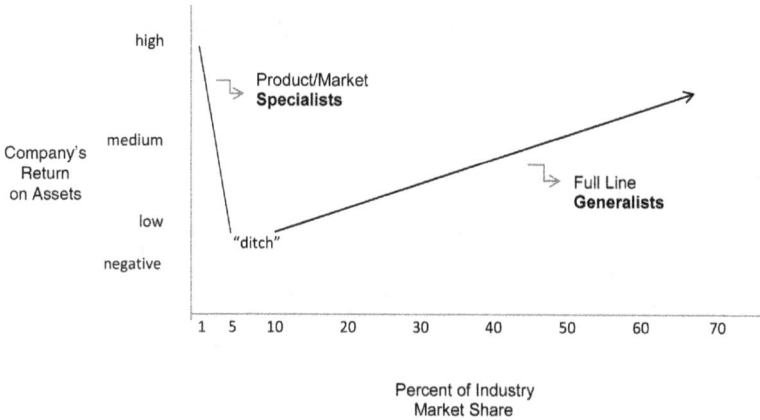

*Figure 4.1  The financial consequences of growth for specialist and generalist companies*

Sheth and Sisodia also found that a number of firms typically operate as large market share specialists (with less than 5 percent of total industry revenues) or small market share generalists (with less than 10 percent of total industry revenues). Both groups suffer from low levels of profitability and poor prospects if they continue to operate as independent firms. As shown in Figure 4.1, these companies are labeled as being in the "ditch." Therefore, the most desirable competitive positions are those furthest away from the ditch.

### Common Elements in Market Evolution

By analyzing the evolution of about 200 competitive markets, Sheth and Sisodia reached many important generalizations.[7] The following seem particularly useful:

1. A typical competitive market starts out in an unorganized way, with only small players serving it. As markets expand, they get organized through consolidation and standardization. This process eventually results in the emergence of a handful of "full-line generalists" surrounded by a number of "product specialists" and "market specialists."

2. With regularity, the number of full-line generalists that survive this transition is three. Typically, the market shares of the three eventually resemble 40, 20, and 10 percent, respectively. Together, they generally serve between 70 and 90percent of the market, with the balance going to product/market specialists. The extent of market share concentration among the three big depends on the extent to which fixed costs dominate the cost structure.

3. The financial performance of the three large players improves with increased market share-up to a point, typically 40 percent.

4. The three big companies are typically valued at a substantial premium (measured by the price–earnings ratio) over those in the ditch.

5. If the top player commands 70 percent or more of the market (usually because of a proprietary technology or strong patent rights), there is often no room for even a second full-line generalist. When the market leader has a share of between 50 and 70 percent, there is often only room for two full-line generalists. Similarly, if the market leader enjoys considerably less than a 40 percent share, there may (temporarily) be room for a fourth generalist player.

6. A market share of 10 percent is the minimum level necessary for a player to be viable as a full-line generalist. Companies that dip below this level must become a specialist to survive; alternatively, they must consider a merger with another company to regain a market share above 10 percent.

7. The No. 1 company is usually the least innovative, though it may have the largest R&D budget. Such companies tend to adopt a "fast follower" strategic posture when it comes to innovation.

8. The No. 3 company is usually the most innovative. However, its innovations are usually "stolen" by the No. 1 company unless it can protect them.

9. The performance of specialist companies deteriorates as they grow market share within the overall market, but improves as they grow their share of a specialty niche.

10. Specialists can make the transition to successful full-line generalists only if there are two or fewer incumbent generalists in the market.

11. Successful product or market specialists typically face only one direct competitor in their chosen specialty.

12. Successful superniche players (that specialize by product and market) are, in essence, monopolists in their niches, commanding 80–90 percent market share.
13. Successful market growth (finding new markets for existing products) requires product strength, and successful product growth (developing new products for existing markets) requires market strength.
14. Companies in the ditch exhibit the worst financial performance and have a very difficult time surviving.
15. The ditch can be a very attractive source of bargains for full-line generalists looking to boost market share rapidly.

These generalizations—and The Rule of Three—are dependable only when market structure is determined by competitive market forces caution.[8] Therefore, we are not likely to see the Rule apply in mature markets with government regulations that:

- greatly restrict consolidation,
- allow exclusive rights to certain companies that enable them to operate like of sub-monopolies,
- construct significant barriers to trade and foreign ownership of assets, or
- support major industries that exhibit combined ownership and management.

Ultimately, the Rule of Three is evidence that the highest operating efficiency is being achieved in a competitive market. Sheth and Sisodia also found that industries with four or more major players, as well as those with two or fewer, tend to be less efficient than those with three major players, and they warn that the role of the government is to ensure that free market conditions prevail so that such efficiency can be achieved and sustained.

### Power Curves

Strategic managers have a new tool that helps them to assess industry structure, which refers to the enduring characteristics that give an industry its distinctive character. According to Michele Zanini of the McKinsey Group, from whose work this discussion is derived, power curves depict the fundamental structural trends that underlie an industry.[9] While major economic events like the worldwide recession of 2007–2009 are extremely disruptive to business activity, they do little to change the relative position of most businesses to one another over the long term.

In many industries, the top firm is best described as a mega-institution—a company of unprecedented scale and scope that has an undeniable lead over competitors. Walmart, Best Buy, McDonalds, and Starbucks are examples. However, even among these firms, there is a clear difference in size and performance. When the distribution of net incomes of the global top 150 corporations in 2005 was plotted, as shown in Figure 4.2, the result was a "power curve," which implies that most companies, even in the set of superstars, are below average in performance.

A power curve is described as exhibiting a small set of companies with extremely large incomes, followed quickly by a much larger array of companies with significantly smaller incomes that are progressively smaller than one another, but only slightly.

As Zanini explains, low barriers to entry and high levels of rivalry are positively associated with an industry's power curve dynamics. The larger the number of competitors in an industry, the larger the gap

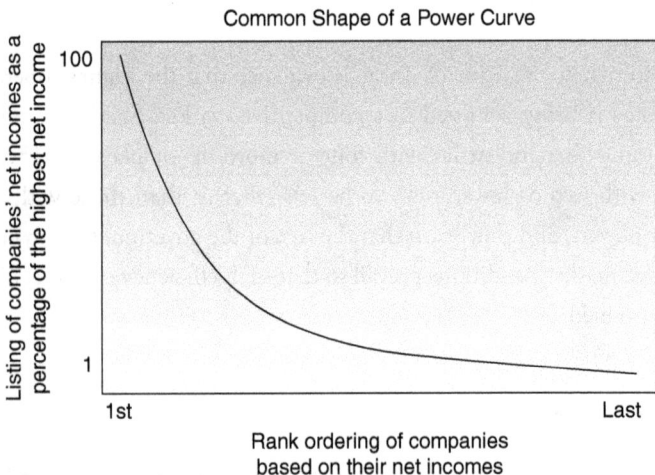

*Figure 4.2 Common shape of a power curve*

on the vertical axis usually is between the top and median companies. When entry barriers are lowered, such as occurs with deregulation, revenues increase faster in the top-ranking firms, creating a steeper power curve. This greater openness seems to create a more level playing field at first, but greater differentiation and consolidation tend to occur over time.

Power curves are also promoted by intangible assets such as software and biotech, which generate increasing returns to scale and economies of scope. By contrast, more labor- or capital-intensive sectors, such as chemicals and machinery, have flatter curves. In industries that display a power curve, including insurance, machinery, and U.S. banks and savings institutions, the intriguing strategic implication is that strategic thrusts rather than incremental strategies are required to improve a company's position significantly.

### Product Life Cycle Analysis

The *product life cycle model*—based on the theory of diffusion of innovations and its logical counterpart, the pattern of acceptance of new ideas—is perhaps the best-known model of industry evolution. It holds that an industry passes through a number of stages: introduction, growth, maturity, and decline. The different stages are defined by changes in the rate of growth of industry sales, generally thought to follow an S-shaped curve, reflecting the cumulative result of first and repeat adoptions of a product or service over time.

The service life cycle can be a useful analytic tool for strategy development. Research has shown that the evolution of an industry or product class depends on the interaction of a number of factors, including the competitive strategies of rival firms, changes in customer behavior, and legal and social influences. Figure 4.3 shows typical competitive responses to the changes that accompany the transition from a market's introduction stage to growth to maturity and, ultimately, to decline.

A high level of uncertainty characterizes the *introductory* or emerging stage of a product or industry life cycle. Competitors are often unsure which segments to target and how. Potential customers are unfamiliar

| Conditions of the Life Cycle of a Service Firm | | | |
|---|---|---|---|
| | Life Cycle Stage | | |
| Condition | Introductory | Growth | Maturity | Decline |
| Barriers to Entry | low | moderate to high | high: capital requirements | low for niche players |
| Barriers to Exit | low | moderate and increasing | high: correlated with size | high: inversely related to asset convertibility |
| Power of Suppliers | high | moderate | low | low |
| Power of Buyers | moderate | decreasing | low | high |
| Rivalry | low: few competitors | rapidly increasing to high; stabilizes at moderate after shakeout* | stable at moderate to low | increasing as industry sales decline |
| Experience Curve Effects | low | high | high but not a differentiator for established firms | low |
| Economies of Scale | few | moderate and increasing | high | high, but declining in value |
| Price Elasticity of Demand | inelastic | more elastic during shakeout | inelastic | elastic: high buyer power |
| Product Differentiation | low | rapidly increasing | high | low |
| Costs Per Unit | high: marketing | high: fixed assets | moderate to low | increasing |
| Cash Flow | low | high but necessary | high | moderate but declining heading low |
| Profits | very low | increasing except during shakeup | high to moderate | low |

*Figure 4.3  Conditions over the life cycle of a service firm[1]*

with the new product or service, the benefits it offers, where to buy it, or how much to pay. Consequently, a substantial amount of experimentation is a hallmark of emerging industries.

*Growth* environments are less uncertain and competitively more intense. At this stage of an industry's evolution, the number of rivals is usually largest. Therefore, competitive shakeouts are common toward the end of the growth phase.

*Mature* industries, although the most competitively stable, are relatively stagnant in terms of sales growth. However, product development can give rise to new spurts of growth in specific segments, technological breakthroughs can alter the course of market development and upset the competitive order, and global opportunities can open avenues for further growth.

*Declining* industries are typically regarded as unattractive, but clever strategies can produce substantial profits. We will return to these different scenarios in Chapter 7 when we consider specific strategies for each life cycle stage.

Although useful as a general construct for understanding how the principle of diffusion can shape industry sales over time, the product life cycle concept has little predictive value. Empirical studies have shown that industry growth does not always follow an S-shaped pattern. In some instances, stages are very brief. More important, the product life cycle concept does not explicitly acknowledge the possibility that companies can affect the shape of the growth curve through strategic actions such as increasing the pace of innovation or repositioning their offerings. Taking an industry growth curve as a given, therefore, can unnecessarily become a self-fulfilling prophecy.

### New Patterns

Many new industries evolve through some convergence in *technological standards*. Competition for standards or formats is frequently waged within a group of companies between the developer of one standard and another group of companies favoring a different standard. Competition for standard or format share is important, because the winning standard will garner for its adopters a substantial share of future profits. Battles for cell phone technologies and set-top box standards, for example, decide the winners in market share.

For industries in which competition for standards is an important determinant of strategic success, C. K. Prahalad has proposed a model that describes industry evolution in three phases.[10] In the first phase, competition is mostly focused on *ideas, product concepts, technology choices, and the building of a competency base.* The primary goal at this stage is to learn more about the potential of the industry and about the key factors that will determine future success or failure. In the second phase, competition is more *about building a viable coalition of partners that will support a standard against competing formats.* Companies cooperating at this stage may compete vigorously in phase three of the process—*the battle for market share for end products and profits.*

As competition becomes more global, industries consolidate, technology becomes more pervasive, and the lines between customers, suppliers, competitors, and partners are increasingly becoming blurred. With greater frequency, companies that compete in one market collaborate with others. At times, they can be each other's customers or suppliers. This complex juxtaposition of roles makes accurately forecasting an industry's future structure extremely difficult and relying on simple, stylized models of industry evolution very dangerous.

As industry boundaries become more permeable, structural changes in *adjacent* industries (industries serving the same customer base with different products or services, or industries using similar technologies and production processes) or *related* industries (industries supplying components, technologies, or complementary services) increasingly influence an industry's outlook for the future. Finally, change sometimes is simply a function of experience. Buyers generally become more discriminating as they become more familiar with a product and its substitutes and, consequently, they are likely to be more explicit in their demands for improvements.

## Methods for Analyzing an Industry

Analyzing an industry is typically done based on a method of strategic segmentation that focuses on a subset of the total customer market, a competitor analysis that concentrates on individual corporations or their major units, or a strategic group analysis of all firms that face similar threats and opportunities.

## Segmentation

*Strategic segmentation* is the process of dividing an industry into relatively homogeneous, minimally overlapping segments that benefit from distinct competitive strategies. Strategic segmentation is the process of identifying segments that offer the best prospects for long term, sustainable results. It considers the long-term defensibility of different segments by analyzing barriers to entry such as capital investment intensity, proprietary technologies and patents, geographical location, tariffs, and other trade barriers.

Segmentation is complex because there are many ways to divide an industry or market. The most widely used categories of segmentation variables are *customer characteristics* and *product- or service-related variables*. Customer descriptors range from geography, size of customer firm, customer type, and customer lifestyle to personal descriptive variables, such as age, income, or sex. Product- or service-related segmentation schemes divide the market based on variables such as user type, level of use, benefits sought, competing offerings, purchase frequency and loyalty, and price sensitivity. After a strategic business unit's (SBU's) preferred segments have been identified, the process of analysis concludes with the strategic targeting of the particular segment and the positioning the firm for competitive advantage within that segment.

## Competitor Analysis

Because industry structures and patterns of evolution are becoming more complex, traditional business assumptions are often not tenable. Many markets are no longer distinct nor are their boundaries well defined; competition is not mainly about capturing market share; customer and competitor profiles are constantly shifting; and competition occurs simultaneously at the business unit and corporate levels.

These new realities call for executives to adopt a broader perspective on strategy and for them to ask new questions. Do consumer companies compete at the business unit level, at the corporate level, or both? Do companies compete as stand-alone entities or as extended families that include their supplier bases? When a firm defines its competition, should executives focus on the corporate portfolio of which the SBU is a part? What are the competitive advantages of a portfolio of businesses against stand-alone businesses? Which is more important to sustainable competitive advantage: access to money or information technology?

As these questions suggest, competitive analysis should be paired with an analysis of the drivers of industry evolution. Consequently, strategies cannot be neatly compartmentalized at the SBU or corporate level. A principal rationale behind the concept of the diversified corporation is that the benefits of a portfolio transcend financial strength. A portfolio of related businesses reflects an integrated set of resources—core competencies that transcend business units—and has the potential for developing a sustainable corporate advantage that must be considered along with competitive factors at the business unit level.

To analyze *immediate competitors*, five key questions are useful:

1. Who are our firm's direct competitors now and in the near term?
2. What are their major strengths and weaknesses?
3. How have they behaved in the past?
4. How might they behave in the future?
5. How will our competitors' actions affect our industry and company?

Developing a solid understanding of who a firm's immediate competitors are and what motivates their competitive behavior is important for strategy formulation. An analysis of key competitors' major strengths and weaknesses and their past behavior, for example, may suggest attractive competitive opportunities or imminent threats. Understanding why a competitor behaves a certain way helps to make a determination of how likely it is to expect a major strategic or retaliatory initiative. Assessing competitors' successes and failures assists in predicting their future behavior. Finally, an analysis of a competitor's organizational structure and culture can be insightful; a cost-driven, highly structured competitor is unlikely to mount a successful challenge with an innovation-driven, market-oriented strategy.

In analyzing competitive patterns, it is often useful to assign roles to particular competitors. In many markets, it is possible to identify a *leader*, one or more *challengers*, and a number of *followers* and *nichers*. Although labeling competitors can be dangerously simplistic, such an analysis can provide insight into the competitive dynamics of the industry.

*Leaders* tend to focus on expanding total demand by attracting new users, developing new uses for their products or services, and encouraging more use of existing products and services. Defending market share is important to them, but they might not want to be aggressive in taking share from their immediate rivals because to do so can be more costly than expanding the market, or because they want to avoid scrutiny by regulatory agencies. Coca-Cola, for example, focuses more on developing new markets overseas than on taking market share from Pepsi Cola in the domestic market.

*Challengers* typically concentrate on a single target—the leader. Sometimes they do so directly, as in the case of Fuji's challenge to Kodak. At other times, they use indirect strategies. Computer Associates, for example, acquired a number of smaller competitors before embarking on directly competitive attacks against larger rivals.

*Followers* and *nichers* compete with more modest strategic objectives. Some followers use a strategy of innovative imitation, whereas others elect to compete selectively in a few segments or with a more limited product or service offering. Nichers typically focus on a narrow slice of the market by concentrating, for example, on specific end users and geographic areas, or offering specialty products or services.

The identification of *potential* competitors is more difficult. Firms that are currently not in the industry but can enter at relatively low cost should be considered. So should companies for whom there is obvious synergy by being in the industry. Customers or suppliers who can integrate backward or forward comprise another category of potential competitors.

## Strategic Groups

Many industries have numerous competitors, far more than can be analyzed individually. In such cases, the application of the concept of *strategic groups* makes the task of competitor analysis more manageable. A strategic group is a set of firms that face similar threats and opportunities, which are different from the threats and opportunities faced by other sets of companies in the same industry.

Rivalry is usually more intense within strategic groups than between them, because members of the same strategic group focus on the same market segments with similar strategies and resources. In the fast food industry, for example, hamburger chains tend to compete more directly with other hamburger chains than with chicken or pizza restaurants. Similarly, in pharmaceuticals, strategic groups can be defined in terms of the disease categories on which companies focus.

Analysis of strategic groups helps to reveal how competition evolves between competitors with a similar strategic focus. Strategic groups can be mapped by using price, product-line breadth, the degree of vertical integration, and other variables that differentiate competitors within an industry.

# CHAPTER 5

# Analyzing a Company's Strategic Resource Base

## Introduction

An assessment of strategic resources and capabilities—and of pressures for and against change—is critical when determining what strategies a company can successfully pursue. An organization's strategic resources include its physical assets; relative financial position; market position, brands, and the capabilities of its people; and specific knowledge, competencies, processes, skills, and culture.

Consider the rapidly increasing reliance of U.S. corporations on analytics to improve data analysis. Data has become a critically important corporate knowledge resource. Data is critical in enabling executives to evaluate their internal processes, their competitors, and the markets in which they operate. Consequently, the demand and availability of data is growing exponentially, with a projected rate of data generation of 40 percent per year through 2020, totally 1,054 percent growth in the period of 2014 to 2020.[1] Firms at the foreground of using this data to analyze their performance and formulate their strategies are estimated to have 6 percent higher profits and 5 percent higher productivity than their competitors.[2] These advantages are widening as the leaders in data utilization see higher growth rates in revenue accompanied by a greater ability to control costs. McKinsey & Company advises that in the retail industry, a company that makes full use of the available data could increase their operating margins by 60 percent.[3] They estimate that a better exploitation of data could add $300 billion a year in value to the U.S. health care industry.

Data acquisition and analysis requires the investment in a lot of bandwidth. While high-speed Internet connections currently allow the transfer of about 25 megabits of data per second, analysts forecast that companies will need connection speeds of 1 gigabit per second by 2020 keeping pace with usage trends.[4] Data storage needs will increase at similar rates. Businesses are increasing their data storage capacity at a rate of 53 percent per year.

Analyzing a company's internal strategic environment has two principal components: (1) cataloging and valuing current resources, including data, and core competencies to create a competitive advantage and (2) identifying internal pressures for change and forces of resistance.

In this chapter, we characterize a company's strategic resource base in terms of physical, financial, human resource, and organizational assets, and describe techniques for analyzing a company's strategic resource base. In the second section, we look at internal organizational change drivers and counterforces that have a major influence on the feasibility of exercising particular strategic options and introduce the company life-cycle model.

## Strategic Resources

A company's strategic resource base consists of its *physical, financial, human resource,* and *organizational* assets. Physical assets such as state-of-the-art manufacturing facilities or plant or service locations near important customers can materially affect a company's competitiveness. Financial strength—excellent cash flow, a strong balance sheet, and a strong financial track record—is a measure of a company's competitive position, market success, and ability to invest in its future. The quality of a company's human resources—strong leadership at the top, experienced managers, and well-trained, motivated employees—may well be its most important strategic resource. Finally, strategic organizational resources are the specific competencies, processes, skills, and knowledge under the control of a corporation. They include qualities such as a firm's manufacturing experience, brand equity, innovativeness, relative cost position, and ability to adapt and learn as circumstances change.

To evaluate the relative worth of a company's strategic resources, four specific questions should be asked:

1. How valuable is a resource? Does it help build and sustain competitive advantage?
2. Is this a unique resource, or do other competitors have similar resources? If competitors have substantially similar resources or capabilities or can obtain them with relative ease, their strategic value is diminished.
3. Is the strategic resource easy to imitate? This is related to uniqueness. Ultimately, most strategic resources, with some exceptions for patents and trademarks, can be duplicated. At what cost? The more expensive it is for rivals to duplicate a strategic resource, the more valuable it is to a company.
4. Is the company positioned to exploit the resource? Possessing a strategic resource is one thing; being able to exploit it is quite another. A strategic resource that has little value to one company might be an important strategic asset for another. The issue is whether a resource can be leveraged for competitive advantage.

## Physical Assets

A company's physical assets, such as state-of-the-art manufacturing facilities and plant or service locations near important customers, can materially affect its competitiveness. For airline companies, the average age of their fleet of aircraft is an important concern. It affects customer perceptions, routing flexibility, and operating and maintenance costs. Infrastructure is a key issue for telecommunication companies. It determines their geographical reach and defines the types of customer service they can provide. In retailing and real estate, the old adage "location, location, location" still applies.

Physical assets do not necessarily need to be owned. Judicious use of outsourcing, leasing, franchising, and partnering can substantially enhance a company's reach with a relatively modest commitment of resources.

### Analyzing a Financial Resource Base

At the corporate level, an evaluation of a company's financial performance and position involves a thorough analysis of the company's current and *pro forma* income statement and cash flows at the divisional or business unit level, with additional consideration of the balance sheet at the corporate level.

*Financial ratio analysis* can provide a quick overview of a company's or business unit's current or past profitability, liquidity, leverage, and activity. *Profitability ratios* measure how well a company is allocating its resources. *Liquidity ratios* focus on cash-flow generation and a company's ability to meet its financial obligations. *Leverage ratios* may suggest potential improvements in the financing of operations. *Activity ratios* measure productivity and efficiency. These ratios can be used to assess (1) the business's position in the industry, (2) the degree to which certain strategic objectives are being achieved, (3) the business's vulnerability to revenue and cost swings, and (4) the level of financial risk associated with the current or proposed strategy.

The *DuPont* formula for analyzing a company or business unit's return on assets (ROA) directly links operating variables to financial performance. For example, ROA is shown to be computed by multiplying earnings, expressed as a percentage of sales, by asset turnover. Asset turnover, in turn, is the ratio of sales to total assets used. A careful analysis of such relationships allows pointed questions about a strategy's effectiveness and the quality of its execution.

Accounting-based measures have generally been found to be inadequate indicators of a business unit's economic value. *Shareholder-value analysis*, in contrast, focuses on cash-flow generation, which is the principal determinant of shareholder wealth. It is helpful in answering the following questions: (1) Does the current strategic plan create shareholder value, and, if so, how much? (2) How does the business unit's performance compare with the performance of others in the corporation? (3) Would an alternative strategy increase shareholder value more than the current strategy?

The use of accounting-based financial measures to assess current performance, such as return on investment (ROI), has been supplanted by that of the broader shareholder-value-based measures of *economic value added* (EVA) and *market value added* (MVA). EVA is a value-based financial performance measure that focuses on economic value creation. Unlike traditional measures based on accounting profit, EVA recognizes that capital has two components: the cost of debt and the cost of equity. Most traditional measures, including ROA and return on equity (ROE), focus on the cost of debt but ignore the cost of equity. The premise of EVA is that executives cannot know whether an operation is really creating value until they assess the complete cost of capital.

In mathematical terms, EVA = profit − [(cost of capital) (total capital)], where *profit* is after-tax operating profit, *cost of capital* is the weighted cost of debt and equity, and *total capital* is book value plus interest-bearing debt. Consider the following example. When buying an asset, executives invest capital from their company and borrowed funds from a lender. Both the stockholders and the lender require a return on their capital. This return is the "cost of capital" and includes both the cost of equity (the company's investment) and the cost of debt (the lender's investment). The company does not generate any meaningful profits until returns generated by the investment exceed the weighted capital charge. Once this occurs, the assets are contributing a positive EVA. If, however, the returns continue to lag the weighted cost of capital, EVA is negative, and change may be needed.

Varity, Inc. used EVA as a basis for reinvigorating its corporate culture and reestablishing its financial health. The company focused employees' attention on its negative $150 million EVA. It established clear objectives to turn EVA positive within a 5-year timeframe. These objectives included revising the firm's capital structure by initiating a stock buyback program, considering strategic opportunities with high EVA prospects, and efficiently managing working capital. By establishing a 20 percent internal cost of capital, managers found attractive strategic opportunities, including the construction of a new manufacturing facility, establishing an Asian presence through a joint venture, and divesting its door-lock actuator business.[5]

Following are two additional benefits of EVA: (1) it can help align employee and owner interests through employee compensation plans and (2) it can be the basis for a single competitive performance measure called MVA. Under EVA-based incentive programs, employees are rewarded for contributing to profits through the efficient use of capital. As employees become conscious of the results of their capital-use decisions, they become more selective in the ways they spend shareholder investment. MVA is equal to market value less capital invested. Thus, EVA can be used as a metric for various internal functions, such as capital budgeting, employee performance evaluation, and operational assessment. In contrast, external shareholder value is measured through MVA, which is equal to the future discounted EVA streams.

Although some analysts have reservations, EVA portrays the true results of a company's strength by considering the cost of debt and equity.[6] Tools such as ROE, ROA, and EPS (earnings per share) measure financial performance, but ignore the cost of equity component of the cost of capital. Therefore, it is possible to have positive earnings and positive returns but a negative EVA. By encouraging an operation to manage indebtedness, a firm that uses EVA maximizes capital efficiency and allocation. If, for example, a business can conserve its assets by improving collections of receivables and inventory turnover, EVA will rise.

*Cost analysis* deals with the identification of strategic cost drivers—those cost factors in the value chain that determine long-term competitiveness in the industry. Strategic cost drivers include variables such as product design, factor costs, scale, scope of operations, and capacity use. To assist in strategy development, cost analysis focuses on those costs and cost drivers that are of strategic importance because they can be influenced by strategic choice.

*Cost benchmarking* is useful in assessing a firm's costs relative to those of competing firms, or for comparing a company's performance against best-in-class competitors. The process involves five steps: (1) selecting areas or operations to benchmark, (2) identifying key performance measures and practices, (3) identifying best-in-class companies or key competitors, (4) collecting cost and performance data, and (5) analyzing and interpreting the results. This technique is extremely practical and versatile. It allows for direct comparisons of the efficiencies with which different tasks in the value chain are performed. It is dangerous, however, to rely heavily on benchmarking for guidance, because it focuses on similarities rather than differences between rival firms' strategic designs and on proven, versus prospective, bases of competitive advantage.

A complete evaluation of a company's financial resources should include a *financial risk* analysis. Most financial models are deterministic. That is, managers specify a single estimate for each key variable. Yet, many of these estimates are made with the recognition that there is a great deal of uncertainty about their true value. Together, such uncertainties can mask high levels of risk. It is important, therefore, that risk be explicitly considered. This involves determining the variables that have the greatest effect on revenues and costs as a basis for assessing different risk scenarios. Some of the variables that are commonly considered are market growth rate, market share, price trends, the cost of capital, and the useful life of the underlying technology.

## Human Capital: A Company's Most Valuable Strategic Resource

Companies are run by and for people. Although some strategic resources can be duplicated, the people who comprise an organization or its immediate stakeholders are unique. Understanding their concerns, aspirations, and capabilities is, therefore, key to determining a company's strategic position and options.

Continuous employee development, through on-the-job training and other programs, is critical to the growth of human capital. FedEx develops its homegrown talent through a commitment to continuous learning. The company puts 3 percent of its total expenses into training—six times the proportion of the average company. All line and staff managers attend 11 weeks of mandatory training in their first year. More than 10,000 employees have been to the "Leadership Institute" and have attended weeklong courses on the company's culture and operations.[7] Many other companies are adopting similar strategies and reaping the benefits. Motorola executives report that their company receives $33 for every $1 invested in employee education.

## Organizational Strategic Resources

A firm's organizational resources include its *knowledge and intellectual capital base; reputation* with customers, partners, suppliers, and the financial community; specific *competencies, processes,* and *skill sets*; and *corporate culture.*

*Knowledge* and *intellectual capital* are the major drivers of competitive advantage. A firm's competitive advantage comes from the value it delivers to customers. Competitive advantage is created and sustained when a company continues to mobilize new knowledge faster and more efficiently than its competitors. Recognizing the importance of knowledge as a strategic asset, Skandia, NASDAQ, Chevron, and Dow Chemical have established director-level positions in charge of intellectual capital.

Additional evidence of the growing importance of knowledge and intellectual capital as strategic resources is provided by the financial markets. Although intellectual capital is difficult to measure and not formally represented on the balance sheet, a company's market capitalization increasingly reflects the value of such resources and the effectiveness with which they are managed. Netscape, before being acquired, had a $4 billion market capitalization based on its stock price, even though the company's sales were only a few million dollars per year. Investors based the high stock price on their assessment of the company's intangibles—its knowledge base and quality of management.

The number of *patents* issued in the United States each year has doubled in the last decade. Increasingly, patents are global. Through a new international patent system organized by the United Nations World Intellectual Property Organization, through the World Trade Organization, and through growing demand from inventors for patents that are protected throughout the world, patenting systems are converging. Landmark court decisions have also made new areas of technology patentable in the United States. A 1980 case opened biotechnology- and gene-related findings for patenting, a 1981 case allowed the patenting of software, and a 1998 case spawned more business method patents.

Strong patent protection can be of great strategic value.[8] For example, to protect its intellectual property and preserve its competitive advantage in the manufacturing and testing processes involved in its build-to-order system, Dell secured 77 patents protecting different parts of the building and testing process. Such protection pays. IBM collected $30 million in a patent infringement suit from Microsoft.

Increasingly, patents are exploited strategically to generate additional revenue. Licensing patents has helped build the market for IBM technology and boosted its licensing revenues. An increasing number of firms practice "strategic patenting"—using patent applications to colonize entire new areas of technology even before tangible products are created.

The largest part of a company's intellectual capital base, however, is not patentable. It represents the total *knowledge* accumulated by individuals, groups, and units within an organization about customers, suppliers, products, and processes, and is made up of a mixture of past experiences, values, education, and insights. As an organization learns, it makes better decisions. Better decisions, in turn, improve performance and enhance learning.

Knowledge becomes an asset when it is managed and transferred. *Explicit knowledge* is formal and objective and can be codified and stored in books, archives, and databases. An intriguing story of how revealing proprietary knowledge resulted in a major strategic blunder is based on Xerox's sale of insider information to Apple.[9] In the early 1970s, Xerox developed world-changing computer technology, including the mouse and the graphical user interface. One of the devices was called the Xerox Alto, a desktop personal computer that Xerox never bothered to market. A decade later, several Apple employees, including Steve Jobs, visited the Xerox PARC research and development facility for 3 days in exchange for $1 million in Apple's still-privately held stock. That educational field trip was well worth the price of admission, given that it helped Jobs build a company worth $110 billion in 2008, using Xerox technology in its Macintosh computers.

*Implicit* or *tacit knowledge* is informal and subjective. It is gained through experience and transferred through personal interaction and collaboration.

A study about how Xerox repair technicians refined their knowledge illustrates the difference.[10] The company's assumption had been that the technicians serviced companies' copying machines by following the documented diagnostic road maps that Xerox provided. Research, however, revealed that technicians often went to breakfast together and, while eating, talked about their work. They exchanged stories, posed problems, offered solutions, constructed answers, and discussed the machines, thereby keeping one another up-to-date about what they had learned. Thus, the approaches that the technicians used to repair the Xerox machines were actually based as much on their informal exchanges as on their formal training. What was thought to be a process based on explicit knowledge was, in fact, based on tacit knowledge, experience, and collaboration.[11]

### The Importance of Brands

A brand is a name, sign, or logo that is identified with the characteristics of a particular good or service. A brand can add value to goods and services and create goodwill through positive associations. Brands are visual shorthand for shoppers that can provide the company with a competitive advantage, simplify and accelerate the customer's buying decision, and reassure the consumer after the purchase.[12] Brand names are a primary cue to consistency and quality for a consumer. Once a brand becomes recognized and trusted by consumers, it becomes a powerful asset that can help build revenues and allow firms to pursue growth opportunities.

A firm's *reputation* with customers, partners, suppliers, and regulatory agencies can be a powerful strategic asset. Physical distance between customers, distributors, and manufacturers created the need for *brands*. They provided a guarantee of reliability and quality. In a global and Internet-based economy, they build trust and reinforce value. Consumers might be reluctant to use their credit cards to purchase products over the Internet if it were not for the trust they accord to companies such as Amazon, Dell, and eBay. Because consumer trust is the basis of all brand values, companies that own the brands have an immense incentive to work to retain that trust.

Thus, *brands* are strategic assets that assist companies in building and retaining customer loyalty. A strong brand can help maintain profit margins and erect barriers to entry. Because a brand is so valuable to a company, it must constantly be nourished, sustained, and protected. Doing so is becoming harder and more expensive. Consumers are busier, more distracted, and have more media options than ever before. Coca-Cola, Gillette, and Nike struggle to increase volumes, raise prices, and boost margins. In addition, failure in support of a brand can be catastrophic. A mistargeted advertising campaign, a drop-off in quality, or a corporate scandal can quickly reduce the value of a brand and the reputation of the company that owns it.

The Nestlé Corporation relies on its company name and logo to generate sales for many of their new product offerings. Nestlé produces a wide variety of products and many of their new offerings are branded with the recognized Nestlé name. However, using the company name may not always be the most effective branding tactic. Field research provided evidence that products carrying the Nestlé brand name generate higher sales volumes than the company's non-Nestle branded products. Many of Nestlé's products with substantially lower comparative sales were less recognizable as Nestlé products.[13] This survey suggested that in Nestlé's case, utilizing a brand name and/or logo to boost sales would be a feasible strategy. The downside of this approach, however, is that a company name can also deteriorate the value of this same wide variety of products if their brand image is damaged.

Using a single company brand can also enable a firm to combine offerings under the same umbrella and project the image of a global firm, which adds a status and prestige to the brand.[14] This survey of consumers worldwide measured the esteem in which consumers hold a particular brand. The results showed that global brands received a higher mean average esteem score than domestic only brands. The study further suggests that global branding creates familiarity and differentiation.

An opposing philosophy is held by global firms with multiple products that choose to market their products under a variety of brand names. To gain market share, these firms apply a tactic of multibranding, which assumes that greater market share can be obtained from multiple offerings that appear to be in competition with one another. This tactic can be effective. Research on consumer behavior shows that few consumers are completely loyal to a specific brand name within a product category. Rather, they choose to select from a variety of select trusted brands.[15]

Brand extension is another tactic for a firm that wants to extend its reach and stimulate new sources of revenue. MK Restaurants, a Southeast Asian company, uses brand extension to provide a separate product offering that is aimed at a different market segment than its existing MK Classic restaurants. Its MK Gold restaurants are targeted at a wealthier demographic that desires an upscale dining setting.[16]

The corporation utilized the same brand extension strategy to reach a younger demographic when they opened MK Trendy. This new line of restaurants was decorated differently, and offered unique aspects that were geared toward a younger demographic, such as a station for downloading free music. Through the Trendy and Gold brand extensions, MK was able to tap into different demographics and broaden their opportunities for revenue growth.

A branding strategy that is gaining popularity is private branding. When a retailer manufactures its own goods rather than relying on out-side vendors, it can sell them under a store brand, usually for an increased profit. For example, Wal-Mart sold McCormick brand spices for many years before switching out McCormick's spices for their own lower priced private label spices.[17] The move to private brands is not isolated to this one case. Private-brand labeled sales made up 17 percent of a basket of U.S. groceries in 2009, up from 13.4 percent in 1994.

### Core Competencies

*Core competencies* represent world-class capabilities that enable a company to build a competitive advantage. 3M has developed a core competency in coat-ings. Canon has core competencies in optics, imaging, and microprocessor controls. Procter & Gamble's (P&G) marketing prowess allows it to adapt more quickly than its rivals to changing opportunities. The development of core competencies has become a key element in building a long-term stra-tegic advantage. An evaluation of strategic resources and capabilities, there-fore, must include assessments of the core competencies a company has or is developing, how they are nurtured, and how they can be leveraged.

Core competencies evolve as a firm develops its business processes and incorporates its intellectual assets. Core competencies are not just things a company does particularly well; rather, they are sets of skills or systems that create a uniquely high value for customers at best-in-class levels. To qualify, such skills or systems should contribute to perceived customer benefits, be difficult for competitors to imitate, and allow for leverage across markets. Honda's use of small-engine technology in a variety of products—including motorcycles, jet skis, and lawn mowers—is a good example.

Core competencies should be focused on creating value and be adapted as customer requirements change. Targeting a carefully selected set of core competencies also benefits innovation. Charles Schwab, for example, successfully leveraged its core competency in brokerage services by expanding its client communication methods to include the Internet, the telephone, branch offices, and financial advisors.

There are three tests for identifying core competencies according to researchers Hamel and Prahalad. First, core competencies should provide access to a broad array of markets. Second, they should help differentiate core products and services. Third, they should be hard to imitate because they represent multiple skills, technologies, and organizational elements.[18]

Experience shows that only a few companies have the resources to develop more than a handful of core competencies. Picking the right ones, therefore, is the key. "Which resources or capabilities should we keep in-house and develop into core competencies and which ones should we outsource?" is a main question to ask. Pharmaceutical companies, for example, increasingly outsource clinical testing in an effort to focus their resource base on drug development. Generally, the development of core competencies should focus on long-term platforms capable of adapting to new market circumstances; on unique sources of leverage in the value chain where the firm thinks it can dominate; on elements that are important to customers in the long run; and on key skills and knowledge, not on products.

## Global Supply-Chain Management

In the global economy, a firm's sourcing approach must be an integral part of its overall corporate strategy. Global competition forces a company to abandon the simplistic approach of developing and producing a product in one country and then taking a country-by-country approach to marketing the product over time. If it took such an approach, global competitors would launch a competing product and with their global reach would be quicker to reach the markets.

Global sourcing captures the benefits of a worldwide integration of engineering, operations, procurement, and logistics into the upstream portion of a firm's supply chain. It involves decisions that determine locations, facilities, capacities, technologies, transportation modes, production planning, the company's response to trade regulations, local government requirements, transfer pricing, taxes, and financial issues. The benefits include improved inventory control, delivery service, quality, and development cycles.

### The Importance of Global Supply-Chain Management

The process of supply-chain management involves a company's coordination of the operations of the suppliers that contribute to the creation and delivery of its product or service. These suppliers can be the providers, distributors, transporters, warehouses, and retailers of a manufactured good, product, or service. The globalization of supply chains, defined as the ratio of a company's value creation outside the home county, is accelerating.

The development and management of an integrated global supply chain is a formidable challenge. An Accenture survey in 2009 found that 95 percent of senior executives doubt that their companies have a global operating model that is fully capable of supporting their international strategy.[19] The most common causes of supply-chain failures are stock-outs, excessive inventories, new product failures, increased product markdowns, and wasted time in engineering and R&D.[20] Reasons for supply-chain dysfunction include poor communication, latent functional silos, short-term perspectives, lack of resources, and ill-defined organizational boundaries. Compounding factors, such as fluctuating materials and logistic costs, increased supply-chain security and quality-control requirements, and dramatic changes in demand patterns add to the complexity of managing a global supply chain.

The market leaders in many industries are companies that have lean and flexible supply chains, end-to end visibility across those supply chains, fair-but-flexible contracts with service providers, and an understanding of how best to monitor and manage supply-chain risks.

### Challenges of a Complex Global Supply-Chain Management

The traditional role of a supply chain was essentially purchasing and inbound logistics to serve manufacturing, shipping, and outbound logistics to fill orders. However, in the new global competitive landscape, supply-chain professionals view the ability to effectively plan for demand, sourcing, production, and delivery requirements as core components of a core competence in supply-chain management. The role of supply-chain management in strategy formulation is evidenced by the results of a survey of leading supply-chain professionals[21]:

- 53 percent indicated that they have an executive officer, such as a chief supply-chain officer, in charge of all supply-chain functions.
- 64 percent have an official supply-chain management group that is responsible for strategy and change management.

To address competitive pressures, market instability, and increased complexity of globalization, companies develop agile supply-chain practices to respond, in real time, to the unique needs of customers and markets. These practices address the top challenges facing supply-chain professionals: cost containment, visibility, risk management, and globalization.[22]

The focus on controlling costs results from rising logistics, labor, and commodity costs. For instance, between 2006 and 2010, transportation costs increased by more than 50 percent. In turn, inventory-holding costs increased by more than 60 percent as companies tried to take advantage of economies of scale by shipping large quantities. During the same years, labor costs in China increased 20 percent year by year on average, causing companies that made production–sourcing decisions 5 years ago based on labor costs to revisit their decisions.[23]

Visibility is another significant challenge to competency in supply-chain management. Although connectivity is easier than ever and more information is available, in many organizations proportionally less information is being effectively captured, managed, analyzed, and made available to people who need it. The most effective initiatives focus on leveraging technology to develop and enhance the extended supply chain. To achieve this goal, companies are deploying advanced modeling tools that consider all costs and provide optimized strategies across a comprehensive supply-chain network of distribution centers, plants, contract manufacturing partners, sourcing options, logistical lanes, and consumer demand.

The use of the reverse logistics process has become an important way for companies to improve visibility and lower costs across the supply chain. Reverse logistics is the process that involves the return/exchange, repair, refurbishment, remarketing, and disposition of products. The process of moving product back through the supply chain to accommodate overstocks, returns, defects, and recalls can cost up to four to five times more than forward logistics.[24] Companies can also leverage the intelligence they gain through reverse logistics to detect or prevent product quality and design problems and to better understand their customers' buying patterns.

The third challenge facing executives is risk management and risk mitigation. As supply chains have grown more global and interconnected, they have increased their complexities and exposure to shocks and disruptions. Dealing effectively with these challenges requires a robust risk monitoring and mitigation process.

The criticality and vulnerability of a core competency in a global supply chain was revealed by the impact of the 2007 to 2009 global recession. The negative impacts included decreased sales volumes, increased supply volatility, elevated risk of supplier defaults, and major strains on cash flow involving difficulty in both inventory management and collections. To mitigate the impact of the resulting instability, supply-chain managers moved to reduce the complexity of global supply chains by simplifying their sales and operations planning, shrinking their global physical footprints, and reducing their product complexity.[25] Additionally, their increased utilization of risk analysis tools helped to refine their assessment of supplier financial viability, through inclusion of bank ratings, liquidity analysis, and business volume. The result was reduced exposure to losses caused by the bankruptcy of key customers and suppliers.

## Strategic Supply-Chain Models

The most commonly used models for organizing and standardizing supply-chain processes are the Supply-Chain Operational Reference (SCOR) model and the Global Supply-Chain Forum (GSCF) model.

The SCOR model prescribes a set of process templates that managers can decompose into a more detailed set of tasks. At the first level of detail, managers classify processes within the supply-chain domain as source, make, deliver, return, plan, or enable processes. The second level gives a list of configurable process templates (e.g., "make-to-order") for modeling a specific supply-chain instance. Level three processes specify task inputs and outputs (process interdependencies), business metrics, and best practices for task implementation.

The GSCF model focuses on collaboration techniques and illustrates the relationships among member firms so they can integrate activities. The relationships outlined include customer-relationship management, customer-service management, demand management, order fulfillment, manufacturing flow management, supplier-relationship management, product development, commercialization, and returns management.

The focus of the SCOR model is to propose efficient management of product flows, whereas the focus of the GSCF model is to provide a structure for stable relationships across the supply chain. Although the underlying process structures are similar, the SCOR model includes an integrated metrics framework while the GSCF model does not. The advantages of the metrics include providing a benchmarking tool that provides a process map and best practices as well as enabling the decomposition of strategic objectives in order to lay a foundation for causal analysis. The main disadvantage is that the complexity required in collecting data might cause an error that would lead to significant differences in the analytical results.

### Supply-Chain Technology Hosting

Outsourced-technology hosting is gaining acceptance globally based on On-demand and Software as a Service (SaaS) or on-demand models. Also called cloud computing, these platforms use supply-chain analytics and Business Intelligence (BI) to help managers make better decisions faster. Specifically, they are able to improve externally oriented processes such as transportation management, supply-chain visibility, collaborative forecasting, inventory optimization, and demand–supply synchronization.

BI refers to computer-based software applications that analyze raw business data that will help companies make decisions. The analytics applications focus on uncovering hidden relationships, identifying the root cause of a problem, and understanding relationships in the data. The result of the analysis leads to knowledge about why a particular business condition occurs.

BI-as-a-service offerings typically import business data in a common format, put a structure around them, apply the appropriate data models, and generate a web-based user interface that allows for the creation and distribution of standardized reports and dashboards across the supply chain. The result enables end-to-end supply-chain visibility and improves the ability to take action with close to real-time access to information.

### Strategic Alliances to Build a Core Competence

With development of global industries and the demands of global sourcing, strategic alliances have become an essential element of many corporate global strategies. Strategic alliances are partnerships of two or more companies that work together to achieve mutually beneficial strategic objectives. They are generally intended to establish and maintain a long-term contractual relationship between the firms and allow them to compete more effectively with external competitors. Alliances are established to allow the alliance partners to share risk and resources, gain knowledge, and obtain access to markets.

There are four principal motivations for companies to form strategic alliances. The first is to combine resources to develop new business or reduce investment. To engage in the global market, a firm needs strategic alliances to help defray the high local fixed costs. In practice, this may mean that rather than investing in an overseas sales force, a firm may utilize an alliance partner's sales force and in exchange use its own sales force to market their partner's products in countries where it has an existing sales force. The second motivation is to eliminate or minimize risks by sharing costs with a partner who possesses a valuable competitive advantage. The third reason is to learn from other members of the alliance, and the fourth motivation is to change the competitive landscape through the alliance of important competitors.

# Forces for Change

## Internal Forces for Change

In Chapter 3, we discussed change forces that emanate from a company's external strategic environment. A second set of drivers for strategic change comes from within the organization or from its immediate stakeholders. Disappointing financial performance, new owners or executives, limitations on growth with current strategies, scarcity of critical resources, and internal cultural changes are examples of drivers that give rise to pressures for change.

Because internal resistance can reduce a company's capacity to adapt and chart a new course, it deserves a strategist's careful attention. Organizational resistance to change can take four basic forms: (1) structural, organizational rigidities; (2) closed mind-sets reflecting support for obsolete business beliefs and strategies; (3) entrenched cultures reflecting values, behaviors, and skills that are not conducive to change; and (4) counterproductive change momentum that is not in tune with current strategic requirements.[26]

The four forms of resistance represent very different strategic challenges. Internal structures and systems, including technology, can be changed relatively quickly in most companies. Converting closed minds to the need for change, or changing a corporate culture, is considerably harder. Counterproductive change is especially difficult to remedy because it typically involves altering all three forms of resistance—structures and systems have to be rethought, mind-sets must change, and new behaviors and skills have to be learned.

## Company Life-Cycle Forces for Change

The forms and strengths of organizational resistance that develop highly depend on a company's history, performance, and culture. Nevertheless, some patterns can be anticipated. Companies go through life cycles. A cycle begins when a founder or founding team organizes a start-up. At this time, a vision or purpose is established, the initial direction for the company is set, and the necessary resources are marshaled to transform this vision into reality. In these early stages, the identities of the founders and that of their company are difficult to separate.

As companies grow, formal systems are needed to handle a widening variety of functions. The transition from informality to a more formal organizational structure can stimulate or hinder strategic change. This passage to organizational maturity, often described as the "entrepreneurial–managerial" transition, poses a dilemma familiar to many companies: How to maintain an entrepreneurial spirit while moving toward an organizational structure increasingly focused on control.

Growth makes organizational learning a requirement for continued success. The evolution of management processes, such as delegation of authority, coordination of effort, and collaboration among organizational units, can have an increasing influence on a company's effectiveness in responding to environmental and internal challenges. In younger companies, the internal operating environment is frequently characterized by greater ambiguity than in established organizations. Often, the ambiguity that encouraged entrepreneurship and innovation also results in a lack of control in a rapidly growing company, which can cause the firm to lose its strategic focus.

Evolving and established companies share the pervasive challenge of finding strategies to manage growth. For some evolving companies, uncontrolled growth is a major concern. As they try to cope with rapid growth, they find that success masks a host of development problems. Dilemmas of leadership can develop, loss of focus becomes an issue, communication becomes harder, skill development falls behind, and stress becomes evident. In established companies, the pressure to grow faster can skew strategic thinking. Ill-considered acquisitions or market expansions, forays into unproven technologies, deviations from developing core skills, and frequent exhortations for more entrepreneurial thinking are indicatives of the challenges experienced in more mature companies.

### Strategic Forces for Change

The increased importance of a firm's capacity to effectively deal with change has made a strategic perspective on this issue essential. As we have seen, a host of internal factors can reduce a company's capacity for change. Sometimes change is inhibited by structural rigidities, a lack of adequate resources, or an adherence to dysfunctional processes. Most often, however, resistance to change can be traced to cultural factors.

One of the early arguments in favor of analyzing the interactive nature of organizational factors such as structure, systems, and style with strategy is the so-called 7-S model, developed at McKinsey & Company.[27] Its central idea is that the organizational effectiveness stems from the interaction of a number of factors, of which strategy is just one.

The model includes seven different variables: strategy, structure, systems, shared values, skills, staff, and style. Intentionally, its design is not hierarchical; it depicts a situation in which it is not clear which factor is the driving force for change or the biggest obstacle to change. The different variables are interconnected—change in one will force change in another, or, put differently, progress in one area must be accompanied by progress in another to effect meaningful change. Consequently, the model holds that solutions to organizational problems that invoke just one or a few of these variables are doomed to fail. Therefore, an emphasis on "structural" solutions ("Let's reorganize") without attention to strategy, systems, and all the other variables can be counterproductive. Style, skills, and superordinate goals—the main values around which a business is built—are observable and even measurable, and can be at least as important as strategy and structure in bringing about a fundamental change in an organization. The key to orchestrating change, therefore, is to assess the potential impact of each factor, align the different variables in the model in the desired direction, and then act decisively on all dimensions.

## Stakeholder Analysis

In assessing a company's strategic position, it is important to identify the key stakeholders inside and outside the organization, the roles they play in fulfilling the organization's mission, and the values they bring to the process. External stakeholders—key customers, suppliers, alliance partners, and regulatory agencies—have a major influence on a firm's strategic options. A firm's internal stakeholders—its owners, board of directors, CEO, executives, managers, and employees—are the shapers and implementers of strategy.

In determining the company's objectives and strategies, executives must recognize the legitimate rights of the firm's stakeholders. Each of these interested parties has justifiable reasons for expecting—and often for demanding—that the company satisfies its claim. In general, stockholders claim competitive returns on their investment; employees seek job satisfaction; customers want what they pay for; suppliers seek dependable buyers; governments want adherence to legislation; unions seek member benefits; competitors want fair competition; local communities want the firm to be a responsible citizen; and the general public expects the firm's existence to improve their nation's quality of life.

The general claims of stakeholders are reflected in thousands of specific demands on every firm—high wages, pure air, job security, product quality, community service, taxes, occupational health and safety regulations, equal employment opportunity regulations, product variety, wide markets, career opportunities, company growth, investment security, high ROI, and so on. Although most, perhaps all, of these claims represent desirable ends, they cannot be pursued with equal emphasis. They must be assigned priorities in accordance with the relative emphasis that the firm will give them. That emphasis results from the criteria that the firm uses in its strategic decision making.

## Creating a Green Corporate Strategy

Seldom do the diverse stakeholders of a corporation coalesce around a mandate as energetically as they have in encouraging companies to improve their action to protect the ecology and provide environmentally friendly products through pollution-reduced processes. Corporate response has been directly forthcoming. Forrester Research found that 84 percent of companies were actively pursuing a "green" strategy, involving environmentally and socially responsible projects. The key drivers for the companies to join the green movement were energy efficiencies, government regulations, and rising consumer demand.

Popular approaches to becoming a green company include adopting sustainability as a core component of the business strategy, embedding green principles in innovation efforts, including green principles in making major decisions, and integrating sustainability into corporate brand marketing.

Many companies have chosen to elevate environmental sustainability to the level of a core component of its strategic plan. In 2005, General Electric (GE) created a green initiative to promote green technologies. By 2006, GE's "Ecomagination" program included a portfolio of 80 new products and services and delivered $100 million in cost savings to GE bottom line.

In 2007, Michael Dell announced his commitment to leading the company to become the "greenest technology company on the planet." By 2008, the carbon intensity of the company was the lowest among *Fortune 500* companies and was less than half of that of closest competitor.

HP demonstrated its commitment to a green company with carefully developed goals, such as reducing combined energy consumption and the greenhouse gas emissions of its products and services to 25 percent below 2005 levels by 2010, improving energy efficiency of servers by 50 percent, and improving recycling and reuse of its electronic products.

### Investors Appreciate Internal Green Initiatives

Companies in diverse areas of operation are making efforts to improve sustainability and reduce adverse effects on environment that results from corporate operations.[28] The purpose of this effort is twofold: Reducing environmental footprint improves the company image and appeals to green consumers; and higher sustainability in operations saves resources. Since the application of green ideas differs greatly within companies, there results are also different. However, as examples illustrate, the outs are often very beneficial for the company.

A company committed to implementing eco-efficient operations is Aetna. Aetna is controlling its carbon footprint by instituting the "telework" program, which involves asking its employees to work at home. Aetna believes that the program will reduce the combined driving of its employees by 65 million miles, save over 2 million gallons of gasoline, and prevent 23,000 metric tons of carbon dioxide emissions per year.

FedEx approach to green is to implement services that are more efficient. The company is investing in renewable energy technology for its operations and shipping facilities. More than 50 percent of the vehicles in FedEx's delivery fleet are powered by hybrid-electric engines. These trucks reduce FedEx's annual fuel usage by 150,000 gallons and its carbon dioxide emissions by 1,521 metric tons.

The efforts of Wal-Mart to eliminate waste by reducing, recycling, or reusing everything that comes into its 4,100 American stores are a good example. Wal-Mart is introducing recyclable and biodegradable packaging and sends its compostable goods to rot in boxes that are turned into mulch. Other efforts include the exclusive use of LED lights and improving the efficiency of heating and air-conditioning units used in all stores. Roofs of all Wal-Mart stores are now painted white to reflect sun light better, since it is more costly to cool buildings in the summer than to heat during winter.

In 2007, Cadbury Schweppes PLC launched its "Purple goes Green" initiative and specified its green targets on its website. The targets included a 50 percent reduction of net absolute carbon emissions by 2020 with a minimum of 30 percent from in-company actions, a 10 percent reduction in packaging used per ton of product, conversion of 60 percent of packaging to biodegradable and environmentally sustainable sources, a 100 percent of secondary packaging being recyclable, and requirement of all "water scarce" sites to have water reduction programs. By 2010, Cadbury was making headway on its goals. For example, its Eco Easter Eggs used 75 percent less plastic than previously, thereby reducing its annual plastic use by 202 tons.

Toyota created a new product with its 2010 Prius car model. It offered carbon dioxide emissions that were 37 percent less than that of a comparable diesel or gasoline vehicle. To achieve the improvement, Toyota evaluated every step of its product design and devised an array of innovative and environmentally friendly features, like a new vehicle design featuring 20 percent lighter drive components, and recycled plastics.

Companies can also become "greener" without incurring the costs of altering their supply chain by making changes internal to their organizations. Common steps include paper recycling or conservation, refurbishing and recycling old equipment, consolidating servers, server virtualization, instituting a lights-out policy, and replacing old equipment with more energy-efficient models.[29]

Many companies enjoy financial benefits of this approach. For example:

- By re-routing their trucks to avoid left turns, which keep trucks idling that wastes time, money, and fuel, UPS reduced routes by 28 million miles.
- By turning off their computers when they are not in use during evenings and weekends (43 percent of the time), various companies save $150 per system per year.
- USEC, a $1.6 billion nuclear fuel company, reduced its power consumption by 40 percent by running its servers on an energy-efficient virtualized environment.
- McDonald's Corp saves 3,200 tons of paper and cardboard annually ever since it eliminated clamshell sandwich containers and replaced them with single-layer flexible sandwich wraps.

### Governments Mandate Adherence to Green Regulations

Regulations in several countries require some companies to adhere to specific green mandates. For example:

- The Comprehensive Environmental Response, Compensation and Liability Act of 1980, also known as the EPA "Superfund," holds companies in the United States accountable for solid and liquid waste disposal, sometimes decades after the disposal occurred.
- Executive Order 12780, issued in 1991, uses the buying power of the U.S. government to force suppliers into greener behavior. The order requires all federal agencies to buy products made from recycled materials when possible and to support suppliers that participate in recovery programs, thereby forcing government suppliers to recognize the long-term environmental effects of both inputs and end products.
- China enacted the first stage of its Restriction of Hazardous Substances in 2007. This regulation is designed to reduce

the use of toxic and hazardous substances in electronic and electric products. Exporters are prohibited from shipping items that contain lead, mercury, cadmium, hexavalent chromium, polybrominated biphenyls (PBB), and polybrominated diphenylether (PBDE). Companies that export to China must engineer their supply chains to meet these regulations or face heavy penalties for noncompliance.

### Customers Endorse External Green Initiatives

Adopting an external green strategy involves analyzing the company's entire value chain to go beyond complying with regulations, reducing their energy use, or marketing ecologically safe products. The goal is to engage their stakeholders in a coordinated program to benefit the environment.

Once a company has defined what it means by the term green means, it has to build processes and products around that vision, it is important to have a marketing strategy to attract consumers' attention. A survey of 6,000 global consumers found that 87 percent believed it was their "duty" to contribute to a better environment, and that 55 percent would pay more for a brand if it supported a cause in which they believed.[30] In turn, retailers and manufacturers are demanding greener products and supply chains. Therefore, marketing strategies are structured and communicated in ways that bolster the corporation's green credibility.[31]

Using its external green strategy, P&G found that 80 percent of the energy used to wash clothes comes from heating the water. P&G calculated that U.S. consumers could save an estimated $63 per year by washing in cold water rather than in warm water. They then created Tide Coldwater, an extension of the Tide brand, which they positioned as a product that would enable customers to save on energy bills. Marketing efforts also reassured consumers of the product's efficacy. P&G designed a dedicated website on which consumers could calculate the amount of energy they could save by using the product. As evidence of the success of the approach, Tide Coldwater generated $2 billion in sales in its first year.

## Society Learns of Sustainability Efforts through Marketing

Companies incorporate their environmental position into communication messages to improve organizational reputation and to attract and inform customers, partners, and investors.

Coca-Cola makes stakeholders aware of its environmental position by issuing news release to the public of its efforts to support of recycling and launch of "Give it back" marketing effort to support recycling. In 2009, Coca-Cola opened the world's largest bottle-to-bottle recycling plant, pledging to recycle 100 percent of its bottles and cans and to ensure sustainability in packaging. The plant produces 100 million pounds of food-grade recycled PET plastic each year, which is equivalent to 2 billion 20-ounce plastic bottles. Additionally, over 10 years, the plant will reduce its emissions of carbon dioxide by 1 million metric tons.

Sustainability reports are used to discuss green activities and highlight strategies and progress. For example, Johnson & Johnson sustainability report has a separate section devoted to environment. The environment section covers how design solutions are used to minimize the size and weight of product packaging and increase the recycled content in packaging. The company also highlights its water management strategy, compliance issues, carbon emissions, waste reduction, and ozone-depletion plans.

# CHAPTER 6

# Formulating Business Unit Strategy

## Introduction

Business unit strategy involves creating a profitable competitive position for a business within a specific industry or market segment. Sometimes called *competitive strategy*, its principal focus is on *how* a firm (or profit center) should compete in a given competitive setting. In contrast, an overarching corporate strategy is concerned with the identification of market arenas *where* a corporation can compete successfully and *how*, as a parent company, it can add value to its strategic business units (SBUs).

Deciding how to compete in a specific market is a complex issue for a business. Optimal strategies depend on many factors, including the *nature of the industry;* the company's *mission, goals,* and *objectives;* its *current position* and *core competencies;* and major *competitors' strategic choices.*

We begin our discussion by examining the *logic* behind strategic thinking at the business unit level. We first address the basic question: What determines relative profitability at the business unit level? We look at the relative importance of the industry in which a company competes and the competitive position of the firm within its industry, and we identify the drivers that determine sustainable competitive advantage. This logic naturally suggests a number of *generic strategy choices*—broad strategy prescriptions that define the principal dimensions of competition at the business unit level. The generic strategy that is most attractive, and the form that it should take, depends on the specific opportunities and challenges. The chapter next deals with the question of how to assess a strategic challenge. A variety of useful techniques is introduced for generating and evaluating strategic alternatives. The final section addresses the issue of designing a profitable business model.

## SBU Disruptions Come from Myriad Sources

When a group of CIOs was asked to predict the ways that technology would disrupt industries by 2525, they gave the following responses:[1]

- The self-driving car will be commonplace.
- There will be a shift to health-record openness.
- Higher education institutions will undergo a massive consolidation.
- Merchants will transition to cashless retailing.
- Home appliances will be remotely controlled.
- Custom-fit clothing will be mainstream.
- Virtual and telemedicine will keep more patients out of the hospital.

Each of these likely changes will disrupt the business plan of countless numbers of corporate SBUs and independent businesses. Each business will need to formulate a revised plan for attracting and serving customers.

## Foundations

### Strategic Logic at the Business Unit Level

What are the principal factors behind a business unit's relative profitability? How important are product superiority, cost, marketing and distribution effectiveness, and other factors? How important is the nature of the industry?

Although there are no simple answers to such questions, and the attractiveness of different strategic options depends on the competitive situation analyzed, much has been learned about what drives competitive success at the business unit level.

We begin with the observation that, at the broadest level, firm success is explained by two factors: the *attractiveness of the industry* in which a firm competes and its *relative position* within that industry. For example, the seemingly insatiable demand for new products in the early days of the software industry guaranteed big profits for the industry leaders and for many of their smaller rivals. In the fiercely competitive beer industry, however, relative positioning is a far more important determinant of profitability, as Budweiser's unprecedented performance has shown.

## How Much Does Industry Matter?

In a comprehensive study of business performance in four-digit Standard Industrial Classification (SIC) code categories, academic research provides an answer to the question: How much does industry matter? Researchers have found that industry, industry segment, and corporate parent accounted for 32 percent, 4 percent, and 19 percent, respectively, of the aggregate variance in business profits, with the remaining variance spread among many other less consequential influences. These results support the conclusion that industry characteristics are an important determinant of profit potential. Industry directly accounted for 36 percent of the explained total variation in profitability.[2]

## Relative Position

The relative profitability of rival firms depends on the *nature of their competitive position* (i.e., on their ability to create a *sustainable competitive advantage* vis-à-vis their competitors). The two generic forms of sustainable competitive positioning are a competitive advantage based on *lower delivered cost* and one based on the ability to *differentiate* products or services from those of competitors and command a price premium relative to the cost incurred.

Whether lowest cost or differentiation is most effective depends, among other factors, on a firm's choice of *competitive scope*. The scope of a competitive strategy includes elements such as the number of product and buyer segments served, the number of different geographic locations in which the firm competes, the extent to which it is vertically integrated, and the degree to which it must coordinate its positioning with related businesses in which the firm is invested.

Decisions about scope and competitive advantage are based on a detailed understanding of customers' values and a company's capabilities and opportunities relative to its competitors. In this sense, strategy reflects a firm's configuration of different elements. Competitive advantage results when a company has a better understanding of what customers' desire, when it learns to meet those customer needs at a lower cost than its rivals, or when it creates buyer value in unique ways that allow it to charge a premium.

### The Importance of Market Share

The relative importance of market share as a strategic goal at the business unit level has been the subject of considerable controversy. Arguing that profitability should be the primary goal of strategy, some analysts believe that executives have been led astray by the principal pursuit of market share.[3] Many failed companies have achieved high market shares, including Great Atlantic & Pacific Tea Company (A&P) in grocery sales, Intel in memory products, and WordPerfect in word processors. Thus, executives must ask themselves: Are we managing for volume growth or value growth?

## Formulating a Competitive Strategy

### Key Challenges

Managers face four key challenges in formulating competitive strategy at the business unit level: (1) analyzing the competitive environment, (2) anticipating key competitors' actions, (3) generating strategic options, and (4) choosing among alternatives.

The first challenge, "analyzing the competitive environment," deals with two questions: With whom will we compete, now and in the future? What relative strengths will we have as a basis for creating a sustainable competitive advantage? Answering these questions requires an analysis of the remote external environment, the industry environment, and internal capabilities.

The second challenge, "anticipating key competitors' actions," focuses on understanding how competitors are likely to react to different strategic moves. Industry leaders tend to behave differently from challengers or followers. A detailed competitor analysis is helpful in gaining an understanding of how competitors are likely to respond and why.

The third challenge, "identifying strategic options," requires a balancing of opportunities and constraints to craft a diverse array of strategic options ranging from defensive to preemptive moves. The fourth challenge, "choosing among alternatives," requires an analysis of the long-term impact of different strategy options as a basis for a final choice.

### What Is Competitive Advantage?

A firm has a *competitive advantage* when it is successful in designing and implementing a value-creating strategy that competitors are not currently using. The competitive advantage is *sustainable* when current or new competitors are not able to imitate or supplant it.

A competitive advantage is often created by combining strengths. Firms look for ways to exploit competencies and advantages at different points in the value chain to add value in different ways. Southwest Airlines' industry-best 15-minute turnaround time for getting airplanes back into the air, for example, is a competitive advantage that saves the firm $175 million annually in capital expenditures and differentiates the firm by allowing it to offer more flights per plane per day. The use of value analysis helps a firm to focus on areas in which it enjoys competitive advantages and to outsource functions in which it does not. To enhance its cost leadership position, Taco Bell outsources many food preparation functions, thereby allowing it to cut prices, reduce employees, and free up 40 percent of its kitchen space.

It is important for executives to understand the nature and sources of a firm's competitive advantages. They should also make sure that middle managers understand the competitive advantages, because the managers' awareness allows for a more effective exploitation of such advantages and leads to increased firm performance. Therefore, building a competitive advantage is rooted in identifying, practicing, strengthening, and instilling throughout the organization those leadership traits that improve the firm's reputation among its stakeholders. As a consequence, a focus on organizational learning and on creating, retaining, and motivating a skilled and knowledgeable workforce may be the best way for executives to foster competitive advantages in a rapidly changing business environment.

### Competitive Advantage in Three Circles

There is considerable appeal and anecdotal evidence that a company must build a distinct competitive advantage to grow and be profitable over the long term. However, it is difficult for many strategists to articulate clearly what their company's competitive advantage is and how it differs from those of competitors. Joel Urbany and James Davis have developed a clever, useful, and simple tool to help in this assessment called "three circle analysis."[4]

The strategizing team of executives should begin their analysis by thinking deeply about what customers of their type of product or service value and why. For example, they might value speedy service because they want to minimize inventory costs with a just-in-time inventory system.

Next, the strategists should draw three circles as shown in Figure 6.1. The first circle (seen on the top right) is to represent the team's consensus of what the most important customers or customer segments needs or wants from the product or service.

Urbany and Davis observe that even in very mature industries customers do not articulate all their wants conversations with companies. For example, there was no consumer demand on Procter & Gamble (P&G) to invent the Swiffer, whose category contributes significantly to the company's recent double-digit sales growth in home care products. Instead, the Swiffer emerged from P&G's careful observation of the challenges of household cleaning. Therefore, in conducting this initial phase of competitive advantage analysis, the consumers' unexpressed needs can often become a growth opportunities.

The second circle represents the team's view of how customers perceive the company's offerings (seen on the top left). The extent to which the two circles overlap indicates how well the company's offerings are fulfilling customers' needs. The third circle represents the strategists' view of how customers perceive the offerings of the company's competitors.

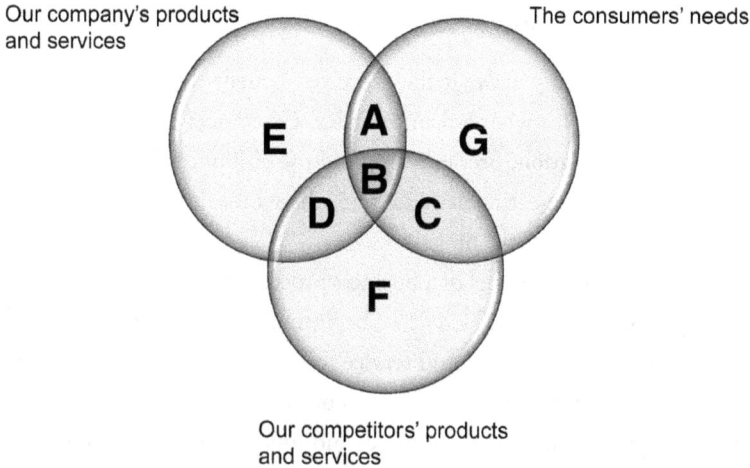

*Figure 6.1 Competitive advantage analysis*

Each area within the circles is important, but areas A, B, and C are critical to building competitive advantage. The planning team should ask questions about each:

- For A: How big and sustainable are our advantages? Are they based on distinctive capabilities?
- For B: Are we delivering effectively in the area of parity?
- For C: How can we counter our competitors' advantages?

As Urbany and Davis explain, the team should form hypotheses about the company's competitive advantages and test them by asking customers. The process can yield surprising insights, such as how much opportunity for growth exists in space G. Another insight might be what value the company or its competitors create that customers do not need (D, F, or F). For example, Zeneca Ag Products discovered that one of its most important distributors would be willing to do more business with the firm only if Zeneca eliminated the time-consuming promotional programs that its managers thought were an essential part of their value proposition. However, the big surprise is often that area A, envisioned as huge by the company, is often quite small in the eyes of the customer.

## Value Chain Analysis

In competitive terms, *value* is the perceived benefit that a buyer is willing to pay a firm for what a firm provides. Customers derive value from product differentiation, product cost, and the ability of the firm to meet their needs. Value-creating activities are, therefore, the discrete building blocks of competitive advantage.

A *value chain* is a model of a business process. It depicts the value creation process as a series of activities, beginning with processing raw materials and ending with sales and service to end users. *Value chain analysis* involves the study of costs and elements of product or service differentiation throughout the chain of activities and linkages to determine present and potential sources of competitive advantage.

The value chain divides a firm's business process into component activities that add value: primary activities that contribute to the physical creation of the product and support activities that assist the primary activities and each other. Charles Schwab successfully used its expertise in a support activity to create value in a primary activity. The firm offers a broad range of distribution channels (primary activity) for its brokerage services and holds extensive expertise in information technology and brokerage systems (support activities). Schwab uses its IT knowledge to create two new distribution channels for brokerage services—E-Schwab on the Internet and the Telebroker touch-tone telephone brokering service—both of which provide value by delivering low-cost services.[5]

Once a firm's primary, support, and activity types are defined, value chain analysis assigns assets and operating costs to all value-creating activities. Activity-based cost accounting is often used to determine whether a competitive advantage exists.

A firm *differentiates* itself from its competitors when it provides something unique that is valuable to buyers beyond a low price. Dell's ability to sell, build to order, and ship a computer to the customer within a few days is a unique differentiator of its value chain. Benetton, the Italian casual wear company, reconfigured its traditional outsourced manufacturing and distribution network to achieve differentiation.[6] Its executives reasoned that the company could improve its flexibility by directly overseeing key business processes throughout the supply chain. If specific activities reduce a buyer's cost or provide a higher level of buyer satisfaction, customers are willing to pay a premium price. Sources of differentiation of primary activities that provide a higher level of buyer satisfaction include build-to-order manufacturing, efficient and on-time delivery of goods, promptness in responding to customer service requests, and high quality.

It is important to identify the value that individual primary and support activities contribute beyond their costs. Different segments of the value chain represent potential sources of profit and, therefore, define *profit pools.*[7] Value chain analysis showed Nike and Reebok how their core competencies in product design (a support activity) and marketing and sales (primary activities) created value for customers. This conclusion led Nike to outsource almost all other activities. In a second case, after completing a detailed value chain analysis, Millennium Pharmaceuticals opted to shift from drug research in the upstream portion of the industry to drug manufacturing downstream, to improve its profitability. This strategy was derived from the firm's clear understanding of the entire pharmaceutical value chain and its newly recognized ability to exploit different profit pools.[8]

Analyzing the value chains of competitors, customers, and suppliers can help a firm add value by focusing on the needs of downstream customers or the weaknesses of upstream suppliers.[9] Dow Chemical captures value from downstream rubber glove producers, to whom it used to sell chemicals, by making the gloves themselves. BASF adds value by leveraging its core competencies in the paint-coating process by painting car doors for automobile manufacturers, instead of just selling them the paint.

Value chain analysis can also be used to shape responses to changing upstream and downstream market conditions through collaboration with customers and suppliers to improve speed, cut costs, and enhance the end customer's perception of value. This is especially true as intercompany links such as electronic data integration systems, strategic alliances, just-in-time manufacturing, electronic markets, and networked companies blur the boundaries of many organizations.

Approaching value chain analysis as a shared process involving the different members of the chain can optimize a firm's value creation by minimizing collective costs. Dell, for example, shares information about its customers with its suppliers. This improves its suppliers' ability to forecast demand, which results in reduced inventory and logistics costs for Dell and the suppliers. Home Depot and General Electric (GE) established an alliance between their value chains that reduces direct and indirect costs for each firm. A web-based application links Home Depot's point-of-purchase data to GE's e-business system and enables Home Depot to ship directly to its customers from GE. The value chain to value chain connection enables Home Depot to sell more GE products and to reduce the inventory in its own warehouses. In addition, GE can use the real-time demand information from Home Depot to adjust the production rate of appliances.

With advances in information technology and the Internet, companies can monitor value creation across many activities and linkages. For purposes of monitoring, it is useful to distinguish between the physical and virtual components of the value chain. The *physical value chain* represents the use of raw materials and labor to deliver a tangible product. The *virtual value chain* represents the information flows underlying the physical activities evident within a firm. Engineering teams at Ford Motor Company optimize the physical design process of a vehicle using real-time collaboration in a virtual workplace. Oracle Corporation is a front-runner in adding virtual value for the customer by using the Internet to directly test and distribute their software products.

## Porter's Generic Business Unit Strategies

### Differentiation or Low Cost?

Earlier, we distinguished between two *generic* competitive strategic postures: *low cost* and *differentiation*. They are called *generic* because in principle they apply to any business and any industry. However, the relative attractiveness of different generic strategies is related to choices about competitive scope. If a company chooses a relatively broad target market (e.g., Walmart), a low-cost strategy is aimed at *cost leadership*. Such a strategy aggressively exploits opportunities for cost reduction through economies of scale and cumulative learning (experience effects) in purchasing and manufacturing and generally calls for proportionately low expenditures on R&D, marketing, and overhead. Cost leaders generally charge less for their products and services than rivals and aim for a substantial share of the market by appealing primarily to budget-sensitive customers. Their low prices serve as an entry barrier to potential competitors. As long as they maintain their relative cost advantage, cost leaders can maintain a defensible position in the marketplace.

With a more narrow scope, a low-cost strategy is based on *focus with low cost*. As with any focus strategy, a small, well-defined market niche— a particular group of customers or geographic region—is selected to the exclusion of others. Then, in the case of cost focus, only activities directly relevant to serving that niche are undertaken, at the lowest possible cost.

Southwest Airlines is renowned for its cost-focus strategy. A low-fare carrier that has the highest-profit margins in the airline industry, Southwest Airlines grew 4,048 percent in the 1990s. Its low-cost, no-frills strategy has been highly successful in the U.S. domestic market.

The cost-focus strategy is based on a narrow scope, with a small, well-defined market niche. Southwest concentrates on short-haul routes with high traffic densities and offers frequent flights throughout the day. Efficiency has been improved by eliminating costs associated with "hub" routes involving large major U.S. airports. Southwest limits the number of U.S. states and cities of operation, and it targets secondary airports because of their lower cost structures.

Southwest's fundamentally different operating structure allows it to charge lower fares than more established airlines. A typical flight, which lasts 1 hour on average, has no assigned seats; in-flight service consists of drinks and snacks only, and the company does not offer transfer of luggage to other airlines.

Southwest's fleet consists of 284 Boeing 737s, which make more than 3,510 flights per day. Having one type of aircraft allows for greater efficiency and easier turnarounds. All Southwest 737s use the same equipment, thereby keeping training and maintenance costs down. Finally, high-asset use, reflected in a turnaround time averaging 20 minutes, which is less than half the industry average, reduces its operating expenses by 25 percent.

The recession of 2007–2009 caused many companies to abandon their growth strategies in favor of a multiyear cost reduction strategy that could improve their survival odds. Because of successful cost cutting at Gap, its shares increased 27 percent in 2008 because of increased profits on declining revenues. Gap's cost savings were achieved through reduced inventory levels and the sell-off of noncore assets such as selected real estate holdings.

Similarly, in the face of sharply declining revenues, Dell undertook cost cutting in 2008, including massive layoffs that totaled 11,000 employees for the year and an aggressive plan to sell its manufacturing facilities worldwide.

Although many firms find it possible to maintain some level of profit by cost cutting for as long as one full year, aggressive cost-cutters must eventually find ways to increase their revenues. Circuit City and Radio Shack cut costs and increased profit margins in 2008, but were undone by sharp declines in their revenues. Circuit City filed for bankruptcy in November 2008, the day after it announced that it would close 155 retail stores, and Radio Shack lost 50 percent of its market value in that year.

Differentiation postures can also be tied to decisions of scope. A *differentiation* strategy aimed at a broad, mass market seeks to create uniqueness on an industry-wide basis. Walt Disney Productions and Nike are examples. Broad-scale differentiation can be achieved through product design, brand image, technology, distribution, service, or a combination of these elements. Finally, like cost focus, a *focus with differentiated* strategy is aimed at a well-defined segment of the market and target customers willing to pay for value added.

### Requirements for Success

The two generic routes—*low cost* and *differentiation*—are fundamentally different. Achieving *cost leadership* requires a ruthless devotion to minimizing costs through continuous improvement in manufacturing, process engineering, and other cost-reducing strategies. Scale and scope effects must be leveraged in all aspects of the value creation process—in the design of products and services, purchasing practices, and distribution. In addition, achieving and sustaining cost leadership require tight control and an organizational structure and incentive system supportive of a cost-focused discipline.

*Differentiation* requires an altogether different approach. Here, the concern is for value added. Differentiation has multiple objectives. The primary objective is to redefine the rules by which customers arrive at their purchase decisions by offering something unique that is valuable. In doing so, companies also seek to erect barriers to imitation. Differentiation strategies are often misunderstood; "spray painting the product green" is *not* differentiation. Differentiation is a strategic choice to provide something of value to the customer other than a low price. One way to differentiate a product or service is to add functionality. However, many other, sometimes more effective, ways to differentiate are possible. R&D aimed at enhancing product quality and durability (Maytag) is a viable element of a differentiation strategy. Investing in brand equity (Coca-Cola) and pioneering new ways of distribution (Avon Cosmetics) are others.

Considerable evidence suggests that the most successful differentiation strategies involve multiple sources of differentiation. Higher-quality raw materials, unique product design, manufacturing that is more reliable, superior marketing and distribution programs, and quicker service all contribute to set a company's offering apart from rival products. The use of more than one source of differentiation makes it harder for competitors to imitate a company's competitive advantage effectively. In addition to using multiple sources, integrating the different dimensions of value added—functionality, and economic and psychological values—is critical. Effective differentiation thus requires explicit decisions about how much value to add, where to add such value, and how to communicate such added value to the customer. Critically for the firm, customers must be willing to pay a premium relative to the cost of achieving the differentiation. Therefore, successful differentiation requires the thorough understanding of what customers value, the relative importance they attach to the satisfaction of their needs and wants, and how much they are willing to pay.

### Risks

Each generic posture carries unique risks. Cost leaders must concern themselves with technological change that can nullify past investments in

scale economics or accumulated learning. In an increasingly global economy, firms that rely on cost leadership are particularly vulnerable to new
entrants from other parts of the world that can take advantage of even
lower factor costs. The biggest challenge to differentiators is *imitation.*
Imitation narrows actual and perceived differentiation. If this occurs,
buyers might change their minds about what constitutes differentiation
and then change their loyalties and preferences.

The goal of each strategic generic posture is to create sustainability.
For cost leaders, sustainability requires continually improving efficiency,
looking for less expensive sources of supply, and seeking ways to reduce
manufacturing and distribution costs. For differentiators, sustainability requires the firm to erect barriers to entry around their dimensions
of uniqueness, to use multiple sources of differentiation, and to create
switching costs for customers. Organizationally, a differentiation strategy calls for strong coordination among R&D, product development and
marketing, and incentives aimed at value creation and creativity.

### Critique of Porter's Generic Strategies

Generic strategies are not always viable. Low-cost strategies are less effective when low cost is the industry norm, and most executives reject
Porter's generic strategies in favor of strategies that combine elements of
cost leadership, differentiation, and flexibility to meet customer needs.[10]

The most common arguments against Porter's generic strategies are
that low-cost production and differentiation are not mutually exclusive
and that when they can exist together in a firm's strategy, they result in
sustained profitability.[11] The preconditions for a cost leadership strategy
stem from the industry's structure, whereas the preconditions for differentiation stem from customer tastes. Because these two factors are independent, the opportunity for a firm to pursue both cost leadership and
differentiation strategies should always be considered.

In fact, differentiation can permit a firm to attain a low-cost position. For example, expenditures to differentiate a product can increase
demand by creating loyalty, which decreases the price elasticity for the
product. Such actions can also broaden product appeal, enabling the firm
to increase market share at a given price, and increases its volume sold.

Differentiation initially increases unit cost. However, the firm can reduce unit cost in the long run if costs fall due to learning economies, economies of scale, and economies of scope. Conversely, the savings generated from low-cost production permit a firm to increase spending on marketing, service, and product enhancement, thereby producing differentiation.

Finally, the possibility of providing both improved quality and lower costs exists within the total quality management framework. High quality and high productivity are complementary, and low quality is associated with higher costs.

## Value Disciplines

"Value disciplines" is a term coined by Michael Treacy and Fred Wiersema to describe different ways companies can create value for customers. Specifically, they are three strategic priorities: *product leadership, operational excellence,* and *customer intimacy.*[12]

### Product Leadership

Companies pursuing *product leadership* produce a continuous stream of state-of-the-art products and services. Such companies are innovation driven, and they constantly raise the bar for competitors by offering more value and better solutions.

The product leadership discipline is based on the following four principles:

1. The encouragement of innovation through small ad hoc working groups, an "experimentation is good" mind-set, and compensation systems that reward success, constant product innovation is encouraged.
2. A risk-oriented management style that recognized that product leadership companies are necessarily innovators, which requires a recognition that there are risks (as well as rewards) inherent in new ventures.
3. Recognition that the company's current success and future prospects lie in its talented product design people and those who support them.

4. Recognition of the need to educate and lead the market regarding the use and benefits of new products.

Examples of companies that use product leadership as a cornerstone of their strategies include Intel, Apple, and Nike.

### Operational Excellence

*Operational excellence*—the second value discipline—describes a strategic approach aimed at better production and delivery mechanisms. Walmart, American Airlines, FedEx, and Starwood Hotels & Resorts Worldwide all pursue operational excellence.

Starwood is one of the largest hotel chains in the world with 742 establishments in 80 countries, including famous brands such as Sheraton, Westin, Four Points, and St. Regis. Following an extended period of subpar performance, the company decided to stylishly renovate its underperforming hotels and focus on doing and presenting everything it already did, much better.

The firm's biggest changes were made to the Sheraton hotel chain, which underwent a $750 million makeover. This renovation was undertaken to restore a reputation for reliability, value, and consistency. The revamping did away with flowered bedspreads in favor of a Ralph Lauren style. Amenities such as ergonomic desk chairs and two-line telephones became standard.

Much of Starwood's Four Points brand underwent renovations with as much as 80 percent of the original hotel structure torn down. Every room was redesigned and redecorated. Twenty-four-hour fitness facilities were opened. Olympic-sized heated swimming pools with outdoor reception areas became standard. Business centers were expanded to include ballrooms and meeting rooms to accommodate groups of all sizes. Management expanded dining options to range from restaurants to pubs. Guestroom hallways and lobbies were brightened and dramatically redesigned in a subtle, Mediterranean style. Wallpaper borders, sconce lighting, and artful signage were added to present the hotel with a bright fresh look.

Starwood's focus on operational excellence was immediately successful. For the four straight quarters following the activation of the changes, Starwood led Marriott and Hilton in North American revenue per available room. Operating income increased 26 percent.

## Customer Intimacy

A strategy based on *customer intimacy* concentrates on building customer loyalty. Nordstrom and Home Depot continually tailor their products and services to changing customer needs. Pursuing customer intimacy can be expensive, but the long-term benefits of a loyal clientele can pay off handsomely.

Because the vast majority of companies worldwide now claim to give top priority to customer concerns, it might be hard to imagine how a firm distinguishes itself through customer intimacy. Home Depot provides an excellent example of a firm that succeeds. It uses customer intimacy initiatives to marginalize competitors. The company's plan began with the creation of its "Service Performance Initiative," which emphasizes changing daily operations to provide a more shopper-friendly store atmosphere. Home Depot added off-hour stocking, which moves merchandise in and out of inventory during late evening hours or after closing for those stores that have not expanded their operating hours to 24 hours per day.

The main benefit of the new stocking method is the ability of employees to focus on customer service and sales. Before the implementation of the initiative, salespeople spent 40 percent of their time with customers and 60 percent on other work-related duties. After the customer intimacy initiatives, salespeople were able to spend 70 percent of their time with customers on sales-oriented tasks and 30 percent on other duties.

Home Depot undertook two additional customer intimacy initiatives. The first was the installation of Linux Info for point-of-sale support systems. With the new system, customers can place orders from home over the Internet and have the purchase processed at the store's register. This process allows customers to enter the store simply for pickup, having already purchased their merchandise. The second initiative involves home improvement classes taught at its stores. Customer intimacy is enhanced when professionals teach customers how to buy and install the proper materials and construction equipment. Home Depot sells products and receives customer feedback as outcomes of the courses.

Most companies try to excel in one of the three value disciplines and be competitive in the others. Explicitly choosing a value discipline and focusing available resources on creating a gap between the company and its immediate competitors with regard to the discipline sharpens a company's strategic focus.

## Designing a Profitable Business Model

Designing a profitable business model is a critical part of formulating a business unit strategy. Creating an effective model requires a clear understanding of how the firm will generate profits and the strategic actions it must take to succeed over the long term.

Adrian Slywotzky and David Morrison have identified 22 business models—designs that generate profits in a unique way. [13] They present these models as examples, believing that others do or can exist. The authors also confirm that in some instances profitability depends on the interplay of two or more business models.

*What is our business model? How do we make a profit?* Slywotzky and Morrison suggest that these are the two most productive questions asked of executives. The classic strategy rule suggested that, "Gain market share and profits will follow." This approach once worked for most industries. However, because of competitive turbulence caused by globalization and rapid technological advancements, the once popular belief in a strong correlation between market share and profitability has collapsed in many industries.

How can businesses earn sustainable profits? The answer is found by analyzing the following questions: Where will the firm be able to make a profit in this industry? How should the business model be designed so that the firm will be profitable?

Slywotzky and Morrison describe the following profitability business models as ways to answer these questions:

1. *Customer Development/Customer Solutions Profit model.* Companies that use this business model make money by finding ways to improve their customers' economics and investing in ways for customers to improve their processes.
2. *Product Pyramid Profit model.* This model is effective in markets where customers have strong preferences for product characteristics, including variety, style, color, and price. By offering a number of variations, companies can build so-called product pyramids. At the base are low-priced, high-volume products, and at the top are high-priced, low-volume products. Profit is concentrated at the top of the pyramid, but the base is the strategic firewall (i.e., a strong, low-priced brand that deters competitor entry), thereby protecting the margins at the top. Consumer goods companies and automobile companies use this model.
3. *Multicomponent System Profit model.* Some businesses are characterized by a production/marketing system that consists of components that generate substantially different levels of profitability. In hotels, for example, there is a substantial difference between the profitability of room rentals and that of bar operations. In such instances, it is often useful to maximize the use of the highest-profit components to maximize the profitability of the whole system.
4. *Switchboard Profit model.* Some markets function by connecting multiple sellers to multiple buyers. The switchboard profit model creates a high-value intermediary that concentrates these multiple communication pathways through one point, or "switchboard," and thereby reduces costs for both parties in exchange for a fee. As volume increases, so, too, do profits.
5. *Time Profit model.* Sometimes, speed is the key to profitability. This business model takes advantage of first-mover advantage. To sustain this model, constant innovation is essential.
6. *Blockbuster Profit model.* In some industries, profitability is driven by a few great product successes. This business model is representative of movie studios, pharmaceutical firms, and software companies, which have high R&D and launch costs and finite product cycles. In this type of environment, it pays to concentrate resource

investments in a few projects rather than to take positions in a variety of products.

7. *Profit Multiplier model.* This business model reaps gains, again and again, from the same product, character, trademark capability, or service. Think of the value that Michael Jordan, Inc. creates with the image of the great basketball legend. This model can be a powerful engine for businesses with strong consumer brands.

8. *Entrepreneurial Profit model.* Small can be beautiful. This business model stresses that diseconomies of scale can exist in companies. They attack companies that have become comfortable with their profit levels, with formal, bureaucratic systems that are remote from customers. As their expenses grow and customer relevance declines, such companies are vulnerable to entrepreneurs who are in direct contact with their customers.

9. *Specialization Profit model.* This business model stresses growth through sequenced specialization. Consulting companies have used this design successfully.

10. *Installed Base Profit model.* A company that pursues this model profits because its established user base subsequently buys the company's brand of consumables or follow-on products. Installed base profits provide a protected annuity stream. Examples include razors and blades, software and upgrades, copiers and toner cartridges, and cameras and film.

11. *De Facto Standard Profit model.* A variant of the Installed Base Profit model, this model is appropriate when the Installed Base model becomes the de facto standard that governs competitive behavior in the industry, as is the case with Oracle.

# CHAPTER 7

# Business Unit Strategy: Contexts and Special Dimensions

## Introduction

Generic strategies are useful for identifying broad frameworks within which a competitive advantage can be developed and exploited. However, to forecast the relative effectiveness of different options, strategists consider the *context* in which a strategy is to be implemented. To see how such analysis is done, in this chapter we examine six types of industry settings. First, we look at three contexts that relate to the various evolutionary stages of an industry: *emerging, growth, mature, and declining*. Next, we discuss four industry environments that pose unique strategic challenges: *fragmented, deregulating, hypercompetitive, and Internet-based* industries. Because hyper-competition is increasingly characteristic of business-level competition in many industries, we then discuss two critical attributes of successful firms in dynamic industries: speed and innovation.

## One Cause to Reconsider an SBU Strategy

As we discussed in the introduction of Chapter 4, the ongoing implementation of the Affordable Care Act (ACA), has immersed the healthcare industry in widespread, disruptive changes. These changes provide growth opportunities for some firms, but they also threaten established firms that may be unseated by competitors who adapt to market changes more quickly or who find innovative new ways to deliver services.

Consequently, every competitor in the disrupted industry must consider the strategic consequences of the ACA at its SBU levels. McKinsey& Company has identified three basic strategies that companies in other industries have used effectively to adjust to disruptions that they faced.[1] The hope is that modeling SBU strategies on the success of companies in similar situation in other industries will be instructive to healthcare firms.

The first basic strategy to consider is for the company to refocus its business portfolio, shifting its attention to those business activities that will benefit from industry changes or will be unaffected by them. Proctor & Gamble (P&G) used this strategy successfully to shift its focus from food products, where profit margins were falling, to branded home, health and beauty products where margins were more attractive. It sold Jif and Crisco in 2002, and Sunny Delight and Punica in 2004, and it continued selling off its remaining food and beverage brands, including Pringles and Folgers. Almost simultaneously, it re-launched its Oil of Olay skincare brand, expanded the product lines under its Mr. Clean brand, launched Swiffer, expanded its fragrance offerings, and acquired Gillette.

A second SBU strategy requires the company to transform its core business model. Charles Schwab, which had made its name as a low-cost stockbroker, undertook such a transformation when online brokers undercut its price. Schwab responded with cut prices and a new online trading platform, but kept its existing offices and customer service staff as competitive advantages against the new online brokers.[2]

The final strategy for dealing with a disruptive industry is to build a new SBU in a different market to make up for losses in the disrupted one. In the early 1990s, IBM, a force in the PC industry that sold end-to-end computing systems to businesses, found itself threatened by low-cost PC manufacturers. The corporation responded by using its connections with clients and its knowledge of company computer systems to develop a services division whose success counterbalanced the declining earnings from IBM's hardware business. It created the IBM Consulting Group, which over the succeeding decade, grew to make up half of IBM's revenue. Growth in the division, known as IBM Global Services, was sparked by its acquisition of PricewaterhouseCoopers management consulting and technical services businesses in 2002.

# Emerging, Growth, Mature, and Declining Industries

## Strategy in Emerging Industries

New industries or industry segments emerge in a variety of ways. Technological breakthroughs can launch entirely new industries or reform old ones, as in the case of changes to the telephone industry with the advent of cellular technology. Sometimes changes in the macro environment spawn new industries. Examples are solar energy and Internet technology.

From a strategic perspective, new industries present new opportunities. Their technologies are typically immature. This means that competitors will actively try to improve existing designs and processes or leapfrog them altogether with next-generation technology. A battle for standards might ensue. Costs are typically high and unpredictable, entry barriers low, supplier relationships underdeveloped, and distribution channels just emerging.

Timing can be critical in determining strategic success in an emerging market. The first company to come out with a new product or service often has a *first mover advantage*. First movers have the opportunity to shape customer expectations and define the competitive rules of the game. In high-technology industries, first movers can sometimes set standards for all subsequent products. Microsoft was able to accomplish this with its Windows operating system. In general, first movers have a relatively brief window of opportunity to establish themselves as industry leaders in technology, cost, or service.

Exercising strategic leadership in the emerging market can be an effective way to reduce risk. In addition to the ability to shape the industry structure based on timing, method of entry, and experience in similar situations, leadership opportunities include the ability to control product and process development through superior technology, quality, or customer knowledge; leverage existing relationships with suppliers and distributors; and leverage access to a core group of early, loyal customers.

## Strategy in Growth Industries

Growth presents a host of challenges. Competitors tend to focus on expanding their market shares. Over time, buyers become knowledgeable and can better distinguish between competitive offerings. As a result, increased segmentation often accompanies the transition to market maturity. Cost control becomes an important element of strategy as unit margins shrink and new products and applications are harder to find. In industries with global potential, international markets become more important. The globalization of competition also introduces new uncertainties as a second wave of global competitors enters the race.

During the early-growth phase, companies tend to add more products, models, sizes, and flavors to appeal to an increasingly segmented market. Toward the end of the growth phase, cost considerations become a priority. In addition, process innovation becomes an important dimension of cost control, as do the redefinitions of supplier and distributor relations. Finally, horizontal integration becomes attractive as a way of consolidating a company's market position or increasing a firm's international presence.

Competing companies that enter the market at this time, often labeled as *followers*, have different advantages than early market leaders. Later entrants have the opportunity to evaluate alternative technologies, delay investment in risky projects or plant capacity, and imitate or leapfrog superior product and technology offerings. Followers also tap into proven market segments rather than take the risks associated with trying to develop latent market demand into ongoing revenue streams.

Firms that consider entry into a growing industry must also face the strategic decision of whether to enter through internal development or acquisition. Entry into a new segment or industry through *internal development* involves creating a new business, often in a somewhat unfamiliar competitive environment. It is also likely to be slow and expensive. Developing new products, processes, partnerships, and systems takes time and requires substantial learning. For these reasons, companies increasingly are turning to *joint ventures, alliances*, and *acquisitions* of existing players as strategies for invading new product–market segments.

Two major issues must be analyzed as part of the decision process to enter a new market: (1) What are the structural barriers to entry? (2) How will incumbent firms react to the intrusion? Some of the most important structural impediments are the level of investment required, access to production or distribution facilities, and the threat of overcapacity.

Potential retaliation is more difficult to analyze. Incumbents will oppose a new player if resistance is likely to pay off. This is more likely to occur in mature markets if growth is low, products or services are not highly differentiated, fixed costs are high, capacity is ample, and the market is of great strategic importance to incumbents. However, the likelihood of competitor resistance at any stage of the life cycle suggests the important issues in the search for new markets. What industries are experiencing disequilibria, where incumbents are likely to be slow to react? In what industries could the firm influence the industry structure? Where do the benefits of entry exceed the costs, including the costs of dealing with retaliation by incumbents?

### Strategy in Mature and Declining Industries

Carefully choosing a balance between differentiation and low-cost postures and deciding whether to compete in multiple- or single-industry segments are critically important issues as maturity sets in and decline threatens. Growth tends to mask strategic errors and let companies survive; a low- or no-growth environment is far less benevolent.

Firms earn attractive profits during the long maturity stage of an industry lifecycle when they do the following:

1. Concentrate on segments that offer chances for higher growth or higher return;
2. Manage product and process innovation aimed at further differentiation, cost reduction, or rejuvenating segment growth;
3. Streamline production and delivery to cut costs; and
4. Gradually "harvest" the business in preparation for a strategic shift to more promising products or industries.

Counterbalancing these opportunities, mature and declining industries contain a number of strategic pitfalls that companies should avoid:

1. An overly optimistic view of the industry or the company's position within it,

2. A lack of strategic clarity shown by a failure to choose between a broad-based and a focused competitive approach,

3. Investing too much for too little return—the so-called "cash trap,"

4. Trading market share for profitability in response to short-term performance pressures,

5. Being unwillingness to compete on price,

6. Resisting industry structural changes or new practices,

7. Placing too much emphasis on new product development compared with improving existing ones, and

8. Retaining excess capacity.[3]

Exit decisions are often extremely difficult, in part because exiting might be actively opposed in the marketplace. Possible exit barriers include government restrictions, labor and pension obligations, and contractual obligations to other parties. Even if a business can be sold, in part or as a whole, a host of issues must be addressed. The negative effects of an exit on customer, supplier, and distributor relations, for example, can ripple throughout the entire corporate structure if the firm is an SBU of a larger corporation. In this case, shared cost arrangements can produce cost increases in other parts of the business, and labor relations can become strained, thereby diminishing the strategic outlook for the corporation as a whole.

## Fragmented, Deregulating, Hypercompetitive, and Internet-Based Industries

### Strategy in Fragmented Industries

Fragmented industries are those in which no single company or small group of firms has a large enough market share to have a strong effect on the industry structure or outcomes. Many areas of the economy share this trait, including retail sectors, distribution businesses, professional services, and small manufacturing. Fragmentation seems to be most prevalent when entry and exit barriers are low; there are few economies of scale or scope; cost structures make consolidation unattractive; products or services are highly diverse or need to be customized; and close, local control is essential.

Thriving in fragmented markets requires creative strategizing. Focus strategies that creatively segment the market based on product, customer, type of order/service, or geographic area, combined with a "no frills" posture, can be effective. Sometimes, scale and scope economies are unrecognized or await new technological breakthroughs. In such instances, a creative strategy can unlock these hidden sources of advantage and dramatically change the dynamics of the industry.

## Strategy in Deregulating Industries

Deregulation has reshaped a number of industries. Some interesting competitive dynamics take place when artificial constraints are lifted and new players are allowed to enter. Perhaps the most important dynamic has to do with the timing of strategic moves. U.S. experience shows that deregulating environments tend to undergo considerable change twice: Once when the market is opened and again about five years later.[4]

Deregulation in the United States became a major issue in 1975 when the Securities and Exchange Commission abolished the brokerage industry and eliminated fixed commissions, which profoundly affected several industries, including airlines, trucking, railroads, banking, and telecommunications. In each instance, a more or less similar pattern developed:

1. Immediately following the opening of the market, a large number of new entrants rushed in—most failing within a relatively short period.
2. Industry profitability deteriorated rapidly as new entrants, often operating from a lower cost basis, destroyed industry pricing for all competitors.
3. The pattern of segment profitability altered significantly. Segments that once were attractive became unattractive because too many competitors entered, whereas previously unattractive segments suddenly became more interesting from a strategic perspective.
4. The variance in profitability between the best and worst players increased substantially, reflecting a wider quality range of competitors.
5. Two waves of merger and acquisition activity ensued. A first wave focused on consolidating weaker players, and a second wave among larger players aimed at market dominance.

6. After consolidation, only a few players remained as broad-based competitors; most were forced to narrow their focus to specific segments or products in a much more segmented industry.

### Strategy in Hypercompetitive Industries

*Hypercompetitive industries* are characterized by intense rivalry. Successful strategies are often based on taking the competitor by surprise (e.g., by introducing a product when least expected) and then moving on as the competition tries to recover. *Hypercompetitive strategies*, therefore, are designed to enable the company to gain an advantage over competitors by disrupting the market with quick and innovative change. The goal is to neutralize previous competitive advantages and create an unbalanced industry segment.[5]

The intense rivalry in a hypercompetitive environment often results in short product life cycles, the emergence of new technologies, competition from unexpected players, repositioning by current players, and major shifts in market boundaries. Personal computers, microprocessors, and software all frequently experience the effects of hypercompetition. The telecommunications industry also provides many examples. Commonly, hypercompetitive strategies involve the bundling of services (e.g., local calling, long-distance calling, Internet access, and even television transmission) to retain current customers and acquire new ones.

In a hypercompetitive market, successful companies are able to manipulate competitive conditions to create advantage for themselves and destroy the advantages enjoyed by others. Within their dynamic and ever-changing environment, firms that stand to benefit are those possessing three major qualities: rapid innovation and speed, superior short-term strategic focus, and market awareness.

Speed and innovation are the foremost requirements for success in a hypercompetitive environment. The focus of companies is on gaining temporary advantage, achieving short-term profitability, and then quickly shifting their strategic focus before competition can react effectively. It is crucial that hypercompetitive companies be able to innovate rapidly and then follow up on that innovation with equally quick manufacturing, marketing, and distribution of their products. In this manner, they are able to rapidly shift the industry dynamics and gain market share at a pace that exceeds that of the competition. Without speed, a company is at a severe disadvantage because its competitors will be first to market, costing it valuable market share.

The second characteristic of successful firms in hypercompetition is superior short-term strategic focus. Firms that have the ability to manipulate the competition into making long-term commitments will find the hypercompetitive marketplace beneficial.

The final requirement for success in a hypercompetitive environment is strong market awareness. Firms must be able to understand consumer markets to deliver high-impact products and provide superior standards of customer support. Having strong customer focus allows firms to identify a customer's needs while uncovering new and previously untapped markets for their products. Once the needs of the customer are identified, firms win temporary market share through a redefinition of quality.

The traditional concept of sustainable competitive advantage centers on the belief that long-term profitability can be achieved through segmented markets and low to moderate levels of competition. However, strategists now recognize another requirement: Over the long term, sustainable profits are possible only when entry barriers restrict competition. Continuous erosion and re-creation of competitive advantage characterize many industries with companies seeking to disrupt the status quo and gain a temporary profitable advantage over larger competitors.

### Competitive Reactions Under Extreme Competition

The pace of competitive change continues to quicken with increasing globalization, technological advancement, and economic liberalization. The consequences include high rivalry in mature undifferentiated industries that results in shrinking profits; shaky dominance by dominant market share firms that are pressured by smaller, more flexible and often more innovative competitors; and shrinking industries with endangered leaders and struggling niche players.

This characterization of extreme competition led Huyett and Viguerie to suggest six actions that established companies could consider to counter the innovative moves of competitors:[6]

1. *Retool strategy and restore its importance.* Strategic planning can be given short shrift when daily pressures for performance are high and the pace of change is great. Therefore, corporate executives are advised to challenge SBU managers to adopt a portfolio view in strategic planning to increase their responsiveness to radical opportunities.

2. *Manage transition economics.* In trying to strike a balance between profit margins and market share, planners should be aware of the importance of building low-cost positions to free funds for innovation efforts that will help fend off aggressive competitors.

3. *Fight aggregation with disaggregation.* Although scale advantages will make some large firms inclined toward aggregation of markets, others will find small, high-profit opportunities by creating differentiated value propositions through disaggregation.

4. *Seek new demand and new growth.* Hypercompetition does not preclude the use of traditional strategies. Particularly when competing with firms that rely on organic growth, external growth through mergers and acquisitions, licensing, joint ventures, and strategic alliances can be successful, even as late entrants work to accelerate the pace of innovation and organizational change.

5. *Use a portfolio of initiatives to increase speed and flexibility.* Strategic managers and planners are encouraged to think of organizational assets as resources that enable the company to launch new products and services, innovate to reduce costs, and provide the basis for price competitiveness in varied markets worldwide. Such a resource-based view is superior to a fixed-commitment approach in extreme competition that places a premium on market responsiveness and innovation.

6. *Assess strategic risk.* Strategists need to be mindful that extreme competition is characterized by volatile corporate earnings and stock prices. Huyett and Viguerie specifically warn of negative consequences if competitors introduce lower-priced products or services, are able to become the low-cost provider, introduce bad-conduct risks (which warn of negative consequences if a price war occurs), or make overly optimistic assumptions.

### Strategic Planning for Internet-Based Industries

Businesses approach Internet-based industries in one of two ways: as pure players that conduct all business online or as click-and-mortar operations that have a physical facility and use the Internet to expand their reach and supplement their activities.

Pure play businesses confront the obstacle of the inability of the customer to examine their product prior to making a decision. This problem can be somewhat offset by a virtual storefront and often counterbalanced by the Internet firm's convenience of being "open" 24/7. Pure play companies are able to interact directly with their customers through the Internet and benefit from the ability to gather information easily about customers and competitors as a means to keeping their prices competitive.

There are special start-up costs that must be considered when launching a company in an Internet-based industry. Most significantly, there are extremely high marketing costs in building a customer base, and most Internet companies do not have an established distribution system to get their products to consumers.

Without a retail presence, pure play companies typically look to build a competitive advantage by becoming "efficiency machines" serving broad markets or "niche leaders" targeting narrow markets.[7] Efficiency machines are characterized by high marketing costs, innovative Web sites, and a highly efficient sourcing and fulfillment process. This set-up creates extremely high fixed costs. Therefore, they must generate very high revenue streams from the very beginning of operations. This model is most competitive in low-margin/high-volume industries.

A good example of an "efficiency machine" is Amazon, which began as a virtual bookstore that generated about $5 million in revenues in their first year of operations. For its first few years, Amazon's focus was on reinvesting to grow sales rapidly. The company then worked to become more efficient, and, in 2003, it had its first profitable year.

Niche players, by contrast, are more limited in number because their business model is built around selling high-priced products or services, including high-end jewelry and travel services. The most successful niche players adapt the traditional direct marketing model into one that can successfully leverage the Internet's advantages. Because most niche leaders are too small to afford large marketing campaigns, they need to rely on targeted online and direct mail campaigns to drive customers to their Web site or catalog.

## Strategic Planning for Click-and-Mortar Businesses

The click-and-mortar model is a hybrid of a pure play online model, where all business activity is conducted online, and a traditional brick-and-mortar model, where all business is done through a physical store. It is estimated that the click-and-mortar model is responsible for 52 percent of all online revenues.[8] The advantage of this strategy is that the physical side of the company has strategic resources that provide a basis for competitive advantage, such as established brands, traditional distribution channels, and vendor relationships.

In the pure play model, technology is the primary driver of growth, forcing many firms to invest heavily in this area to stay ahead of the curve. Click-and-mortar firms are less dependent on technology for competitive position, allowing them to spread their investments to develop a number of strengths. They are also able to allocate their resources more efficiently by choosing to have a product available online and in the store, or through just one option, as is commonly done in disposing of clearance items. Customers also benefit by gaining the ability to choose how they are most comfortable interacting with the company. Examples include the ability to return products in the store versus having to ship them back, and the opportunity to view products in the store and then order the item online if a size or color they like is not available.

## Customer Service

Customer service has applications to the three business models in an Internet-based industry. Pure play firms like Expedia.com, the world's largest leisure-travel agency, can use the Internet as a differentiator or as their core competency. Because there are no inventories to manage and no physical locations to maintain, firms are able to operate efficiently.

Future e-commerce strategies are expected to move from the current focus of online sales to increased engagement with customers. Such a shifting of the focus from sales driven to service driven will allow companies that are not typically users of the Internet to leverage their capabilities to meet the customers' needs. In new customer service-centered e-commerce models, strategies include marketing, selling, customer decision support, and retail partnership components.[9] Dell has developed a system that breaks customers down into subsets such as home and small business customers to match them with the appropriate product line. Once customers are in the correct subset, Dell is able to direct them to an appropriate product line based on their computer use in areas such as multimedia or basic word processor functions.

Other companies are also finding ways to leverage their online capabilities to help support their customers and improve efficiency. Metalco, a manufacturer of specialty metal products, uses the Internet to enable customers to make inquiries and requests, receive quotations, place orders, and manage the ongoing manufacturing and billing process. The system was designed to automate the process between Metalco and their customers, thereby improving efficiency, reducing errors, and increasing customer loyalty. This system is consistent with a marketing-driven approach designed to focus on a niche market. Metalco differentiates its product offerings through improved customer service.

### Competitive Superiority

While the evidence available indicates there is little difference between the profit performance of click-and-mortar and brick-and-mortar models, there does appear to be an advantage of click-and-mortar firms over pure play firms in an Internet-based industry. Customers favor the click-and-mortar model since it provides them with options in where they conduct business—on the Internet or at a physical store.[10] Research has shown that mere presence of an Internet alternative to traditional stores is a significant marketing advantage. An e-commerce element of a company strategy is necessary because of the accessibility benefit the Internet provides to customers.[11]

### Internet-Based Business Models

*Supply Chains of Internet Business Models.*    Internet businesses can be distinguished by the way they sell through the supply chain, including direct sales channels, intermediary channels, or marketplace channels. In direct sales channels, product and service providers deal directly with their customers during Internet business transactions. In intermediary channels, portals serve to build a community of consumers and play a role in driving traffic to the Web sites for product and service providers. In a marketplace channel, market makers build a community of customers or suppliers of products and service and facilitate secure business transactions between the buyer and the supplier.

*Revenue Business Models.*    Revenue business models generate sales through the direct transaction of goods or services, where a business adds value by acquiring products and reselling them to consumers, or through production-based methods where companies manufacture, customize, and sell products to consumers. Companies can also provide free content or services to visitors and earn revenue by selling advertising to businesses that want to reach those visitors.

*Business-to-Business and Business-to-Consumer Models.*    Internet businesses can be distinguished through the markets they serve, whether the markets are business-to-consumer (B2C) or business-to-business (B2B) models. B2C involves the marketing and delivery of a service directly to a customer, while B2B involves the marketing and delivery of goods and services to other businesses.

### Internet-Based Firm Inventory and Fulfillment

The Internet has enabled firms to separate the sales process from inventory management and fulfillment through drop shipping. Internet drop shipping is the method where Internet firms receive customer orders and send the customer orders to the supplier over the Internet using vendor software, and the supplier packages and ships the orders to the customers using the Internet firm's logo and label. Internet firms benefit by saving warehouse space, reducing inventory carrying costs, and gaining time to spend on other business functions.

A drop-shipping method is most appropriate for younger firms with larger, low-margin products, higher levels of variety, and higher levels of demand uncertainty.[12] The study also found that firms making inventory and fulfillment decisions within these guidelines were less likely to go bankrupt, suggesting that the firm's inventory and fulfillment decisions are related to its economic performance.

eBags.com is an Internet firm that uses drop shipping due to its great variety of products and low demand certainty. The company sells 8,000 different bags, including backpacks, purses, and suitcases. Offering a large variety of bags is important to the business, but holding all of the items in physical inventory would result in unacceptably high inventory holding and handling costs. Therefore, the company adopted drop shipping. eBags advertises the bags, but its suppliers actually keep them in their possession until orders are placed by eBags to have them shipped to customers. This tactic enables eBags to be almost free of inventory while offering a larger selection of bags than the small specialty bag stores with whom they compete.

## Business Unit Strategy: Special Dimensions

### Speed

Speed in innovation, manufacturing, distribution, and a host of other areas is emerging as a key success factor in a growing number of industries, especially those characterized by transitional or habitual hypercompetition.[13] Coupled with trends toward globalization, the multiplying business applications of the Internet have led to the elevation of speed as a strategic priority. The unprecedented growth in B2C and B2B Internet connections made speed almost as important as quality and a customer orientation in some markets. Yet, it is the newest and least understood of the critical success factors.

In a competitive context, *speed* is the pace of progress that a company displays in responding to current or anticipated business needs. It is gauged by a firm's response times in meeting customer expectations, innovating and commercializing new products and services, changing strategy to benefit from emerging market and technological realities, and continuously upgrading its transformation processes to improve customer satisfaction and financial returns.

Responding to industry challenges to increase their customer responsiveness are *speed merchants* who built their strategies on the rapid pace of their operations. Their accelerated change activities become a hallmark for the progress of the industry. Speed merchants modify their environments to convert their core competencies into competitive advantages. Therefore, competitive landscapes are altered in their favor. The public images of a growing number of firms are synonymous with the speed that they exhibit: AAA with fast emergency road service, Dell with fast computer assembly, Domino's with fast pizza delivery, and CyberGate with fast Internet access. A critical assessment of the strategies of these high-profile companies provides three important insights: (1) distinct and identifiable sources of pressure that create the demand on a company to accelerate its speed; (2) an emphasis on speed places new cost, cultural, and change process requirements on a company; and (3) several implementation methods to accelerate a firm's speed of operations.

There are four elements of a model to guide executives in the acceleration of their companies' speed. They are the (1) pressures to increase speed, (2) requirements of speed, (3) methods to increase speed, and the (4) consequences of speed. Taken together, these elements remind us that pressures to increase company speed can be generated both externally and internally. Firms can assume a reactive posture and await an increase in speed by competitors before making their own investment, or they can gamble on a payoff from a proactive "move to improve."

*Pressures to Increase Speed.*    Speed is almost universally popular. Customers in nearly every product–market segment seek immediate need satisfaction, and they reward quick-acting companies with market share growth. Because employees of speed-oriented companies enjoy the job flexibility and heightened individual responsibility that are required to maintain the strategy, they reward their employers with the loyalty and commitment that is so highly prized in competitive environments.

Suppliers to fast-moving companies are willing to bear extra costs and responsibilities to earn partnerships with firms that seem destined to overtake competitors that conduct business in time-tested rather than time-conscious ways.

Pressures for speed come from customers' expectations, from competitors who accelerate their own pace, from the company itself when it seeks to establish a new competitive advantage, and from the adjusting priorities of a changing industry.

*Requirements of Speed.*   As a strategic weapon, a speed initiative requires that every aspect of an organization be focused on the pace at which work is accomplished. Executives must foster a "fast" culture within their organizations. The agility that comes from a speed orientation and carefully tailored resource investments provides the prerequisite competitive means to change and accelerate a firm's strategic course. Specifically, action must be taken on the following issues: refocusing the business mission, creating a speed-compatible culture, upgrading communications within the business, focusing business process reengineering (BPR), and committing to new performance metrics.

*Methods to Increase Speed.*   The development of speed as a competitive advantage begins with an internal analysis by a firm to determine where speed exists and where it does not. Companies then look to eliminate any "speed gaps." Three categories of methods dominate corporate option lists: streamlining operations, upgrading technology, and forming partnerships.

*Streamlining Operations.*   Many companies enter new markets with a level of competitive information that would have traditionally been labeled as insufficient to support investment. However, most of these firms are not marginalizing quality; they have adopted a new strategic schema. With a speed-enhanced ability to obtain quick post-implementation feedback from the marketplace and respond with unparalleled speed in making adjustments, successful innovations no longer need to be flawless at introduction.

*Upgrading Technology.*   Using the latest informational technologies to create speed, companies are able to roll out new product information faster. The common goal of speed-focused IT is to connect manufacturers with retailers to enhance information sharing and streamline, and accelerate product distribution. In turn, shortening pipelines speeds products to shelves and satisfies customers with less costly inventories. Doubling back, technology enables companies to learn customers' buying patterns to better anticipate their preferences.

*Forming Partnerships.*   Sharing business burdens is a proven way to shorten the time needed to improve market responsiveness (i.e., "partners collapse time"). Ford Motor Company's partnership with General Motors and DaimlerChrysler provides a front-page example. The three major auto manufacturers joined to develop an Internet portal that links their purchasing organizations with 30,000 raw material suppliers. These Web-based exchanges also increase the speed with which the automobile companies respond to customer inquiries at every stage along the supply chain.

The evidence from business practice supports the emergence of speed as a critical success factor as a primary element in business unit strategy. The company goal of accelerating speed to satisfy consumer needs is becoming less of an option and more of a mandate for financial survival. Fortunately, businesses can be systematic in evaluating the pressures and requirements for change that they face in accelerating their speed. Methods available for implementing upgrades are gaining widespread acceptance and are backed by the records of success that faster firms enjoy.

*Consequences of Speed.*   In planning to increase the company's speed, executives need to consider the consequences of a successful implementation. The firm's pre-emotive capability will improve, but demands on the firm to innovate will simultaneously increase—since innovation both creates and justifies the need to invest in speed.

The firm's response time will improve, with a result that its competitive defensive capability will be strengthen, but to be able to produce and maintain the new level of speed, executives will need to enlist fast-moving and responsive suppliers and distributors. Furthermore, when the benefits of speed are essential but not distinguishing characteristics of a company in hypercompetitive arenas that are characterized by rapid and diversified change, executives need to view increased speed as essential benefit, but not necessarily as an advantage.

With consumer expectations in many industries constantly on the rise, a company's ability to increase rates and forms of speed in the future is critical. However, no challenge should be more appealing to executives that use speed to leverage a firm's core competencies than to operate in a competitive arena where success is based on a high rate of change.

### Innovating to Gain or Retain an Advantage

Innovation is the initial commercialization of invention that is achieved by producing and selling a new product, service, or process. Because every product has a lifespan that flattens out and eventually declines, creating new products that are able to backfill a company's revenue streams is vital to sustaining a successful business model.

Innovation can come in the form of a breakthrough that revolutionizes and creates new industries. Sony's Bravia LCD TVs, Blu-ray Disc products, and Playstation 3 gaming consoles allowed consumers to experience 3D in their homes.

The goal of companies that pursue a breakthrough innovation is to create a disruptive product that revolutionizes an industry or creates a new one. In 2010, Microsoft Office offered a free Web-based version of their software. The software was stored on Microsoft's servers and delivered to end users online. This concept is "cloud computing" and goes against Microsoft's historical business model. Cloud computing is the concept of assigning computing tasks to a remote location rather than a desktop computer, handheld machine, or a company's own servers. Traditionally, Microsoft sold their software programs to consumers and the software was stored directly on the consumer's computer. This new business model required Microsoft to provide a higher level of support to their customers after the initial sale of the software package. This innovation can be seen as self-destructive, but Microsoft chose to treat it as an opportunity to tackle the next big innovation in software.

Breakthrough innovations can require substantial investment in R&D and patience. As an alternative, many companies pursue cost-saving approaches to developing innovations that attempt to minimize the risks involved. For example, joint ventures can be utilized as a means of cost savings when two or more companies are looking to share the costs of an investment that may yield an innovation. Hulu.com, which is a joint venture between GE's NBC and News Corp., provides an online, streaming Web television service that is supported by advertising. It allows consumers to watch television shows from a variety of networks on their computers.[14] Hulu.com dramatically increased its revenues and gave its partner companies a chance to share in a product that could be an innovation in the way consumers watch television shows, while only bearing partial risk of the investment.

Outsourcing innovation can also be used to reduce the risk of failure of innovation. U.S. firms have pursued this strategy in the electronics and retail markets, and a 2009 survey found that 90 percent of all innovations in the service industry were generated by outsourcing.[15] For example, half of Proctor & Gamble's (P&G) new product ideas are generated from outside resources.[16]

### Creating Value Through Innovation

Value creation greatly depends on innovation. Sustained profitable growth requires more than judicious acquisitions or careful "subtraction" by shedding unprofitable operations or downsizing. Many companies recognize their need to generate more value from core businesses and leverage their core competencies more effectively. These strategic initiatives, in turn, increase the demand for innovation.[17]

Innovation is a major strategic challenge for most companies. Clayton Christensen coined the concepts of *disruptive* and *sustaining innovation* to describe what he calls the "Innovators' Dilemma"—how successful companies with established products can keep from being pushed aside by competitors with newer, cheaper products that will, over time, get better and become a serious threat.[18]

He notes that incumbent industry leaders and competitors mostly engage in *sustaining innovation*—innovation that focuses on improving their existing products. Some sustaining advancements are simple, incremental, year-to-year improvements; others are dramatic, breakthrough technologies, such as the transition from analog to digital and from digital to optical. The effect of these technological advances was to bring a better product into the market that could be sold for higher margins to the best customers served by the industry leaders.

New entrants and challengers have greater freedom to launch products that may have all of the attributes of the existing products and, therefore, not attractive to current customers, but that are simple, and often more affordable. These new entrants find acceptance in undemanding and underserved segments of the market and create a beachhead for competition for mainstream customers with improved products later. Christensen calls this *disruptive innovation* not because it defines a technological breakthrough, but because it disrupts the established basis of competition.

The computer hardware industry offers many examples of disruptive innovation. The introduction of the minicomputer disrupted the mainframe industry. The personal computer disrupted minicomputer sales. Wireless handheld devices, such as Blackberries and Palm Pilots, disrupted notebook computers.

Sustaining innovation can keep a company viable for many years; targeting current customers exclusively can be damaging in the long run. To start a new growth business, noncustomers often are the most important customers to understand. Discovering why they are not customers encourages innovation and stimulates growth.

A focus by incumbents firms on profit rather than growth can impede innovation, thereby inhibiting growth.[19] Public companies, under pressure from Wall Street to produce steady returns, face a particularly strong challenge. Investors and industry analysts are likely to expect the company to generate more of its earnings growth from profitability, whereas company executives tend to prefer earnings to come from increasing revenue. However, there is empirical evidence that the more a company's earnings come from either profitability improvement or revenue growth at the expense of the other, the more likely it is that the company's strategy is inherently flawed.[20] The differing emphases between investors and executives suggest why private companies often have better opportunities to invest for the long term and pursue disruptive innovations, which require a long time to develop and mature and might produce short-term losses in the early stages of development.

Creating a culture of innovation eludes many companies because it transcends traditional strategic planning practices. Strategic planning too often centers on existing or closely related products and services rather than on opportunities to drive future demand. In contrast, innovation is a product of anticipating, assessing, and fulfilling potential customer needs in a creative manner. Sometimes innovation is technology based, but often it springs from the firm's recognition of explicit or latent customer needs. Innovation can be directed at any point in the customer or company value chain, from sourcing raw materials to value-added, after-sale services.

Although many businesses pursue innovation, for almost 100 years Minnesota Mining & Manufacturing (3M) has succeeded because its business model is based on a culture that is geared to producing innovative products. Best known for Post-it Notes, Scotch Guard, and Scotch Tape, 3M's business segments include industrial, transportation, graphics and safety, health care, consumer and office, electronics and communications, and specialty materials.

Because of the company's unparalleled success as an innovator, its approach deserves broader consideration. Fundamentally, six mandates drive innovation at 3M:

1. Support innovation from R&D to customer sales and support.
2. Understand the future by trying to anticipate and analyze future trends. 3M has developed a program called "Foresight" in which industry experts survey the remote and external environments for changes in technology and other trends to identify new market opportunities, called "Greenfields."
3. Establish stretch goals. This driver is important to 3M because it is a measure that encourages growth. One example of a stretch goal is the new product sales target. This target is that 40 percent of sales will be from products introduced in the past four years. In addition, 10 percent of sales will be from products introduced in the current year.
4. Empower employees to meet goals. At 3M, this is accomplished through its 40-year-old "15 percent rule." This gives 3M researchers

the opportunity to devote 15 percent of their time to any creative idea or project, and management approval is not required.

5. Support broad networking across the company. This driving force calls for the sharing of discoveries within the company. A 3M corporate policy states that technologies belong to the company, which signals that research results are to be shared across all of its six business segments.

6. Recognize and reward innovative people. An innovative program at 3M rewards innovative people through peer-nominated award programs and a corporate "hall of fame."

Fostering a culture of innovation takes time and effort. Although there is no universal model for creating an innovating environment, a look at successful companies reveals certain common characteristics. First, a business needs a *top-level commitment to innovation*. Commitment to innovation is evident in the attitudes of top executives, through their communication of their belief to all levels of the organization in the benefits of innovation, and in their willingness to sponsor and guide new product activity.

Second, a business needs a *long-term focus*. "Quarteritis," the preoccupation with the next quarter's results, is one of the most common stumbling blocks to innovation. Innovation is an investment in the future, not a rescue mission for current top- or bottom-line problems.

Third, a business needs a *flexible organization structure*. Innovation rarely flourishes in a rigid structure, with complicated approval processes or with bureaucratic delays and bottlenecks.

Fourth, a business needs a combination of *loose and tight planning and control*. Allocating all direct, indirect, overhead, and other costs to a development project virtually guarantees its demise. Few innovative ideas immediately translate into commercial ventures that cover all of their own costs or meet conventional payback requirements.

Finally, to create an environment for innovation a business needs a system of *appropriate incentives*. Reward systems in many companies are oriented toward existing businesses, with short-term considerations outweighing longer-term innovation and market development objectives. Innovation can flourish only when risk taking is encouraged, occasional failure is accepted, and managers are accountable for missing opportunities as well as exploiting them.

## Framework for Innovation

A company's approach to innovation differs depending upon its product–market strategy. Low-cost leaders often focus their innovation efforts on new production and delivery processes and procedures, while differentiators primarily work on product innovations.

The "first movers" in an industry also benefit from product and technology efforts, while industry "followers" are best served by innovation in services and supply chain upgrades, and industry "laggards" need to focus on operational process innovation to help assure low costs.

A firm that emphasizes innovation usually takes a portfolio approach in which it undertakes an array of R&D projects that promote the company's strategic objectives. The firm will mix projects that focus on core improvements, logical extensions of current brands, and new growth initiatives in a way that will meet its risk and growth targets. Both incremental innovations and breakthroughs are important to the firm because incremental innovations extend the current revenue streams from prior innovations and breakthroughs create a new product life cycle that will provide a strong competitive advantage.[21]

## Leveraging External Partners as a Part of Overall Innovation Strategy

Historically, a company that emphasizes innovation maintained large patent portfolios to bolster growth and discourage competitors. However, adopting a more selective approach, Hitachi will only file for a patent if it can clearly define the value that the patent will provide for the firm. One result is that the number of patent applications Hitachi has submitted has declined steadily over the past two decades, while its income from licensing patents has more than doubled.[22]

Another way for innovating firms to derive value from their R&D investments is to give away free access to patented technology. IBM earns more than $1 billion per year from licensing a select subset of its patents, but it allows free access to most of the technology that it has patented, so that other technology companies can build systems that are compatible with IBM's products and thus create a user environment that is readily adaptable to IBM's core products.

A third way for businesses to optimize their R&D investment is to partner with companies that are interested in sharing a high-risk, high-reward undertaking. For example, Apple benefited from a joint venture with AT&T, which became the sole service provider of the iPhone. The terms of the agreement provided that both companies would share the cost and risk of the innovation. Because of this JV, Apple could focus on providing a world-class phone, and AT&T could focus on using their expertise as a service provider to handle customers' service requirements.

### Proctor & Gamble

P&G began a strategic intent program called "Connect and Develop" in 2002. It was designed to transform a company that had been highly secretive and protective of its technologies into a company that was openly looking for partners to develop cutting edge solutions to business problems. P&G doubled its revenue in the eight years following this initiative by committing to this new strategy that aimed to develop 50 percent of all innovations from collaborative efforts with external firms.[23]

In addition, P&G has a group called FutureWorks that is dedicated to investing in breakthrough technologies, a fund to provide supplemental capital above the budget for investment in innovation, and a training group that works with engineers to focus on disruptive technologies. P&G makes and commits 4 percent sales to innovation projects.[24] The company attempts to spend two times as much on innovation as its competitors, which has helped it build a product portfolio of 23 brands, each with a value of at least $1 billion, and another 20 brands that are each worth at least $500 million. These brands drive approximately 90 percent of P&G's profit, which was in excess of $4.6 billion in 2009.[25]

Over 50 percent of P&G's products utilize at least one component that was developed in conjunction with an external partner. This collaboration drives profits because most all of its organic sales growth comes from new brands or improved products. P&G uses only 10 percent of its patents, but spends millions of dollars each year to renew the other 90 percent in hopes that the technology will be of later use or will block to progress of its competitors.[26] In 2004, the company partnered with Clorox on Glad Press'n Seal bags to maximize the revenue from a then unused patent that P&G held for a plastic wrap. Since Clorox's Glad brand was too strong to make a new product launch worthwhile, the two companies formed a joint venture that allowed each to profit handsomely by making full use of its strengths.[27]

By 2010, P&G was promoting efforts to make its products more environmentally sustainable through innovation. It targeted products for the "sustainable mainstream," which consists of consumers that are interested in improvements to sustainability but are not willing to sacrifice value or features. The company estimates this segment makes up 75 percent of the global marketplace, in comparison to 15 percent of "niche" consumer who are willing to give up one of those two factors for improved sustainability, and the 10 percent of "basic living" consumers who do not make any decisions based upon sustainability factors.

### Innovation and Profitability

Innovating is difficult, as evidenced by the 50 percent of executives who say that they are not pleased with their companies' return on investment from innovation initiatives due to long development times, a risk adverse corporate culture, difficulty in choosing the right products to commercialize, and lack of coordination within the company.[28]

Research suggests that executives lack confidence in their companies' ability to use innovation to drive profits. In a Forrester Research study, 67 percent of respondents from manufacturing firms considered themselves more innovative than competitors, but only 7 percent identified themselves as very successful in meeting their innovation performance goals.[29] Respondents in the BCG *Innovation* survey questioned the effectiveness of their R&D spending; 48 percent of those surveyed were unsatisfied with the financial returns on their companies' investments in innovation.

The reason for the lack of success in translating innovation into profitable performance surfaced in a study of the growth records of the *Fortune*

50 sponsored by HP and the Corporate Executive Board. The study concluded that the single biggest growth inhibitor for large companies was "mismanagement of the innovation process."[30]

When R&D investments fail to generate successful products and financial gains it is attributed to one of three main reasons: failure to develop truly innovative products, failure to commercialize innovative products successfully, and failure to market innovative products in a timely manner. Statistics differ but research indicates that the probability of success with innovations is small:

- It takes 125 to 150 new initiatives to generate one marketplace success.[31]
- Eighty-five percent of new product ideas never make it to market, and of those that do, 50 to 70 percent fail.[32]
- In a global study of 360 industrial firms launching 576 new industrial products, the overall success rate was 60 percent from launch.[33]
- Newly launched products suffering from failure rates often reach 50 percent or greater.[34]
- Delays in getting a product to market can be extremely costly. McKinsey & Co. found that a product that is six months late to market misses 33 percent of the potential profits over the product's lifetime.[35]

*Recommendations for Improving Performance Through Innovation.*   An overall evaluation of the research on the impact of innovation investments on company financial performance leads to six recommendations for strategic managers:

1. *Link strategy and innovation.* Firms that innovate toward achieving a specific strategic goal improve their chances of success.[36]
2. *Areas where new opportunities and competitive advantage exist provide a firm's best chances to profit from innovation.* Product and service offerings, customers served, processes employed, and core competencies must be considered in innovation decisions.[37]

3. *Profits from innovation in business systems can match those from product development.*[38] Firms relying on new products alone might exclude the investments required to strengthen business systems, which will leave them vulnerable to competitors who strengthen business processes in the areas of marketing, and information and financial systems. Benefits of broad-based innovation include a system wide supporting infrastructure for product innovation, the development of an entry barrier to would-be competitors, and other opportunities for innovation in the functions and processes.

4. *Look outside of the company's internal environment to increase the likelihood of success and reduce the risks of innovation.* Open-business models enable organizations to be more effective in creating value by leveraging many more ideas via the inclusion of external concepts and capture greater value through more effective utilization of firm assets in the organization's operations and in other companies' businesses.[39]

5. *Alliances and corporate venture capital programs allow a firm to share the risks associated with exploration investments.*[40] Corporate venturing has the potential to furnish reliable, practical, near-term solutions to the innovation challenge by providing the opportunity for sourcing complementary and strategic intellectual property, additional financial resources, and skills.[41]

6. *Involve customers early and often in the innovation process.* Through co-development, the customer takes an active role in the innovation process by helping to define product requirements, components, and materials.[42] It can help companies avoid costly product failures by soliciting new product concepts from existing customers, pursuing the most popular of those ideas, and asking for commitments from customers to purchase a new product before commencing final development and production.[43] The use of co-development is particularly effective in testing innovative products and developing products for relatively small and heterogeneous market segments.

# CHAPTER 8

# Global Strategy: Fundamentals

## Introduction

To create a global vision, a company must carefully define what globalization means for its particular businesses. This depends on the industry, the products or services, and the requirements for global success. For Coca-Cola, it meant duplicating a substantial part of its value creation process—from product formulation to marketing and delivery—throughout the world. Intel's global competitive advantage is based on attaining technological leadership and preferred component supplier status on a global basis. For a midsize company, it may mean setting up a host of small foreign subsidiaries and forging numerous alliances. For others, it may mean something entirely different. Thus, although it is tempting to think of global strategy in universal terms, globalization is a highly company- and industry-specific issue. It forces a company to rethink its strategic intent, global architecture, core competencies, and entire current product and service mix. For many companies, the outcome demands dramatic changes in the way they do business—with whom, how, and why.

## Global Strategy as Business Model Change

To craft a global strategy, a company therefore must take its *business model* apart and consider the impact of global expansion on every single component of the model. For example, with respect to its value proposition a company must decide whether or not to modify its company's core strategy as it moves into new markets? This decision is intimately linked to a choice of what markets and/or regions to enter and why? Once decisions

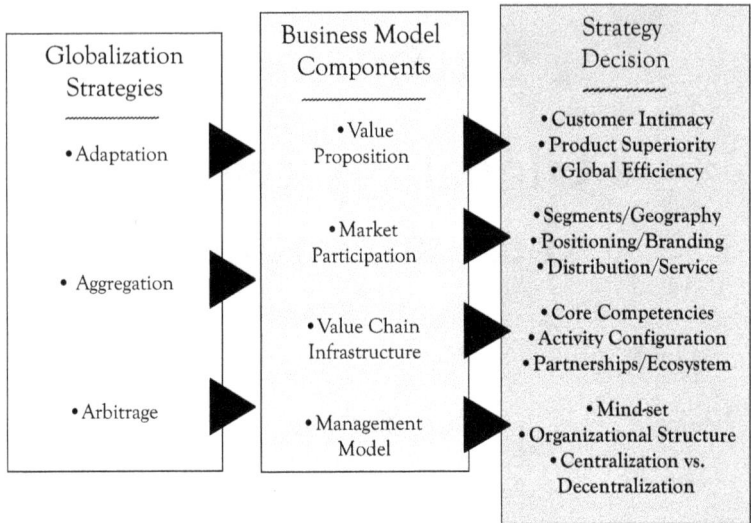

*Figure 8.1  Array of globalization decisions*

have been made about the *what* (the value proposition) and *where* (market coverage) of global expansion, choices need to be made about the *how*—whether or not to adapt products and services to local needs and preferences or standardize them for global competitive advantage, whether or not to adopt a uniform market positioning worldwide, which value-adding activities to keep in-house, which to outsource, which to relocate to other parts of the world, and so on. Finally, decisions need to be made about *how to organize and manage* these efforts on a global basis. Together, these decisions define a company's global strategic focus on a continuum from a truly global orientation to a more local one. Figure 8.1 shows the full array of globalization decisions a company needs to make when it expands globally.

> *Crafting a global strategy therefore is about deciding how a company should change or adapt its core (domestic) business model to achieve a competitive advantage as the firm globalizes its operations.*

## Ghemawat's Generic "AAA" Global Strategy Framework

Ghemawat offers three generic approaches to global value creation. *Adaptation* strategies generate revenues and market share by tailoring one

or more components of a company's business model to suit local requirements or preferences. *Aggregation* strategies focus on achieving economies
of scale or scope by creating regional or global efficiencies; they typically
involve standardizing a significant portion of the value proposition and
grouping together development and production processes. *Arbitrage* is
about exploiting economic or other differences between national or regional markets, usually by locating separate parts of the supply chain in
different places.

## Adaptation

Adaptation—creating global value by changing one or more elements of
a company's offer to meet local requirements or preferences—is probably
the most widely used global strategy. The reason for this will be readily apparent; some degree of adaptation is essential or unavoidable for
virtually all products in all parts of the world. The taste of Coca-Cola in
Europe is different from that in the United States reflecting differences in
water quality and the kind and amount of sugar added. The packaging of
construction adhesive in the United States informs customers how many
square feet it will cover; the same package in Europe must do so in square
meters. Even commodities, such as cement, are not immune; their pricing
in different geographies reflects local energy and transportation costs and
what percentage is bought in bulk.

Adaptation strategies typically fall into one of five categories: *variation, focus, externalization, design*, and *focus* (Figure 8.2).

*Variation* strategies not only include decisions to make changes in *products and services* but also adjustments to *policies, business positioning*, and
even redefine *expectations for success*. The *product* dimension will be obvious: Whirlpool, for example, offers smaller washers and dryers in Europe
than those in the United States reflecting the space constraints prevalent
in many European homes. The need to consider adapting *policies* is less
obvious. An example is Google's dilemma in China to conform to local
censorship rules. Changing a company's overall *positioning* in a country
goes well beyond changing products or even policies. Initially, Coke did
little more than "skim the cream" off big emerging markets, such as India
and China. To boost volume and market share, it had to reposition itself

| Adaptation | Aggregation | Arbitrage |
|---|---|---|
| Variation | | |
| Focus: Reduce Need for Adaptation | Economies of Scale | Performance Enhancement |
| Externalization: Reduce Burden of Adaptation | Economies of Scope | Cost Reduction |
| Design: Reduce Cost of Adaptation | | Risk Reduction |
| Innovation: Improve on Existing Adaptation | | |

*Figure 8.2  Adaptation, aggregation, and arbitrage*

to a "lower margin–higher volume" strategy that involved lowering price points, reducing costs, and expanding distribution. Changing *expectations* for say, the rate of return on investment in a country, while a company is trying to create a presence, is also a prevalent form of variation.

A second type of adaptation strategy uses a *focus* on particular *products, geographies, vertical stages* of the value chain or *market segments* as a way of reducing the impact of differences across regions. A *product focus* takes advantage of the fact that wide differences can exist *within* broad product categories in the degree of variation required to compete effectively in local markets—action films need far less adaptation than local newscasts. Restriction of *geographic* scope can permit a focus on countries where relatively little adaptation of the domestic value proposition is required. A *vertical focus* strategy involves limiting a company's direct involvement to specific steps in the supply chain while outsourcing others. Finally, a *segment focus* involves targeting a more limited customer base: Rather than adapting a product or service, a company using this strategy accepts that without modification its products will appeal to a smaller market segment or different distributor network from those in the domestic market. Many luxury goods manufacturers use this approach.

Whereas focus strategies overcome regional differences by narrowing scope, *externalization strategies* transfer—through *strategic alliances, franchising, user adaptation*, or *networking*—responsibility for specific parts of a company's business model to partner companies to accommodate local requirements, lower cost, or reduce risk. For example, Eli Lilly extensively uses *strategic alliances* abroad for drug development and testing. McDonald's growth strategy abroad uses *franchising* as well as company-owned stores. And software companies depend heavily on both *user adaptation and networking* for the development of applications for their basic software platforms.

A fourth type of adaptation focuses on *design* to reduce the cost of, rather than the need for, variation. Manufacturing costs can often be achieved by introducing design *flexibility* so as to overcome supply differences. Introducing standard production *platforms* and *modularity* in components also helps to reduce cost. A good example of a company focused on design is Tata Motors, which has successfully introduced a car in India that is affordable to a significant number of citizens.

A fifth approach to adaptation is *innovation,* which, given its crosscutting effects, can be characterized as improving the effectiveness of adaptation efforts. For instance, IKEA's flat-pack design, which has reduced the impact of geographic distance by cutting transportation costs, has helped that retailer expand into three dozen countries.

## Aggregation

Aggregation is about creating *economies of scale or scope* as a way of dealing with differences (Figure 8.1). The objective is to exploit similarities among geographies rather than adapt to differences but stop short of complete standardization that would destroy concurrent adaptation approaches. The key is to identify ways to introduce economies of scale and scope into the global business model without compromising local responsiveness.

Adopting a *regional* approach to globalizing the business model—as Toyota has done effectively—is probably the most widely used aggregation strategy. *Regionalization* or *semiglobalization* applies to many aspects of globalization—from investment and communication patterns to trade. And even when companies do have a significant presence in more than one region, competitive interactions are often regionally focused.

Examples of different *geographic* aggregation approaches are not hard to find. Xerox centralized its purchasing, first regionally, later globally, to create a substantial cost advantage. Dutch electronics giant Philips created a global competitive advantage for its Norelco shaver product line by centralizing global production in a few strategically located plants. And the increased use of global (corporate) branding over product branding is a powerful example of creating economies of scale and scope. As these examples show, *geographic* aggregation strategies have potential application to every major business model component.

Geographic aggregation is not the only avenue for generating economies of scale or scope, however. The other, nongeographic dimensions of the CAGE framework introduced in Chapter 3—*cultural, administrative or political, and economic*—also lend themselves to aggregation strategies. Major book publishers, for example, publish their best sellers in but a few languages, counting on the fact that readers are willing to accept a book in their second language (*cultural* aggregation). Pharmaceutical companies seeking to market new drugs in Europe must satisfy the regulatory requirements of a few, selected countries to qualify for a license to distribute throughout the European Union (*administrative* aggregation). As for *economic* aggregation, the most obvious examples are provided by companies that distinguish between developed and emerging markets and, at the extreme, focus on one or the other.

### Arbitrage

A third generic strategy for creating a global advantage is *arbitrage* (Figure 8.1). Arbitrage is based on *exploiting* differences rather than *adapting* to them or bridging them and defines the original global strategy: buying low in one market and selling high in another. Outsourcing and offshoring are modern day equivalents; Wal-Mart saves billions of dollars a year by buying goods from developing countries. Other economies can be created through greater differentiation with customers and partners, improved corporate bargaining power with suppliers or local authorities, reduced supply chain and other market and nonmarket risks, and through the local creation and sharing of knowledge.

Since arbitrage focuses on exploiting differences between regions, the CAGE framework described in Chapter 3 is of particular relevance and helps define a set of substrategies for this generic approach to global value creation.

Favorable effects related to country or place of origin have long supplied a basis for *cultural arbitrage*. For example, an association with French culture has long been an international success factor for fashion items, perfumes, wines, and foods. Similarly, fast-food products and drive-through restaurants are mainly associated with U.S. culture. Another example of cultural arbitrage—real or perceived—is provided by Benihana of Tokyo, the "Japanese steakhouse." Although heavily American—the company has only one outlet in Japan, out of more than one hundred worldwide—it serves up a theatrical version of teppanyaki cooking that the company describes as "Japanese" and "eatertainment."

Legal, institutional, and political differences between countries or regions create opportunities for *administrative* arbitrage. One well-known version of this strategy consists of creating a holding company in the Cayman Islands, which allows a company to deduct interest payments on the debt used to finance acquisitions from profits generated elsewhere in the world. Through this and other, similar actions, companies can significantly lower their tax liabilities.

With steep drops in transportation and communication costs in the last 25 years, the scope for *geographic* arbitrage—the leveraging of geographic differences—has been diminished but not fully eliminated. Consider what is happening in medicine, for example. It is quite common today, for doctors in the United States to take x-rays during the day, send them electronically to radiologists in India for interpretation overnight, and for the report to be available the next morning in the United States again. In fact, reduced transportation costs sometimes create new opportunities for geographic arbitrage. Every day, for instance, at the international flower market in Aalsmeer, the Netherlands, more than 20 million flowers and 2 million plants are auctioned off and flown to customers in the United States.

Although all arbitrage strategies that add value are "economic" in some sense, the term *economic* arbitrage is primarily used to describe strategies that do not directly exploit *cultural, administrative,* or *geographic differences.* Rather, they are focused on leveraging differences in the costs of labor and capital, as well as variations in more industry-specific inputs (such as knowledge) or in the availability of complementary products.

## Which "A" Strategy Should a Company Choose?

A company's financial statements can be a useful guide to signaling which of the "A" strategies will have the greatest potential to create global value. Firms that rely heavily on branding and do a lot of advertising, such as food companies, often need to engage in considerable adaptation to local markets. Those that do a lot of R&D—think pharmaceutical firms—may want to aggregate to improve economies of scale, since many R&D outlays are fixed costs. For firms whose operations are labor intensive, such as apparel manufacturers, arbitrage will be of particular concern because labor costs vary greatly from country to country.

Which "A" strategy a company emphasizes also depends on its globalization history. Companies that start on the path of globalization on the supply side of their business model, that is, seeking to lower cost or access new knowledge, typically first focus on aggregation and arbitrage approaches to creating global value, whereas companies that start their globalization history by taking their value propositions to foreign markets are immediately faced with adaptation challenges. Regardless of their starting point, most companies will need to consider all "A" strategies at different points in their global evolution, sequentially or sometimes simultaneously.

Nestlé's globalization path, for example, started with the company making small related acquisitions outside its domestic market and therefore had early exposure to adaptation challenges. For most of their history IBM also pursued an adaptation strategy, serving overseas markets by setting up a mini-IBM in each target country. Every one of these companies operated a largely local business model, which allowed it to adapt to local differences as necessary. Inevitably, in the 1980s and 1990s, dissatisfaction with the extent to which country-by-country adaptation curtailed opportunities to gain international scale economies led to the overlay of a regional structure on the mini-IBMs. IBM aggregated the countries into regions in order to improve coordination and thus generate more scale economies at the regional and global levels. More recently, however, IBM has also begun to exploit differences across countries (arbitrage). For example, it has increased its workforce in India while reducing its headcount in the United States.

Procter & Gamble's (P&G) early history parallels that of IBM, with the establishment of mini-P&Gs in local markets, but it has evolved differently. Today company's global business units now sell through market development organizations that are aggregated up to the regional level. P&G has successfully evolved to a company that uses all three "A" strategies in a coordinated manner. It adapts its value proposition to important markets, but ultimately competes—through global branding, R&D, and sourcing—on the basis of aggregation. Arbitrage, while important—mostly through outsourcing activities that are invisible to the final consumer—is less important to P&G's global competitive advantage because of its relentless customer focus.

## From "A" to "AA" to "AAA"[1]

Although most companies will focus on just one "A" at any given time, leading-edge companies—GE, P&G, IBM, Nestlé, to name a few—have embarked on implementing two, or even all three of the As. Doing so presents special challenges because there are inherent tensions between all three foci. As a result, the pursuit of "AA" strategies or even an "AAA" approach requires considerable organizational and managerial flexibility.

There are serious constraints on the ability of any one company to use all three As simultaneously with great effectiveness. Such attempts stretch a firm's managerial bandwidth, force a company to operate with multiple corporate cultures, and can present competitors with opportunities to undercut a company's overall competitiveness. Thus, to even contemplate an "AAA" strategy, a company must be operating in an environment in which the tensions among adaptation, aggregation, and arbitrage are weak or can be overridden by large-scale economies or structural advantages, or in which competitors are otherwise constrained. Ghemawat cites the case of GE Healthcare (GEH). The diagnostic imaging industry has been growing rapidly and has concentrated globally in the hands of three large firms, which together command an estimated 75 percent of revenues in the business worldwide: GEH, with 30 percent; Siemens Medical Solutions (SMS), with 25 percent; and Philips Medical Systems (PMS), with 20 percent. This high degree of concentration is probably related to the fact that the industry ranks in the 90th percentile in terms of R&D intensity.

Research shows that the aggregation-related challenge of building global scale has proven particularly important in the industry in recent years. GEH, the largest of the three firms in the earlier example, has consistently been the most profitable, reflecting its success at aggregation, through (1) economies of scale (for example, GEH has higher total R&D spending than its competitors but its R&D-to-sales ratio is lower), (2) acquisition prowess (GEH has made nearly 100 acquisitions under Jeffrey Immelt before he became GE's CEO), and (3) economies of scope (the company strives to integrate its biochemistry skills with its traditional base of physics and engineering skills; it finances equipment purchases through GE Capital).

GEH has even more clearly outpaced its competitors through arbitrage. It has become a global product company by migrating rapidly to low-cost production bases. Today, GEH purchases more than 50 percent of its materials directly from low-cost countries and has significant manufacturing capacity in such countries.

In terms of adaptation, GEH has invested heavily in country-focused marketing organizations. It also has increased customer appeal with its emphasis on providing services as well as equipment—for example, by training radiologists and providing consulting advice on post–image processing. Such customer intimacy obviously has to be tailored by country. And recently, GEH has cautiously engaged in some "in China, for China" manufacture of stripped-down, cheaper equipment aimed at increasing penetration there.

### Pitfalls and Lessons in Applying the "AAA" Framework

Most companies would be wise to (1) *Focus on one or two of the As.* While it is possible to make progress on all three As—especially for a firm that is coming from behind—companies (or, often more to the point, businesses or divisions) usually have to focus on one or at most two As in trying to build competitive advantage; (2) *Make sure the new elements of a strategy are a good fit organizationally.* If a strategy does embody nontrivially new elements, companies should pay particular attention to how well they work with other things the organization is doing. IBM has grown its staff in India much faster than other international competitors (such as Accenture) that have begun to emphasize India-based arbitrage. But quickly molding this workforce into an efficient organization with high delivery standards and a sense of connection to the parent company is a critical challenge: Failure in this regard might even be fatal to the arbitrage initiative; (3) *Employ multiple integration mechanisms.* Pursuit of more than one of the As requires creativity and breadth in thinking about integration mechanisms. Given the stakes, these factors cannot be left to chance. Essential to making such integration work is an adequate supply of leaders; (4) *Think about externalizing integration.* Not all the integration that is required to add value across borders needs to occur within a single organization. IBM and other firms illustrate that some externalization is a key part of most ambitious global strategies. It takes a diversity of forms: joint ventures in advanced semiconductor research, development, and manufacturing; links to and support of Linux and other efforts at open innovation; (some) outsourcing of hardware to contract manufacturers and services to business partners; IBM's relationship with Lenovo in personal computers; and customer relationships governed by memoranda of understanding rather than detailed contracts; (5) *Know when not to integrate.* Some integration is always a good idea, but that is not to say that more integration is always better.

## The Need for Global Strategic Management

The judicious globalization of a company's *management model* is critical to unlocking the potential for global competitive advantage. But globalizing a company's management model can be ruinous if conditions are not right or the process for doing so is flawed. Key questions include: When and to what extent should a company globalize its decision-making processes and its organizational and control structure, what are some of the key implementation challenges, and how does a company get started?

As firms increase their revenue by expanding into more countries and by extending the lives of existing products by bringing them into emerging markets, costs can often be reduced through global sourcing and better asset utilization. But capitalizing on such profit opportunities is hard, because every opportunity for increased globalization has a cost and carries a danger of actually reducing profit. For example, the company's customer focus may blur, as excessive standardization makes products appeal to the lowest common denominator, alienating key customer segments and causing market share to fall. Or a wrong globalization move makes innovation slow down, and causes price competition to sharpen.

The best executives in a worldwide firm often are country managers who are protective of "their" markets and value delivery networks. Globalization shrinks their power. Some rise to new heights within the organization by taking extra global responsibilities. Some leave. Many fight globalization, making it tough for the CEO. Sometimes they win and the CEO loses. Overcoming organizational resistance is therefore key to success.

### The Importance of a Global Mind-set

A common challenge that many corporations encounter as they move to globalize their operations can be summed up in one word: mind-set. Successful global expansion requires corporate leaders who think proactively, sense and foresee emerging trends and act upon them in a deliberate, timely manner. To accomplish this, they need a global mind-set and an enthusiasm to embrace new challenges, diversity, and a measure of ambiguity. Simply having the right product and technology is not sufficient; it is the caliber of a company's global leadership that makes the difference.

Herbert Paul defines a mind-set as "a set of deeply held internal mental images and assumptions, which individuals develop through a continuous process of learning from experience."[2] These images exist in the subconscious and determine how an individual perceives a specific situation, and his or her reaction to it. In a global context, a global mind-set is "the ability to avoid the simplicity of assuming all cultures are the same, and at the same time, not being paralyzed by the complexity of the differences."[3] Thus, rather than being frustrated and intimidated by cultural differences, an individual with a global mind-set enjoys them and seeks them out because they are fascinated by them and understand they present unique business opportunities.

The concept of a mind-set does not just apply to individuals; it can be logically extended to organizations as the aggregated mind-set of all of its members. Naturally, at the organizational level mind-set also reflects how its members interact and such issues as the distribution of power within the organization. Certain individuals, depending on their position in the organizational hierarchy, will have a stronger impact on the company's mind-set than others. In fact, the personal mind-set of the CEO sometimes is the single most important factor in shaping the organization's mind-set.

A corporate mind-set shapes the perceptions of individual and corporate challenges, opportunities, capabilities, and limitations. It also frames how goals and expectations are set and therefore has a significant impact on what strategies are considered and ultimately selected and how they are implemented. Recognizing the diversity of local markets and seeing them as a source of opportunity and strength, while at the same time pushing for strategic consistency across countries lies at the heart of global strategy development. To become truly global, therefore, requires a company to develop two key capabilities: (1) the capability to enter any market in the world it wishes to compete in. This requires that the company constantly looks for market opportunities worldwide, processes information on a global basis and is respected as a real or potential threat by competitors even in countries/markets it has not yet entered; (2) the capability to leverage its worldwide resources. Making a switch to a lower cost position by globalizing the supply chain is a good example. Leveraging a company's global know-how is another.

To understand the importance of a corporate mind-set to the development of these capabilities, consider two often quoted corporate mantras: "Think global and act local" and its opposite: "Think local and act global." The "think global and act local" mind-set is indicative of a global approach in which management operates under the assumption that a powerful brand name with a standard product, package, and advertising concept serves as a platform to conquer global markets. The starting point is a globalization strategy focused on standard products, optimal global sourcing, and the ability to react globally to competitors' moves. While sometimes effective, this approach can discourage diversity and puts a lot of emphasis on uniformity. Contrast this with a "think local and act global" mind-set that is based on the assumption that global expansion is best served by adaptation to local needs and preferences. In this mind-set, diversity is looked upon as a source of opportunity, whereas strategic cohesion plays a secondary role. Such a "bottom-up" approach can offer greater possibilities for revenue generation, particularly for companies wanting to grow rapidly abroad. However, it may require greater investment in infrastructure necessary to serve each market and can produce global strategic inconsistency and inefficiencies.

C.K. Prahalad and Kenneth Lieberthal first exposed the Western (which they refer to as "imperialist") bias that many multinationals have brought to their global strategies, particularly in developing countries and note that they would perform better—and learn more—if they tailored their operations more effectively to the unique conditions of emerging markets. Arguing that literally hundreds of millions of people in China, India, Indonesia, and Brazil are ready to enter the marketplace they observe that multinational companies typically target only a tiny segment of affluent buyers in these emerging markets—those who most resemble Westerners. This kind of myopia—thinking of developing countries simply as new places to sell old products—is not only shortsighted and the direct result of a Western "imperialist" mind-set; it causes these companies to miss out on much larger market opportunities further down the socioeconomic pyramid, which are often seized by local competitors.[4]

Companies with a genuine global mind-set do not assume that they can be successful by simply exporting their current business models around the globe. Citicorp, for example, knew it could not profitably serve a client in Beijing or Delhi whose net wealth is less than $5,000 with its U.S. business model and attendant cost structure. It therefore had to create a new business model—which meant rethinking every element of its cost structure—to serve average citizens in China and India.

To become truly global, multinational companies will also increasingly have to look to emerging markets for talent. India is already recognized as a source of technical talent in engineering, sciences, and software, as well as in some aspects of management. High-tech companies recruit in India not only for the Indian market but also for the global market. China, Brazil, and Russia will surely be next. Philips, the Dutch electronics giant, is downsizing in Europe and already employs more Chinese than Dutch workers. Nearly half of the revenues for companies, such as Coca-Cola, P&G, Lucent, Boeing, and GE, come from Asia, or will do so shortly.

As corporate globalization advances, the composition of senior management will also begin to reflect the importance of the BRIC and other emerging markets. At present, with a few exceptions, such as Citicorp and Unilever, C-suites are still filled with nationals from the company's home country. As the senior managements for multinationals become more diverse, however, decision-making criteria and processes, attitudes toward ethics and corporate responsibility, risk taking, and team building all will likely change, reflecting the slow but persistent shift in the center of gravity in many multinational companies toward Asia. This will make the clear articulation of a company's core values and expected behaviors even more important than it is today. It will also increase the need for a single company culture as more and more people from different cultures have to work together.

### Organization as Global Strategy[5]

Organizational design should be about developing and implementing corporate strategy. In a global context, the balance between local and central authority for key decisions is one of the most important parameters in a company's organizational design. Companies that have partially or fully globalized their operations typically have migrated to one of four organizational structures: (1) an *international*, (2) a *multidomestic*, (3) a *global*, or (4) a so-called *transnational* structure. Each occupies a well-defined position in the global aggregation/local adaptation matrix first developed by Bartlett and Ghoshal and usefully describes the most salient characteristics of each of these different organizational structures (Figure 8.3).[6]

The *international* model characterizes companies that are strongly dependent on their domestic sales and that export opportunistically. International companies typically have a well-developed domestic infrastructure and additional capacity to sell internationally. As their globalization

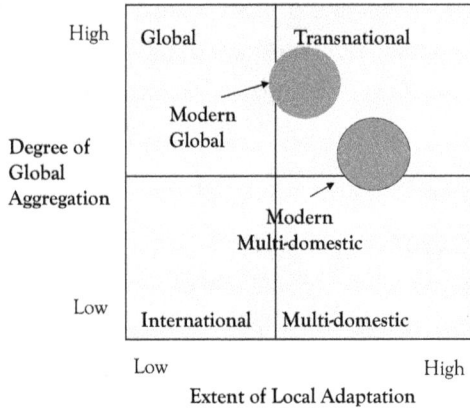

*Figure 8.3  Global aggregation/local adaptation matrix*

develops further, they are destined to evolving into multidomestic, global, or transnational companies. The international model is fairly unsophisticated, unsustainable if the company further globalizes and therefore usually transitory in nature. In the short-term, this organizational form may be viable in certain situations where the need for localization and local responsiveness is very low (i.e., the domestic value proposition can be marketed internationally with very minor adaptations), and the economies of aggregation (i.e., global standardization) are also low.

The *multidomestic* organizational model describes companies with a portfolio of independent subsidiaries operating in different countries as a decentralized federation of assets and responsibilities under a common corporate name.[7] Companies operating with a multidomestic model typically employ adopt country-specific strategies with little international coordination or knowledge transfer from the center headquarters. Key decisions about strategy, resource allocation, decision making, knowledge generation and transfer, and procurement reside with each country subsidiary with little value added from the center (headquarters). The pure multidomestic organizational structure is positioned as high on local adaptation and low on global aggregation (integration). Like the international model, the traditional multidomestic organizational structure is not well suited to a global competitive environment in which standardization, global integration, and economies of scale and scope are critical. However, this model is still viable in situations where local responsiveness, local differentiation, and local adaptation are critical while the opportunities for efficient production, global knowledge transfer, economies of scale, and economies of scope are minimal. As with the international model, the pure multidomestic company often represents a transitory organizational structure. An example of this structure and its limitations is provided by Philips during the last 25 years of the last century; in head-to-head competition with its principal rival, Matsushita, Philips' multidomestic organizational model became a competitive disadvantage against Matsushita's centralized (global) organizational structure.

The traditional *global* company is the antithesis of the traditional multidomestic company. It describes companies with globally integrated operations designed to take maximum advantage of economies of scale and scope by following a strategy of standardization and efficient production.[8] By globalizing operations and competing in global markets these companies seek to reduce cost of R&D, manufacturing, production, procurement, and inventory, improve quality by reducing variance, enhance customer preference through global products and brands, and obtain competitive leverage. Most, if not all, key strategic decisions—about corporate strategy, resource allocation, and knowledge generation and transfer—are made at corporate headquarters. In the global aggregation/ local adaptation matrix, the pure global company occupies the position of extreme global aggregation (integration) and low local adaptation (localization). An example of a pure global structure is provided by the aforementioned Japanese company Matsushita in the latter half of the last century. Since a pure global structure also represents an (extreme) ideal, it frequently is also transitory.

The *transnational* model is used to characterize companies that attempt to simultaneously achieve high global integration and high local responsiveness. It was conceived as a theoretical construct to mitigate the limitations of the pure multidomestic and global structures and occupies the fourth cell in the aggregation/adaptation matrix. This organizational structure focuses on integration, combination, multiplication of resources and capabilities, and managing assets and core competencies as a network of alliances, as opposed to relying on functional or geographical division. Its essence, therefore, is matrix management: The ultimate objective is to have access and make effective and efficient use of all the resources the company has at its disposal globally, including both global and local knowledge. As a consequence, it requires management intensive processes and is extremely hard to implement in its pure form and is as much a mind-set, idea, or ideal rather than an organization structure found in many global corporations.[9]

Given the limitations of each of the above structures in terms of either their global competitiveness or their implementability, many companies have settled on matrix-like organizational structures that are more easily managed than the pure transnational model but still target the simultaneous pursuit of global integration and local responsiveness. Two of these have been labeled the *modern multidomestic* and *modern global* models of global organization.

The *modern multidomestic* model is an updated version of the traditional (pure) multidomestic model, which includes a more significant role for the corporate headquarters. Accordingly, its essence no longer consists of a loose confederation of assets, but rather a matrix structure with a strong culture of operational decentralization, local adaptation, product differentiation, and local responsiveness. The resulting model, with national subsidiaries with significant autonomy, a strong geographical dimension, and empowered country managers, allows companies to maintain their local responsiveness and their ability to differentiate and adapt to local environments. At the same time, in the modern multidomestic model the center is critical to enhancing competitive strength. Whereas the role of the subsidiary is to be locally responsive, the role of the center is to enhance global integration by developing global corporate and competitive strategies, and to play a significant role in resource allocation, selection of markets, developing strategic analysis, mergers, and acquisitions, decisions regarding R&D and technology matters, eliminating duplication of capital intensive assets, and knowledge transfer. An example of a modern multidomestic company is Nestlé.

The *modern global* company is rooted in the tradition of the traditional (pure) global form but gives a more significant role in decision making to the country subsidiaries. Headquarters targets a high level of global integration by creating low-cost sourcing opportunities, factor cost efficiencies, opportunities for global scale and scope, product standardization, global technology sharing and IT services, global branding, and an overarching global corporate strategy. But unlike the traditional (pure) global model, the modern global structure makes more effective use of the subsidiaries in order to encourage local responsiveness. As traditional global firms evolve into modern global enterprises, they tend to focus more on strategic coordination and integration of core competencies worldwide, and protecting home country control becomes less important. Modern global corporations may disperse R&D, manufacture and production, and marketing around the globe. This helps ensure flexibility in the face of changing factor costs for labor, raw materials, exchange rates, as well as hiring talent worldwide. P&G is an example of a modern global company.

### Realigning and Restructuring for Global Competitive Advantage

Creating the right environment for a global mind-set to develop and re-aligning and restructuring a company's global operations, at a minimum, require *(1) a strong commitment by the right top management, (2) a clear statement of vision and a delineation of a well-defined set of global decision-making processes, (3) anticipating and overcoming organizational resistance to change, (4) developing and coordinating networks, and (5) a global perspective on employee selection and career planning.*

*A Strong Commitment by the Right Top Management.*   Shaping a global mind-set starts at the top. The composition of the senior management team and the board of directors should reflect the diversity of markets in which the company wants to compete. In terms of mind-set, a multicultural board can help operating managers by providing a broader perspective and specific knowledge about new trends and changes in the environment. A good example of a company with a truly global top management team is the Adidas Group, the German-based sportswear company. Its executive board consists of two Germans, an American, and a New Zealander; the CEO is German. The company's supervisory board includes German nationals, a Frenchman, and Russians. Adidas is still an exception. Many other companies operating on a global scale still have a long way to go to make the composition of their top management and boards reflects the importance and diversity of their worldwide operations.

*A Clear Statement of Vision and a Delineation of a Well-Defined Set of Global Decision-Making Processes.*   For decades it has been general management's primary role to determine corporate strategy and the organization's structure. In many global companies, however, top management's role has changed from its historical focus on strategy, structure, and systems to a one on developing purpose and vision, processes, and people. This new philosophy reflects the growing importance of developing and nurturing a strong corporate purpose and vision in a diverse, global competitive environment. Under this new model, middle and upper-middle managers are expected to behave more like business leaders/entrepreneurs rather than administrators/controllers. To facilitate this role change, companies must spend more time and effort engaging middle management in developing strategy. This process gives middle and upper-middle managers an opportunity to make a contribution to the (global) corporate agenda and, at the same time, helps create a shared understanding and commitment of how to approach global business issues. Instead of traditional strategic planning in a separate corporate planning department Nestlé, for example, focuses on a combination of bottom-up and top-down planning approach involving markets, regions, and strategic product groups. That process ensures that local managers play an important part in decisions to pursue a certain plan and the related vision. In line with this approach headquarters does not generally force local units to do something they do not believe in. The new philosophy calls for development of the organization less through formal structure, and more through effective management processes.

*Anticipating and Overcoming Organizational Resistance to Change.*   The globalization of key business processes, such as IT, purchasing, product design, and R&D, is critical to global competitiveness. Decentralized, siloed local business processes simply are ineffective and unsustainable in today's intense global competitive environment. In this regard, creating the right "metrics" is important. When all of a company's metrics are focused locally or regionally, locally or regionally inspired behaviors can be expected. Until a consistent set of global metrics is adopted, designed to encourage global behaviors, globalization is unlikely to take hold, much less succeed. Resistance to such global process initiatives runs deep, however. As many companies have learned, country managers will likely invoke everything from the "not invented here" syndrome to respect for local culture and business heritage to defend the status quo.

*Developing and Coordinating Networks.*    Globalization has also brought greater emphasis on collaboration, not only with units inside the company but also with outside partners, such as suppliers and customers. Global managers must now develop and coordinate networks, which give them access to key resources on a worldwide basis. Network building helps to replace nationally held views with a collective global mind-set. Established global companies, such as Unilever or GE, have developed a networking culture, in which middle managers from various parts of the organization are constantly put together in working, training, or social situations. They range from staffing multicultural project teams, sophisticated career path systems encouraging international mobility to various training courses and internal conferences.

*A Global Perspective on Employee Selection and Career Planning.*    Recruiting from diverse sources worldwide supports the development of a global mind-set. A multicultural top management, as described previously, might improve the company's chances of recruiting and motivating high-potential candidates from various countries. Many companies now hire local managers and put them through intensive training programs. Microsoft, for example, routinely brings foreign talent to the United States for intensive training. P&G runs local courses in a number of countries and then sends trainees to its headquarters in Cincinnati or to large foreign subsidiaries for a significant period of time. After completion of their training they are expected to take over local management positions.

Similarly, a career path in a global company must provide for recurring local and global assignments. Typically, a high-potential candidate will start in a specific local function, for example, marketing or finance. A successful track record in the chosen functional area provides the candidate with sufficient credibility in the company and, equally important, self-confidence to take on more complex and demanding global tasks, usually as a team member where he or she gets hands-on knowledge of the workings of a global team. With each new assignment, managers should broaden their perspectives and establish informal networks of contact and relationships. Whereas international assignments in the past were primarily demand-driven to transfer know-how and solve specific problems, they are now much more learning-oriented and focus on giving the expatriate the opportunity to understand and benefit from cultural differences as well as to develop long-lasting networks and relationships. Exposure to all major functions, rotation through several businesses, and different postings in various countries are critical in creating a global mind-set, both for the individual manager and for the entire management group. In that sense, global human resource management is probably one of the most powerful medium- and long-term tools for global success.

# CHAPTER 9

# Global Strategy: Adapting the Business Model

## Introduction

Few companies can afford to enter all markets open to them. Even the world's largest companies such as General Electric or Nestlé must exercise strategic discipline in choosing the markets they serve. They must also decide when to enter them, and weigh the relative advantages of a direct or indirect presence in different regions of the world. Small and midsize companies are often constrained to an indirect presence; for them the key to gaining a global competitive advantage often is creating a worldwide resource network through alliances with suppliers, customers, and sometimes competitors. What is a good strategy for one company, however, might have little chance of succeeding for another.

The track record shows that picking the most attractive foreign markets, the best time to enter them and selecting the right partners and level of investment has proven difficult for many companies, especially when it involves large emerging markets such as China. For example, it is now generally recognized that Western car makers entered China far too early, and overinvested believing a "first-mover advantage" would produce superior returns. Reality was very different. Most lost large amounts of money, had trouble working with local partners, and saw their technological advantage erode due to "leakage". None achieved the sales volume needed to justify their investment.

Even highly successful global companies often first sustain substantial losses on their overseas ventures, and occasionally have to trim back their foreign operations or even abandon entire countries or regions in the face of ill-timed strategic moves or fast-changing competitive circumstances.

Not all of Wal-Mart's global moves have been successful, for example— a continuing source of frustration to investors. In 1999 the company spent $10.8 billion to buy British grocery chain Asda. Not only was Asda healthy and profitable—it was already positioned as "Wal-Mart lite." Today, Asda is lagging well behind its No.1 rival, Tesco. Even though Wal-Mart's UK operations are profitable, sales growth has been down in recent years, and Asda has missed profit targets for several quarters running, and is in danger of slipping further in the UK market.

This result comes on top of Wal-Mart's costly exit from the German market. In 2005, it sold its 85 stores there to rival Metro at a loss of $1 billion. Eight years after buying into the highly competitive German market, Wal-Mart executives, accustomed to using Wal-Mart's massive market muscle to squeeze suppliers, admitted they had been unable to attain the economies of scale it needed in Germany to beat rivals' prices, prompting an early and expensive exit.

### Global Market Selection

What makes global market selection and entry so difficult? Research shows there is a pervasive "the grass is always greener" effect that infects global strategic decision making in many, especially globally inexperienced, companies and causes them to overestimate the attractiveness of foreign markets.[1] As noted in Chapter 3 "distance", broadly defined, unless well-understood and compensated for, can be a major impediment to global success: cultural differences can lead companies to overestimate the appeal of their products or the strength of their brands; administrative differences can slow expansion plans, reduce the ability to attract the right talent and increase the cost of doing business; geographic distance impacts the effectiveness of communication and coordination; and economic distance directly influences revenues and costs.

A related issue is that developing a global presence takes time and requires substantial resources. Ideally, the pace of international expansion is dictated by customer demand. Sometimes it is necessary, however, to expand ahead of direct opportunity in order to secure a long-term competitive advantage. But, as many companies that entered China in anticipation of its membership in the World Trade Organization (WTO) have learned, early commitment to even the most promising long-term market makes earning a satisfactory return on invested capital difficult. As a result, an increasing number of firms, particularly smaller and midsize ones, favor global expansion strategies that minimize direct investment. Strategic alliances have made vertical or horizontal integration less important to profitability and shareholder value in many industries. Alliances boost contribution to fixed cost while expanding a company's global reach. At the same time, they can be powerful windows on technology, and greatly expand opportunities to create the core competencies needed to effectively compete on a worldwide basis.

Finally, a complicating factor is that a global evaluation of market opportunities requires a multidimensional perspective. In many industries we can distinguish between *"must"* markets—markets in which a company must compete in order to realize its global ambitions—and *"nice-to-be-in"* markets—markets in which participation is desirable but not critical. "Must" markets include those that are critical from a *volume* perspective, markets that define *technological leadership*, and markets in which key *competitive* battles are decided. In the cell phone industry, for example, Motorola looks to Europe as a primary competitive battleground, but it derives much of its technology from Japan and sales volume from the United States.

### Measuring Global Market Attractiveness

Four key factors in selecting global markets are (1) a *market's size and growth rate*, (2) a particular country or region's *institutional contexts*, (3) a region's *competitive environment,* and (4) a market's *cultural, administrative, geographic and economic distance* from other markets the company serves.

*Market Size and Growth Rate.*   A wealth of country-level economic and demographic data is available from a variety of sources including governments, multinational organizations such as the United Nations or the World Bank, and consulting firms specializing in economic intelligence or risk assessment. However, while valuable from an overall investment perspective, such data often reveal little about the prospects for selling products or services in foreign markets to local partners and end users or about the challenges associated with overcoming other elements of distance. Yet, many companies still use this information as their primary guide to market assessment simply because country-market statistics are readily available, whereas real product-market information is often difficult and costly to obtain.

What is more, a country/regional approach to market selection may not always be the best. Even though Theodore Levitt's vision of a global market for uniform products and services has not come to pass and global strategies exclusively focused on the "economics of simplicity" and the selling of standardized products all over the world rarely payoff, research increasingly supports an alternative "global segmentation" approach to the issue of market selection, especially for branded products. In particular, surveys show that a growing number of consumers, especially in emerging markets, base their consumption decisions on attributes beyond direct product benefits such as their perception of the global brands behind the offerings.

Companies that use a "global segment" approach to market selection such as Coca-Cola, Sony or Microsoft to name a few, therefore must manage two dimensions for their brands. They must strive for superiority on basics like the brand's price, performance, features, and imagery and, at the same time, they must learn to manage brands' global characteristics, which often separate winners from losers. A good example is provided by Samsung, the South Korean electronics maker. In the late 1990s, Samsung launched a global advertising campaign that showed the South Korean giant excelling time after time in engineering, design, and aesthetics. By doing so, Samsung convinced consumers that it could compete successfully directly with technology leaders like Nokia and Sony across the world. As a result, Samsung was able to change the perception that it was a downmarket brand, and it became known as a global provider of leading-edge technologies. This brand strategy, in turn, allowed Samsung to use a global segmentation approach to making market selection and entry decisions.

*Institutional Contexts.*    Khanna et al.[2] developed a five dimensional framework to map a particular country or region's institutional contexts.

Specifically, they suggest careful analysis of a country's (1) *Political and Social Systems,* (2) *Openness,* (3) *Product Markets,* (4) *Labor Markets, and* (5) *Capital Markets.*

A country's *political system* affects its product, labor, and capital markets. In socialist societies like China, for instance, workers cannot form independent trade unions in the labor market, which affects wage levels. A country's *social* environment is also important. In South Africa, for example, the government's support for the transfer of assets to the historically disenfranchised native African community has affected the development of the capital market.

Even though developing countries have *opened* up their *product* markets during the past 20 years, multinational companies struggle to get reliable information about consumers. Market research and advertising often are less sophisticated and, because there are no well-developed consumer courts and advocacy groups in these countries, people can feel they are at the mercy of big companies.

*Labor markets* also present ongoing challenges. Recruiting local managers and other skilled workers in developing countries can be difficult. The quality of local credentials can be hard to verify, there are relatively few search firms and recruiting agencies, and the high-quality firms that do exist focus on top-level searches, so companies scramble to identify middle-level managers, engineers, or floor supervisors.

Finally, *capital and financial* markets in developing countries often lack sophistication. Reliable intermediaries like credit-rating agencies, investment analysts, merchant bankers, or venture capital firms may not exist and multinationals cannot count on raising debt or equity capital locally to finance their operations. Nurturing strong relationships with government officials often is necessary to succeed. Even then, contracts may not be well enforced by the legal system.

*Competitive Environment.* The number, size, and quality of competitive firms in a particular target market comprise a third set of factors that affect a company's ability to successfully enter and compete profitably. While country-level economic and demographic data are widely available for most regions of the world, competitive data is much harder to come by, especially when the principal players are subsidiaries of multinational corporations. As a consequence, competitive analysis in foreign countries, especially in emerging markets, is difficult and costly to perform and its findings do not always provide the level of insight needed to make good decisions. Nevertheless, a comprehensive competitive analysis provides a useful framework for developing strategies for growth, and for analyzing current and future primary competitors and their strengths and weaknesses.

*Distance.*    Explicitly considering the four dimensions of distance introduced in Chapter 3 can dramatically change a company's assessment of the relative attractiveness of foreign markets. In his book *The Mirage of Global Markets,* David Arnold describes the experience of Mary Kay Cosmetics (MKC) in entering Asian markets. MKC is a direct marketing company that distributes its products through independent "beauty consultants" who buy and resell cosmetics and toiletries to contacts either individually or at social gatherings. When considering market expansion in Asia, the company had to choose: Enter Japan or China first? Country-level data showed Japan to be the most attractive option by far: it had the highest per capita level of spending of any country in the world on cosmetics and toiletries, disposable income was high, it already had a thriving direct marketing industry, and it had a high proportion of women who did not participate in the workforce. MKC learned, however, after participating in both markets, that the market opportunity in China was far greater, mainly because of economic and cultural distance: Chinese women were far more motivated than their Japanese counterparts to boost their income by becoming beauty consultants. Thus, the entrepreneurial opportunity represented by what MKC describes as "the career" (i.e., becoming a beauty consultant) was a far better predictor of the true sales potential than high-level data on incomes and expenditures. As a result of this experience, MKC now employs an additional business-specific indicator of market potential within its market assessment framework: The average wage for a female secretary in a country.[3]

MKC's experience underscores the importance of analyzing distance. It also highlights the fact that different product-markets have different success factors; some are brand-sensitive while in others pricing or intensive distribution are key to success. Country-level economic or demographic data do not provide much help in analyzing such issues; only locally gathered marketing intelligence can provide true indications of a market's potential size and growth rate and its key success factors.

## Entry Strategies: Modes of Entry

What is the best way to enter a new market? Should a company first establish an export base or license its products to gain experience in a newly targeted country or region? Or does the potential associated with first-mover status justify a bolder move such as entering an alliance, making an acquisition, or even starting a new subsidiary? Many companies move from exporting to licensing to a higher investment strategy, in effect treating these choices as a learning curve. Each has distinct advantages and disadvantages.

*Exporting* is the marketing and direct sale of domestically produced goods in another country. Exporting is a traditional and well-established method of reaching foreign markets. Since it does not require that the goods be produced in the target country, no investment in foreign production facilities is required. Most of the costs associated with exporting take the form of marketing expenses.

While relatively low risk, exporting entails substantial costs and limited control. Exporters typically have little control over the marketing and distribution of their products, face high transportation charges and possible tariffs, and must pay distributors for a variety of services. What is more, exporting does not give a company first-hand experience in staking out a competitive position abroad, and it makes it difficult to customize products and services to local tastes and preferences.

*Licensing* essentially permits a company in the target country to use the property of the licensor. Such property usually is intangible, such as trademarks, patents, and production techniques. The licensee pays a fee in exchange for the rights to use the intangible property and possibly for technical assistance.

Because little investment on the part of the licensor is required, licensing has the potential to provide a very large Return on Investment (ROI). However, because the licensee produces and markets the product, potential returns from manufacturing and marketing activities may be lost. Thus, licensing reduces cost and involves limited risk. However, it does not mitigate the substantial disadvantages associated with operating from a distance. As a rule, licensing strategies inhibit control and produce only moderate returns.

*Strategic alliances* and *joint ventures* have become increasingly popular in recent years. They allow companies to share the risks and resources required to enter international markets. And although returns also may have to be shared, they give a company a degree of flexibility not afforded by going it alone through direct investment.

There are several motivations for companies to consider a partnership as they expand globally, including (1) facilitating market entry, (2) risk/reward sharing, (3) technology sharing, (4) joint product development (PD), and (5) conforming to government regulations. Other benefits include political connections and distribution channel access that may depend on relationships. Such alliances often are favorable when (1) the partners' strategic goals converge while their competitive goals diverge; (2) the partners' size, market power, and resources are small compared to the industry leaders; and (3) partners are able to learn from one another while limiting access to their own proprietary skills.

The key issues to consider in a joint venture are ownership, control, length of agreement, pricing, technology transfer, local firm capabilities and resources, and government intentions. Potential problems include (1) conflict over asymmetric new investments, (2) mistrust over proprietary knowledge, (3) performance ambiguity—how to split the pie, (4) lack of parent firm support, (5) cultural clashes, and (6) if, how, and when to terminate the relationship.

*Acquisitions* or *greenfield* start-ups. Ultimately, most companies will aim at building their own presence through company-owned facilities in important international markets. Acquisitions or greenfield start-ups represent this ultimate commitment. Acquisition is faster but starting a new, wholly owned subsidiary might be the preferred option if no suitable acquisition candidates can be found.

Also known as *Foreign Direct Investment*, acquisitions and Greenfield start-ups involve the direct ownership of facilities in the target country, and therefore the transfer of resources including capital, technology, and personnel. Direct ownership provides a high degree of control in the operations and the ability to know better the consumers and competitive environment. However, it requires a high level of resources and a high degree of commitment.

### Entry Strategies: Timing

In addition to selecting the right mode of entry, timing of entry is critical. Just as many companies have overestimated market potential abroad and underestimated the time and effort needed to create a real market presence, so have they justified their overseas' expansion on the grounds of an urgent need to participate in the market early. Arguing that there existed a limited window of opportunity in which to act that would reward only those players bold enough to move early, many companies made sizable commitments to foreign markets even though their own financial projections showed they would not be profitable for years to come. This dogmatic belief in the concept of a first-mover advantage (sometimes referred to as pioneer advantage), became one of the most widely established theories of business. It holds that the first entrant in a new market enjoys a unique advantage that later competitors cannot overcome, that is, that the competitive advantage so obtained is structural, and therefore sustainable.

Some companies have found this to be true. Procter & Gamble, for example, has always trailed rivals such as Unilever in certain large markets, including India and some Latin American countries, and the most obvious explanation is that its European rivals were participating in these countries long before Proctor & Gamble (P&G) entered. Given that history, it is understandable that Procter & Gamble erred on the side of urgency in reacting to the opening of large markets such as Russia or China. For many other companies, however, the concept of pioneer advantage was little more than an article of faith, and applied indiscriminately and with disastrous results to country-market entry, to product-market entry, and, in particular, to the "new economy" opportunities created by the Internet.

The "get in early" philosophy of pioneer advantage remains popular. And while there clearly are examples of its successful application—the advantages gained by European companies from being early in "colonial" markets provide some evidence of pioneer advantage—first-mover advantage is overrated as a strategic principle. In fact, in many instances there are disadvantages to being first. First, if there is no real first-mover advantage, being first often results in poor business performance as the large number of companies that rushed into Russia and China attests. Second, pioneers may not always be able to recoup their investment in marketing required to "kick-start" the new market. When that happens, a "fast follower" can benefit from the market development funded by the pioneer, and leapfrog into earlier profitability.[4]

This ability of later entrants to free-ride on the pioneer's market development investment is the most common source of first-mover disadvantage, and suggests two critical conditions necessary for real first-mover advantage to exist. First, there must be a scarce resource in the market that the first entrant can acquire. Second, the first-mover must be able to lock up that scarce resource in such a way that it creates a barrier to entry for potential competitors. A good example is provided by markets in which it is necessary for foreign firms to obtain a government permit or license to sell their products. In such cases, the license, and perhaps government approval more generally, may be a scarce resource that will not be granted to all comers. The second condition is also necessary for first-mover advantage to develop. Many companies believed that brand preference created by being first constituted a valid source of first-mover advantage, only to find later that in most cases consumers consider the alternatives available at the time of their first purchase, not which came first.

## Globalizing the Value Proposition

Managers sometimes assume that what works in their home country will work just as well in another part of the world. They take the same product, the same advertising campaign, even the same brand names and packaging, and expect instant success. The result in most cases is failure. Why? Because the assumption that one approach works everywhere fails to consider the complex mosaic of differences that exists between countries and cultures.

Of course, marketing a standardized product with the same positioning and communications strategy around the globe—the purest form of *aggregation*—has considerable attraction because of its cost effectiveness and simplicity. It is also extremely dangerous, however. Simply assuming that foreign customers will respond positively to an existing product can lead to costly failure. Consider the following classic examples of failure:

- Coca-Cola had to withdraw its 2-liter bottle in Spain after discovering that few Spaniards owned refrigerators with large enough compartments to accommodate it.
- General Foods squandered millions trying to introduce packaged cake mixes to Japanese consumers. The company failed to note that only 3 percent of Japanese homes were equipped with ovens.
- General Foods' Tang initially failed in France because it was positioned as a substitute for orange juice at breakfast. The French drink little orange juice and almost none at breakfast.

With a few exceptions the idea of an identical, fully standardized global value proposition is a myth and few industries are truly global. How to adapt a value proposition in the most effective manner therefore is a key strategic issue.

### Value Proposition Adaptation Decisions

Value proposition adaptation deals with a whole range of issues, ranging from the quality and appearance of products to materials, processing, production equipment, packaging, and style. A product may have to be adapted to meet the physical, social or mandatory requirements of a new market. It may have to be modified to conform to government regulations or to operate effectively in country specific geographic and climatic conditions. Or it may be redesigned or repackaged to meet the diverse buyer preferences, or standard of living conditions. A product's size and packaging may also have to be modified to facilitate shipment or to conform to possible differences in engineering or design standards in a country or regional markets. Other dimensions of value proposition adaptation include changes in brand name, color, size, taste, design, style, features, materials, warranties, after sale service, technological sophistication, and performance.

The need for some changes such as accommodating different electricity requirements will be obvious. Others may require in-depth analysis of societal customs and cultures, the local economy, technological sophistication of people living in the country, and customers' purchasing power and purchase behavior. Legal, economic, political, technological, and climatic requirements of a country market all may dictate some level of localization or adaptation.

As tariff barriers (tariffs, duties, and quotas) are gradually reduced around the world in accordance with World Trade Organization rules, other, *nontariff, barriers,* such as *product standards*, are proliferating. Take regulations for food additives. Many of the U.S. so-called "Generally Recognized as Safe" additives are banned today in foreign countries. In marketing abroad, documentation is important not only for the amount of additive, but also its source, and often additives must be listed on the label of ingredients. As a result, product labeling and packaging must often be adapted to comply with another country's legal and environmental requirement.

Many products must be adapted to local *geographic and climatic* conditions. Factors such as topography, humidity, and energy costs can affect the performance of a product or even define its use in a foreign market. The cost of petroleum products along with a country's infrastructure, for example, may mandate the need to develop products with a greater level of energy efficiency. Hot dusty climates of countries in the Middle East and other emerging markets may force the automakers to adapt the automobiles with different types of filters and clutch systems than those used in North America, Japan, and Europe countries. Even shampoo and cosmetic product makers have to chemically reformulate their shampoo and cosmetic products to make them more suited for people living in hot humid climates.

The availability, performance, and level of sophistication of a *commercial infrastructure* will also warrant a need for adaptation or localization of products. For example, a company may decide not to market its frozen line of food items in countries where retailers do not have adequate freezer space. Instead, it may choose to develop dehydrated products for such markets. Size of packaging, material used in packaging, before and after sale service and warranties may have to be adapted in view of the scope and level of service provided by the distribution structure in the country markets targeted. In the event post sale servicing facilities are conspicuous by their absence, companies may need to offer simpler, more robust products in overseas markets to reduce the need for maintenance and repairs.

Differences in *buyer preferences* also are a major driver behind value proposition adaptation. Local customs, such as religion or the use of leisure time, may affect market acceptance. The sensory impact of a product, such as taste or its visual impression, may also be a critical factor. The Japanese consumers' desire for beautiful packaging, for example, has led many U.S. companies to redesign cartons and packages specifically for this market. At the same time, to make purchasing mass marketed consumer products more affordable in lesser developed countries, makers of products such as razor blades, cigarettes, chewing gum, ball point pens and candy bars repackage them in small single units rather than multiple units prevalent in the developed and more advanced economies.

Expectations about *product guarantees* also can vary from country to country depending on the level of development, competitive practices, and degree of activism by consumer groups, local standards of production quality, and prevalent product usage patterns. Strong warranties may be required to break into a new market, especially if the company is an unknown supplier. In other cases warranties similar to those in the home country market may not be expected.

As a general rule, *packaging design* should be based on the customer needs. For industrial products packaging is primarily functional and should consider needs for storage, transportation, protection, preservation, reuse, and so on. For consumer products packaging has additional functionality and should be protective, informative, appealing, conform to legal requirements, and reflect buying habits (e.g., Americans tend to shop less frequently than Europeans, so larger sizes are more popular in the United States).

In analyzing adaptation requirement, careful attention to *cultural differences* between the target customers in home (country of origin) and those in the host country is extremely important. The greater the cultural differences between the two target markets the greater the need for adaptation. Cultural considerations and customs may influence branding, labeling, and package considerations. Certain colors used on labels and packages may be found unattractive or offensive. Red, for example, stands for good luck and fortune in China and parts of Africa; aggression, danger, or warning in Europe, America and Australia/New Zealand; masculinity in parts of Europe; mourning (dark red) in the Ivory Coast; and death in Turkey. Blue denotes immortality in Iran while purple denotes mourning in Brazil and is a symbol of expense in some Asian cultures. Green is associated with high-tech in Japan, luck in the Middle East, connotes death in South America and countries with dense jungle areas, and is a forbidden color in Indonesia. Yellow is associated with femininity in the United States and many other countries, but denotes mourning in Mexico and strength and reliability in Saudi Arabia. Finally, black is used to signal mourning as well as style and elegance in most Western nations but it stands for trust and quality in China while white is the symbol for cleanliness and purity in the West and denotes mourning in Japan and some other Far Eastern nations.

When potential customers have limited purchasing power, companies may need to develop an entirely new product designed to address the market opportunity at a price point that is within the reach of a potential target market. Conversely companies in lesser developed countries that have achieved local success may find it necessary to adopt an "up-market strategy" whereby the product may have to be designed to meet world class standards.

### Adaptation or Aggregation: The Value Proposition Globalization Matrix

A useful construct for analyzing the need to adapt the product/service and message (positioning) dimensions is the *value proposition globalization matrix* shown in Figure 9.1. It illustrates four generic global strategies: (1) a pure aggregation approach (also sometimes referred to as a "global marketing mix" strategy) under which both the offer and the message are the same, (2) an approach characterized by an identical offer (product/service

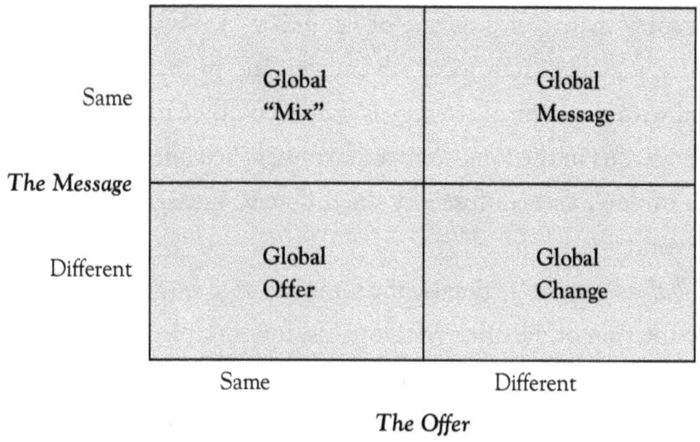

Figure 9.1  The value proposition globalization matrix

aggregation) but different positioning (message adaptation) around the world (also called a "global offer" strategy), (3) an approach under which the offer might be different in various parts of the world (product adaptation) but the message is the same (message aggregation) (also referred to as a "global message" strategy), and (4) a "global change" strategy under which both the offer and the message are adapted to local market circumstances.

*Global mix* or pure aggregation strategies are relatively rare because only a few industries are truly global in all respects. They apply (1) when a product's usage patterns and brand potential are homogeneous on a global scale, (2) when scale and scope cost advantages substantially outweigh the benefits of partial or full adaptation, and (3) when competitive circumstances are such that a long-term, sustainable advantage can be secured using a standardized approach. The best examples are found in industrial product categories such as basic electronic components or certain commodity markets.

*Global offer* strategies are feasible when the same offer can advantageously be positioned differently in different parts of the world. There are several reasons for considering a differential positioning in different parts of the world. When fixed costs associated with the offer are high, when key core benefits offered are identical, and when there are natural market boundaries, adapting the message for stronger local advantage is tempting. Although such strategies increase local promotional budgets, they give country managers a degree of flexibility in positioning the product or service for maximum local advantage. The primary disadvantage associated with this type of strategy is that it could be difficult to sustain or even dangerous in the long-term as customers become increasingly global in their outlook and confused by the different messages in different parts of the world.

*Global message* strategies use the same message worldwide but allow for local adaptation of the offer. McDonalds, for example, is positioned virtually identically worldwide, but it serves vegetarian food in India and wine in France. The primary motivation behind this type of strategy is the enormous power behind a global brand. In industries in which customers increasingly develop similar expectations, aspirations, and values, in which customers are highly mobile, and in which the cost of product or service adaptation is fairly low, leveraging the global brand potential represented by one message worldwide often outweighs the possible disadvantages associated with factors such as higher local R&D costs. As with global offer strategies, however, global message strategies can be risky in the long run; global customers might not find elsewhere what they expect and regularly experience at home. This could lead to confusion or even alienation.

*Global change* strategies define a "best fit" approach and are by far the most common. As we have seen, for most products, some form of adaptation of both the offer and the message is necessary. Differences in a product's usage patterns, benefits sought, brand image, competitive structures, distribution channels, and governmental and other regulations all dictate some form of local adaptation. Corporate factors also play a role. Companies that have achieved a global reach through acquisition, for example, often prefer to leverage local brand names, distribution systems, and suppliers rather than embark on a risky global one-size-fits-all approach. As the markets they serve and the company itself become more global, selective standardization of the message and/or the offer itself can become more attractive.

### Combining Aggregation and Adaptation: Global Product Platforms

One way around the trade-off between creating global efficiencies and adapting to local requirements and preferences is to design a global product and/or communication platform that can be adapted efficiently to different markets. This modularized approach to global product design has become particularly popular in the automobile industry. One of the first "world car platforms" was introduced by Ford in 1981. The Escort was assembled simultaneously in three countries—the United States, Germany, and the UK—with parts produced in 10 countries. The U.S. and European models were distinctly different but shared standardized engines, transmissions, and ancillary systems for heating, air conditioning, wheels and seats, thereby saving the company millions of dollars in engineering and development costs.

### Combining Adaptation and Arbitrage: Global Product Development[5]

Globalization pressures have changed the practice of product development in many industries in recent years. Rather than using a centralized or local, cross-functional model, companies are moving to a mode of global collaboration in which skilled development teams dispersed around the world collaborate to develop new products. Today, a majority of global corporations have engineering and development operations outside of their home region. China and India offer particularly attractive opportunities; Microsoft, Cisco, and Intel all have made major investments there.

The old model was based on the premise that colocation of cross-functional teams to facilitate close collaboration among engineering, marketing, manufacturing, and supply-chain functions was critical to effective PD. Co-located PD teams were thought to be more effective at concurrently executing the full range of activities involved, from understanding market and customer needs, through conceptual and detailed design, testing, analysis, prototyping, manufacturing engineering, and technical product support/engineering. Such co-located concurrent practices were thought to result in better product designs, faster time to market, and lower-cost production. They were generally located in corporate research and development centers, which maintained linkages to manufacturing sites and sales offices around the world.

Today, best practice emphasizes a highly distributed, networked, and digitally supported development process. The resulting global product development process combines centralized functions with regionally distributed engineering and other development functions. It often involves outsourced engineering work as well as captive offshore engineering. The benefits of this distributed model include greater engineering efficiency (through utilization of *lower-cost* resources), *access to technical expertise* internationally, more *global input to product design* and greater *strategic flexibility.*

### Combining Aggregation, Adaptation, and Arbitrage: Global Innovation[6]

A core competency in global innovation—the ability to leverage new ideas all around the world—has become a major source of global competitive advantage, as companies such as Nokia, Airbus, SAP, and Starbucks demonstrate. They realize that the principal constraint on innovation "performance" is knowledge. Accessing a diverse set of sources of knowledge is therefore a key challenge, and critical to successful differentiation. Companies whose knowledge pool is the same as that of its competitors likely will develop uninspired "me too" products; access to a diversity of knowledge allows a company to move beyond incremental innovation to attention grabbing designs and breakthrough solutions.

To reap the benefits of global innovation, companies must do three things: (1) *prospect* (find the relevant pockets of knowledge from around the world), (2) *assess* (decide on the optimal "footprint" for a particular innovation), and (3) *mobilize* (use cost-effective mechanisms to move distant knowledge without degrading it).[7]

*Prospecting,* that is, finding valuable new pockets of knowledge to spur innovation may well be the most challenging task. The process involves knowing what to look for, where to look for it, and how to tap into a promising source. Santos et al. cite the efforts of the cosmetics maker Shiseido Co. Ltd. in entering the market for fragrance products. Based in Japan, a country with a very limited tradition of perfume use, Shiseido was initially unsure of the precise knowledge it needed to enter the fragrance business. But the company did know where to look for it. So it bought two exclusive beauty boutique chains in Paris, mainly as a way to experience, firsthand, the personal-care demands of the most sophisticated customers of such products. It also hired the marketing manager of Yves Saint Laurent Parfums and built a plant in Gien, a town located in the French perfume "cluster." France's leadership in that industry made the *where* fairly obvious to Shiseido. The *how* had also become painfully clear because the company had previously flopped in its efforts to develop perfumes in Japan. Those failures convinced Shiseido executives that, to access such complex knowledge—deeply rooted in local culture and combining customer information, aesthetics, and technology—the company had to immerse itself in the French environment and learn by doing. Having figured out the *where* and *how,* Shiseido would gradually learn *what* knowledge it needed to succeed in the perfume business.

*Assessing* new sources of innovation, that is, incorporating new knowledge into and optimizing an existing innovation network, is a second major challenge. If a semiconductor manufacturer is developing a new chip set for mobile phones, for example, should it access technical and market knowledge from Silicon Valley, Austin, Hinschu, Seoul, Bangalore, Haifa, Helsinki, and Grenoble? Or should it restrict itself to just some of those sites? At first glance determining the best footprint for innovation does not seem fundamentally different from the trade-offs companies face in optimizing their global supply chains: Adding a new source might reduce the price or improve the quality of a required component, but more locations also may mean additional complexity and cost. Similarly, every time a company adds a source of knowledge into the innovation process it might improve its chances of developing a novel product, but it also increases costs. Determining an optimal innovation footprint is more complicated, however, because the direct and indirect cost relationships are far more imprecise.

*Mobilizing* the footprint, that is, integrating knowledge from different sources into a virtual melting pot from which new products or technologies can emerge, is the third challenge. To accomplish this, companies must bring the various pieces of (technical) knowledge together that are scattered around the world and provide a suitable organizational form for innovation efforts to flourish. More important, they would have to add the more complex, contextual (market) knowledge to integrate the different pieces into an overall innovation blueprint.

# Globalizing the Sourcing Dimension

## To Outsource or Not to Outsource[8]

Few companies, especially ones with a global presence, are self-sufficient in all of the activities that make up their value chain. Competitive pressures force companies to focus on those activities that they judge critical to their success and excel at—core capabilities in which they have a distinct competitive advantage—and that can be leveraged across geographies and lines of business. Which activities should be kept in-house and which ones can effectively be outsourced depends on a host of factors, most prominently the nature of the company's core strategy, partner network, and asset base.

Firms tend to concentrate their investments in global value chain activities that contribute directly to their competitive advantage and, at the same time, help the company retain the right amount of strategic flexibility. Making such decisions is a formidable challenge; capabilities that may seem unrelated at first glance can turn out to be critical for creating an essential advantage when they are combined. As an example consider the case of a leading consumer packaged goods company that created strong embedded capabilities in sales. Its smaller brands showed up on retailers' shelves far more regularly than comparable brands from competitors. It was also known for the efficacy of its short-term R&D in rapidly bringing product variations to market. These capabilities are worth investing in separately, but together they add up to a substantial advantage over competitors, especially in introducing new products.

Outsourcing and offshoring of component manufacturing and support services can offer compelling strategic and financial advantages including *lower costs, greater flexibility, enhanced expertise, greater discipline,* and *the freedom to focus on core business activities.*

*Lower Costs.*    Savings may result from lower inherent, structural, systemic or realized costs. A detailed analysis of each of these cost categories can identify the potential sources of advantage. For example, larger suppliers may capture greater scale benefits than the internal organization. The risk is that efficiency gains lead to lower quality or reliability.

Offshoring typically offers significant infrastructure and labor cost advantages over traditional outsourcing. In addition, many offshoring providers have established very large-scale operations not economically possible for domestic providers.

*Greater Flexibility.*    Using an outside supplier can sometimes add flexibility to a company such that it can adjust the scale and scope of production rapidly at low cost. As we have learned from the Japanese keiretsu and Korean chaebol conglomerates, networks of organizations can often adjust to demand more easily than fully integrated organizations.

*Enhanced Expertise.*    Some suppliers may have proprietary access to technology or other intellectual property advantages that a firm cannot access by itself. Such technology may improve operational reliability, productivity, efficiency or long-term total costs and production. The significant scale of today's offshore manufacturers, in particular, allows them to invest in technology that may be cost prohibitive for domestic providers.

*Greater Discipline.*    Separation of purchasers and providers can assist with transparency and accountability to identify true costs and benefits of certain activities. This can enable transactions under market-based contracts where the focus is on output not input. At the same time, competition among suppliers creates choice for purchasers and encourages the adoption of innovative work practices.

*Focus on Core Activities.*    The ability to focus frees up resources internally to concentrate on those activities where the company has distinctive capability and scale, experience or differentiation to yield economic benefits. In other words, focus allows a company to concentrate on creating *relative* advantage to maximize total value and allow others to produce supportive goods and services.

While outsourcing is largely about scale and the ability to provide services at a more competitive cost, offshoring is primarily driven by the dramatic wage-cost differentials that exist between developed and developing nations. However, cost should not be the only consideration in making offshoring decisions; other relevant factors include the quality and reliability of labor continuous process improvements, environment, and infrastructure. Political stability and broad economic and legal frameworks should also be taken into account. In reality, even very significant labor cost differentials between countries cannot be the sole driver of offshoring decisions. Companies need to be assured of quality and reliability in the services they are outsourcing. This is the same whether services are outsourced domestically or offshore.

### Risks Associated with Outsourcing[9]

Outsourcing can have significant benefits but is not without risk. Some risks, such as potentially higher overall costs due to the eroding value of the U.S. dollar, can be anticipated and addressed through contracts by employing financial hedging strategies. Others, however, are harder to anticipate or deal with.

Risks associated with outsourcing typically fall into four general categories: *loss of control, loss of innovation, loss of organizational trust, and higher-than-expected transaction costs*:

*Loss of Control.*   Managers often complain about loss of control over their own process technologies and quality standards when specific processes or services are outsourced. The consequences can be severe. When tasks previously performed by company personnel are given to outsiders over whom the firm has little or no control, quality may suffer, production schedules may be disrupted or contractual disagreements may develop. If outsourcing contracts inappropriately or incorrectly detail work specifications outsourcers may be tempted to behave opportunistically— for example, by using subcontractors, or by charging unforeseen or unwarranted price increases to exploit the company's dependency. Control issues can also be exacerbated by geographic distance, particularly when the vendor is offshore. Monitoring performance and productivity can be challenging, and coordination and communication maybe difficult with offshore vendors. The inability to engage in face-to-face discussions, brainstorm, or explore nuances of obstacles could cripple a project's flow.

Distance, too, can increase the likelihood of outages disabling the communication infrastructure between the vendor and the outsourcing firm. Depending on where the outsourced work is performed, there can be critical cultural or language-related differences between the outsourcing company and the vendor. Such differences can have important customer implications. For example, if customer call centers are outsourced, the manner in which an agent answers, interprets, and reacts to customer telephone calls (especially complaints) may be affected by local culture and language.

*Loss of Innovation.*   Companies pursuing innovation strategies recognize the need to recruit and hire highly qualified individuals, provide them a long-term focus and minimal control, and appraise their performance for positive long-run impact. When certain support services—such as IT, software development, or materials management—are outsourced, innovation may be impaired. Moreover, when external providers are hired for the purposes of cutting costs, gaining labor pool flexibility, or adjusting to market fluctuations, long-standing cooperative work patterns are interrupted which may adversely affect the company's corporate culture.

*Loss of Organizational Trust.*   For many firms, a significant nonquantifiable risk occurs because outsourcing, especially of services, can be perceived as a breach in the employer–employee relationship. Employees may wonder which group or what function will be the next to be outsourced. Workers displaced into an outsourced organization often feel conflicted as to who their "real" boss is: The new external service contractor, or the client company by which they were previously employed?

*Higher-than-Expected Transaction Costs.*   Some outsourcing costs and benefits are easily identified and quantified because they are captured by the accounting system. Other costs and benefits are decision-relevant but not part of the accounting system; such factors cannot be ignored simply because they are difficult to obtain or require the use of estimates. One of the most important and least understood considerations in the make-or-buy decision is the cost of outsourcing risk.

There are many other factors to consider in selecting the right level of participation in the value chain and the location for key value-added activities. Factor conditions, the presence of supporting industrial activity, the nature and location of the demand for the product, and industry rivalry all should be considered. In addition, such issues as tax consequences, the ability to repatriate profits, currency, and political risk, the ability to manage and coordinate in different locations, and synergies with other elements of the company's overall strategy should be factored in.

## Partnering

Formulating cooperative strategies—*joint ventures, strategic alliances, and other partnering* arrangements—is the complement of outsourcing. Globalization is an important factor in the rise of cooperative ventures. In a global competitive environment, going it alone often means taking extraordinary risks. Escalating fixed costs associated with achieving global market coverage, keeping up with the latest technology, and increased exposure to currency and political risk all make risk-sharing a necessity in many industries. For many companies, a global strategic posture without alliances would be untenable.

Cooperative strategies take many forms and are considered for many different reasons. However, the fundamental motivation in every case is the corporation's ability to spread its investments over a range of options, each with a different risk profile. Essentially, the corporation is trading off the likelihood of a major payoff against the ability to optimize its investments by betting on multiple options. The key drivers that attract executives to cooperative strategies include the need for *risk-sharing*, the corporation's *funding limitations*, and the *desire to gain market* and *technology access*.

*Risk Sharing.*   Most companies cannot afford "bet the company" moves to participate in all product markets of strategic interest. Whether a corporation is considering entry into a global market or investments in new technologies, the dominant logic dictates that companies prioritize their strategic interests and balance them according to risk.

*Funding Limitations.*   Historically, many companies focused on building sustainable advantage by establishing dominance in *all* of the business' value creating activities. Through cumulative investment and vertical integration, they attempted to build barriers to entry that were hard to penetrate. However, as the globalization of the business environment accelerated and the technology race intensified, such a strategic posture became increasingly difficult to sustain. Going it alone is no longer practical in many industries. To compete in the global arena, companies must incur immense fixed costs with a shorter payback period and at a higher level of risk.

*Market Access.*   Companies usually recognize their lack of prerequisite knowledge, infrastructure, or critical relationships necessary for the distribution of their products to new customers. Cooperative strategies can help them fill the gaps. For example, Hitachi has an alliance with Deere & Company in North America and with Fiat Allis in Europe to distribute its hydraulic excavators. This arrangement makes sense because Hitachi's product line is too narrow to justify a separate distribution network. What is more, customers benefit because the gaps in its product line are filled with quality products such as bulldozers and wheel loaders from its alliance partners.

*Technology Access.*   A large number of products rely on so many different technologies that few companies can afford to remain at the forefront of all of them. Carmakers increasingly rely on advances in electronics; application software developers depend on new features delivered by Microsoft in its next generation operating platform, and advertising agencies need more and more sophisticated tracking data to formulate schedules for clients. At the same time, the pace at which technology is spreading globally is increasing, making time an even more critical variable in developing and sustaining competitive advantage. It is usually beyond the capabilities, resources, and good luck in R&D of any corporation to garner the technological advantage needed to independently create disruption in the marketplace. Therefore, partnering with technologically compatible companies to achieve the prerequisite level of excellence is often essential. The implementation of such strategies, in turn, increases the speed at which technology diffuses around the world.

Other reasons to pursue a cooperative strategy are a lack of particular *management skills;* an *inability to add* value in-house; and a *lack of acquisition opportunities* because of size, geographical, or ownership restrictions.

Cooperative strategies cover a wide spectrum of nonequity, cross-equity, and shared-equity arrangements. Selecting the most-appropriate arrangement involves analyzing the nature of the opportunity, the mutual strategic interests in the cooperative venture, and prior experience with joint ventures of both partners. The essential question is: How can we structure this opportunity to maximize the benefit(s) to both parties?

# CHAPTER 10

# The Board's Role in Strategic Management[1]

## Introduction

Twenty years ago, boards of directors might have rubber-stamped their CEO's strategic plan without involving itself in significant ways in its formulation. They were often content with rewarding profitability or mopping up after the occurrence of losses—all based on a rear-view mirror perspective of financial performance. The GM bailout, the global financial crisis, the BP oil spill and similar debacles clearly demonstrate that a hindsight view is not good enough to avoid catastrophes from occurring. That requires more meaningful involvement up front in "strategic planning." Only when strategy involved acquisitions and mergers to accomplish growth, boards historically were deeply involved along with major shareholders. But in today's environment, as shareholders and regulators alike demand greater accountability, all aspects of a company's strategy receive much closer scrutiny by directors. Corporate boards now want to be assured as much about the planning process itself as the content of the strategy, to make sure risks are properly addressed in a comprehensive fashion with a robust strategic planning framework.

## What is the Proper Role of the Board in Strategy Development?

Deloitte reports that in 2012 54 percent of public companies reported discussing strategy at every board meeting. Moreover, boards spend some of their time specifically discussing risks associated with the company's strategy. Is this number low given that strategy and its continual monitoring are key areas of board responsibility? If evaluating the quality of management's strategic and business plans, including the likelihood of realizing the intended results, is a key board responsibility, should it not determine for itself whether the company has the capacity to implement and deliver?

It is a good but intricate question. How might a board do this? What, for example, should a board do if management presents a bold plan for spinning off or acquiring strategic assets worldwide? Assume that the logic is consistent, that the plan makes sense, that the numbers look good, and that management has a convincing answer for every tough question asked by the board. Has the board met its fiduciary responsibility or should it seek an independent opinion to "audit" the strategic assumptions made by management and its consultants? After all, directors do not have the equivalent time and resources to review the details of strategies presented to them.

A strong argument can be made that if the board feels compelled to retain outside experts to review corporate strategy, it probably has lost confidence in the CEO and should simply fire him or her. Conversely, one can argue that hiring outside consultants is the most cost-effective way for the board to prove its independence and positively challenge top management. What is the right answer?

In attempts to provide guidance on this issue, numerous "codes of best practice" have been proposed in recent years urging boards to define their responsibilities with respect to strategy development as "setting the ultimate direction for the corporation; reviewing, understanding, assessing, and approving specific strategic directions and initiatives; assessing and understanding the issues, forces, and risks that define and drive the company's long-term performance".

As the simple example above demonstrates, however, reality is considerably more complex. Traditionally, boards have become involved in strategy mainly when there were specific reasons for them to do so. The most common are the retirement of an incumbent CEO, a major investment decision or acquisition proposal, a sudden decline in sales or profits, or an unsolicited takeover bid. In recent years, however, as regulatory and other pressures increased, many boards have sought to become more deeply involved and create an ongoing strategic role, for example, by participating in annual strategy retreats or through the CEO performance evaluation process. Still, in most companies even today boards limit their involvement to *approving* strategy proposals and to *monitoring progress* toward strategic goals; *very few participate in shaping and developing the company's strategic direction.*

There are a number of reasons for this. First, there is a long-standing concern on the part of both executives and directors regarding where to draw the line between having directors involved through contributing ideas about the company's strategic direction and having directors who try to manage the company.[2] Specifically, there is a widely shared belief that strategy formulation is fundamentally a management responsibility and that the role of the board should be confined to making sure that an appropriate strategic planning process is in place and the actual development—and approval—of strategy is left to the CEO. Even those who do favor greater director involvement in strategy say that the degree of involvement should depend on the specific circumstances at hand. A significant acquisition proposal or a new CEO, for example, may indicate the needs for greater board involvement.

Second, in the aftermath of recent governance scandals, many boards had to focus on internal issues and on digesting the new accounting compliance rules of the landmark Sarbanes-Oxley Act. In a number of companies, this turning inward has had the undesirable side effect that the board's decision making has become so focused on compliance issues that strategic considerations have taken a backseat.

Third, some CEOs simply do not want their boards involved in strategy discussions; they view the board's engagement in developing strategy as interference into their managerial responsibilities and a threat to their sense of personal power. Of course, the downside of this posture is that the board may not fully understand or buy into the organization's strategy and that board talent is underutilized. Taking this approach sometimes backfires on CEOs when formerly disengaged boards become overly engaged and then make their CEOs "walk through fire" on tactics.

Fourth, there is the delicate question of how knowledgeable even the most capable directors are to assist with strategy development. Most are quite effective in dealing with short-term financial data. Strategy development, however, also demands a detailed understanding of more future- and long-term-oriented issues, such as changing customer preferences, competitive trends, technological developments, and the firm's core competencies. A typical board of directors is poorly designed and ill-equipped for this task. According to a McKinsey survey, more than a quarter of directors have, at best, a limited understanding of the current strategy of their companies. Only 11 percent claim to have a complete understanding. More than half say that they have a limited or no clear sense of their companies' prospects 5 to 10 years down the road. Only 4 percent say that they fully understand their companies' long-term position. More than half indicate that they have little or no understanding of the 5 to 10 key initiatives that their companies need in order to secure the long-term future.[3]

Finally, while board meetings are conducive to questioning specific strategic assumptions and monitoring progress toward strategic goals, they are not a good forum for the more creative, elaborate, and nonlinear process of crafting strategy. Board discussions tend to focus on the implementation and tactics of an ongoing strategic direction. Revealing serious reservations about the underlying strategic assumptions sometimes not only is seen as distracting and inappropriate but also may be interpreted as a vote of no confidence in the current management.

*The bottom line is that carving out a significant role for the board in strategy formulation is extremely difficult.* First, as we have seen, there is the nature of the strategy development process itself. Characterizing a board's involvement in strategy on a continuum from "passive" to "active" is a dangerous oversimplification. A passive posture assumes that strategic decisions are both separate and sequential, that managers generate options that boards choose from, and that managers then implement the chosen option and boards evaluate the outcomes. An active conception assumes that boards and management formulate strategy in a partnership approach and that management then implements the strategy and then both groups evaluate its results. As we have seen, in reality strategic decisions often evolve through complex, nonlinear, and fragmented processes. What is more, a board can be actively involved in strategy without being involved in its formulation. For example, a board can "shape" strategy through a process of influence over management in which it guides strategic thinking but never actually participates in the development of the strategies themselves.[4]

Second, as noted, certain situations dictate a more influential strategy role for the board than others. For example, at times of crisis, such as a sudden decline in performance, a new CEO, or some other major organizational change, boards tend to become more actively involved in strategy. Other determinants of the degree of board engagement in strategy issues include firm size; the nature of the core business; directors' skills and experience; board size; occupational diversity; board tenure and board member age; board attention to strategic issues; and board processes, such as the use of strategy retreats, prior firm performance, and the relative power between the board and the CEO, particularly in terms of board involvement in monitoring and evaluating this position. External factors include the concentration and level of engagement of the firm's ownership and the degree of environmental uncertainty.[5]

Third, many directors lack the relevant industry expertise to participate effectively in shaping strategy—much less to reshape it in an increasingly fast-paced business climate. What is more, even as the business landscape is becoming more complex, many boards continue to give priority to compliance-oriented appointments rather than visionary ones.[6]

Finally, there are the ever-present constraints on time and knowledge. To become meaningfully engaged in strategy formulation, boards must become much more efficient, particularly since their time has already been stretched in recent years: The average commitment of a director of a U.S.-listed company increased from 13 hours a month in 2001 to more than twice that today, according to Korn/Ferry.[7] Directors also need to become far more knowledgeable and proactive about grasping the company's current strategic position and challenges more clearly. To understand the long-term health of a company, directors must pay attention not only to its current financials but also to a broader range of indicators: market performance, network positioning, organizational performance, and operational performance. Similarly, a broader appreciation of risk—including credit, market, regulatory, organizational, and operational risk—is vital. Without this knowledge, directors will have only a partial understanding of a company. While boards receive and discuss all sorts of "strategic information," financial measures—probably the least valuable component of a board member's strategic information requirements—still dominate. Even with better information, time constraints may prevent a broader role for the board. Boards typically perform their strategic governance role in the course of a couple of hours at every third board meeting—annually supplemented by a 2-day strategy retreat. A more active role in strategy development requires much more time.

## Creating a Meaningful Role for the Board

Despite these difficulties, Nadler (2004) argues that companies should try hard to create a meaningful role for their boards in the strategy development process. The key is to create a process in which directors participate in strategic thinking and strategic decision making but do not infringe on the CEO's and senior executive team's fundamental responsibilities. In such a process, the CEO and management should lead and develop strategic plans with directors' input, while the board approves the strategy and the metrics to assess progress. The direct benefits of such an engagement are many, including a *deeper understanding* by directors of the company and its strategic environment, a *sense of ownership* of the process and the resulting strategy, *better decisions* reflecting the broader array of perspectives, *greater collaboration* between the board and the management on other initiatives and decisions, *increased board satisfaction,* and *more effective external advocacy.*[8]

But, as Nadler notes, while the benefits can be significant, broader board participation in strategy development also comes with its own costs. First, directors must have a thorough understanding of the company—its capital allocation, debt levels, risks, business unit strategies, and growth opportunities, among many issues—and that takes time and commitment. Importantly, they must engage management on the major challenges facing the company and have a firm grasp on the trade-offs that must be made. A second potential cost is that increased board participation can result in less management control over outcomes. Real participation means influence, and influence means the ability to change outcomes. A well-designed process yields the benefits of participation while limiting the amount of time and potential loss of control.[9]

To create a workable framework for board engagement, Nadler (2004) distinguishes between four, roughly sequential, types of strategic activity:

1. *Strategic thinking.* The collection, analysis, and discussion of information about the environment of the firm, the nature of competition, and business models.

2. *Strategic decision making.* Making a set of core directional decisions that define fundamental choices concerning the business portfolio and the dominant business model, which serve as the platform for the future allocation of limited resources and capabilities.

3. *Strategic planning.* Identifying priorities, setting objectives, and securing and allocating resources to execute the chosen directional decisions.

4. *Strategy execution.* Implementing and monitoring results and appropriate corrective action. This phase of strategy development can involve the allocation of funds, acquisitions, and divestitures.[10]

It will be apparent that the board's role can and should differ dramatically in these four development phases. Early in the process, the board's focus should be on providing advice and counsel about issues, such as the process followed, perspectives taken, the inside–outside balance of environmental and competitive analyses, and presentation formats. Later, when key directional choices must be made, the board's role becomes more evaluative and decision focused. Once directional decisions have been taken, reviewing and monitoring progress should become the board's primary focus.

Following this logic, the various discussions and decisions the board needs to undertake can be organized into a multistep "strategic choice process"[11]:

1. *Agreeing on the company vision.* This step entails restating or confirming the company's vision—a description of its aspirations in relation to multiple stakeholders, including investors, customers, suppliers, employees, legislative and regulatory institutions, and communities. Such a vision statement should be aspirational and paint a picture of what the company hopes to accomplish in tangible and measurable terms. Good vision statements talk about measures of growth, relative positions in markets or industries, or returns to

shareholders. They provide a benchmark against which to assess strategic alternatives.

2. *Viewing the opportunity space.* This second step focuses on an analysis of the full array of strategic options the company should consider from different perspectives. For example, the analysis might look at different emerging markets, the range of available technologies to meet a customer need, the potential set of customers, or the constellation of competitors. Each of these presents a different set of "lenses" through which to look at the environment.

3. *Assessing the company's business design and internal capabilities.* This third step looks inward, focusing on an assessment of the company itself, including its current business design and organization. The objective is to analyze the relative strengths and weaknesses of the firm, including its human capital, technologies, financial situation, and work processes, among others.

4. *Determining the company's future strategic intent.* In this fourth step, the vision, the view of the opportunity space, and the assessment of the current business or organization are brought together to identify a future strategic intent. The purpose is to identify the most attractive opportunities for their vision and their capabilities.

5. *Developing a set of business design prototypes.* Having identified a strategic intent, the next step is to develop prototypes for each business design. It is useful to consider a number of distinct, viable options to provide the opportunity for real comparison, contrasting approaches, and true choice. The final decision should be made against a set of criteria developed in the strategic intent stage. The leading choices should also be tested against current organizational capabilities to understand the nature of the challenges inherent in executing each strategy. When this choice is made, initial planning of execution is complete.

This process unfolds over a period of months, with numerous meetings, work sessions, and rounds of data collection and feedback, and provides a way of building board engagement. Perhaps more importantly, management will benefit from the board's informed point of view.[12]

# Dealing with Special Situations

Two dimensions of strategy formulation merit special attention because they require substantial board involvement and typically are subject to detailed scrutiny by investors and other stakeholders—crafting a capital structure for the corporation and dealing with a takeover, merger, or acquisition proposal.

## Deciding on a Capital Structure

Deciding on an appropriate capital structure is a strategic board responsibility. Businesses adopt various capital structures to meet both internal needs for capital and external requirements for returns on shareholders' investments. A company's capitalization shapes its balance sheet and is constructed from three sources of capital:

1. *Long-term debt.* Debt consisting mostly of bonds or similar obligations, including notes, capital lease obligations, and mortgage issues, with a repayment horizon of more than one year.
2. *Preferred stock.* Equity (ownership) interest in the corporation with claims ahead of the common stock and normally with no rights to share in the increased worth of a company if it grows.
3. *Common stockholders' equity.* The firm's principal ownership is made up of (a) the nominal par or stated value assigned to the shares of outstanding stock, (b) the capital surplus or the amount above par value paid to the company whenever it issues stock, and (c) the earned surplus (also called retained earnings), which consists of the portion of earnings a company retains after paying out dividends and similar distributions. Thus, common stock equity is the net worth after all the liabilities (including long-term debt), as well as any preferred stock, are deducted from the total assets shown on the balance sheet.

*Debt versus Equity.* In deciding a company's financial structure, management often seeks to minimize the cost of capital, whereas investors look for the greatest possible return. While these desires can conflict with each other, they are not necessarily incompatible, especially with equity investors. This is because the cost of capital can be kept low and the opportunity for return on common stockholders' equity enhanced through what is called "leverage"—creating a high percentage of debt relative to common equity. Doing so, however, increases risk. This is the inescapable trade-off both management and investors must factor into their respective decisions.

The leverage provided by debt financing is further enhanced because the interest that corporations pay is a tax-deductible expense, whereas dividends to both preferred and common stockholders must be paid with after-tax dollars. Thus, it is argued, the lower net cost of bond interest helps accrue more value for the common stock.

Higher debt levels increase a firm's fixed costs that must be paid in good times and bad, and can severely limit a company's flexibility. Specifically, as leverage is increased, (a) the risk of bankruptcy grows; (b) access to the capital markets, especially during times of tight credit, may diminish; (c) management will need to spend more time on finances and raising additional capital at the expense of focusing on operations; and (d) the cost of any additional debt or preferred stock capital the company may have to raise increases.

Because of its tax advantages and stability relative to equity capital (common stock), some finance experts have argued that higher proportions of debt capital may be advantageous to corporations. Their advice is not always heeded, however. Although periodically companies use debt to buy back common shares, a practice that can improve stock performance, most large companies rely heavily on equity financing.

Companies tend to use debt under certain circumstances more than others. For example, the decision whether or not to use debt is often related to the nature and risks of the cash flows associated with the capital investment. When diversifying into new lines of business, companies that are moving into related fields tend to use equity capital and those entering unrelated fields tend to use debt. Ownership structure is another factor. Firms with a high degree of management ownership, for example, are less likely to carry high levels of debt, as are corporations with significant institutional ownership.

*Changing Patterns.* In earlier days, a debt-free structure was often considered a sign of strength, and companies that were able to finance their growth with an all-common capitalization prided themselves on their "clean" balance sheet.

The advent of *leveraged buyouts* (LBOs) of the 1980s brought a new twist to the capitalization issue. Because of their low degree of leverage, large corporations with conservative, low-debt capitalizations became vulnerable to capture. Corporate raiders with limited financial resources were successful in raising huge amounts of noninvestment grade ("junk") debt to finance the deals. The captured companies often would then be dismembered and stripped of cash holdings so the raiders could pay down their borrowings. In effect, the prey's own assets were used to pay for its capture. As a takeover defense, potential targets began to assume heavy debt themselves, often to finance an internal buyout by its own management.

By purposely leveraging their prey so highly (at times with current income insufficient to meet current interest requirements) that the company could not continue to conduct business as usual, raiders forced cuts in low-return growth avenues and the sale of those divisions, which are more valuable outside the firm. In the process, a significant amount of intrinsic firm value was distributed to stockholders—especially those who had bought in for just that purpose—at the expense of other stakeholders and the company's long-term needs. They justified their actions by stating that managers who operated with low leverage were either inept or feathering their own nest, or both.

### Takeovers, Mergers and Acquisitions[13]

Takeovers, mergers, and acquisitions are an integral part of corporate strategy and not only provide important external growth opportunities for companies but also involve considerable risks for the firm and its shareholders. A merger signifies that two companies have joined to form one company. An acquisition occurs when one firm buys another. To outsiders, the difference might seem small and related less to ownership control than to financing. However, the critical difference is often in management control. In acquisitions, the management team of the buyer tends to dominate decision making in the combined company.

The advantages of buying an existing player can be compelling. An acquisition can quickly position a firm in a new business or market. It also eliminates a potential competitor and therefore does not contribute to the development of excess capacity.

Acquisitions, however, are also generally expensive. Premiums of 30 percent or more than the current value of the stock are not uncommon. This means that, although sellers often pocket handsome profits, acquiring companies frequently lose shareholder value. The process by which merger and acquisition (M&A) decisions are made contributes to this problem. In theory, acquisitions are part of a corporate growth strategy based on the explicit identification of the most suitable players in the most attractive industries as targets to be purchased. Acquisition strategies should also specify a comprehensive framework for the due diligence assessments of targets, plans for integrating acquired companies into the corporate portfolio, and a careful determination of "how much is too much" to pay.

In practice, the acquisition process is far more complex. Once the board has approved plans to expand into new businesses or markets, or once a potential target company has been identified, the time to act is typically short. The ensuing pressures to "do a deal" are intense. These pressures emanate from senior executives, directors, and investment bankers who stand to gain from *any* deal, shareholder groups, and competitors bidding against the firm. The environment can become frenzied. Valuations tend to rise as corporations become overconfident in their ability to add value to the target company and as expectations regarding synergies reach new heights. Due diligence is conducted more quickly than is desirable and tends to be confined to financial considerations. Integration planning takes a backseat. Differences in corporate cultures are discounted. In this climate, even the best designed strategies can fail to produce a successful outcome, as many companies and their shareholders have learned.

Most studies carried out in this area show that the probability of a major acquisition or merger failing (as measured in terms of financial return) is greater than the probability of success. Empirically, the probability of failure increases with the size and complexity of the merger and with the degree of unfamiliarity with the target business. They also show that the buyer often pays too much for the target company because it is overoptimistic in terms of its ability to (a) do better than the existing management, (b) implement the synergies identified, and (c) integrate the target within its own company in a timely manner.

The application of new international accounting standards (and, more particularly, International Accounting Standard [IAS] 36 on impairment of assets) forces companies to examine the value of their assets, especially that of their intangible assets, on a recurring basis. As a result, each overpaid acquisition will inevitably result in impairment of goodwill, and, sooner or later, the board and management will have to publicly admit that their decision has destroyed shareholder value. This new regulation alone is a powerful reason for boards to go beyond merely approving major transactions and become much more actively involved in merger and acquisition (M&A) activity than in the past.

The very nature of the M&A process makes the board's involvement a particularly sensitive issue, however. An acquisition frequently results from a long, confidential negotiation process, often involving extremely technical issues, and its outcome is largely uncertain. These factors lead management to present the board with only summary and high-level information on the opportunity and to wait for the outcome of the process before organizing in-depth discussions with the board.

This is unfortunate because M&A activity represents a unique opportunity for a board to add value. Outside directors may have unique experience with the M&A process, particularly intermediaries, or with all too often overlooked merger integration challenges. At the very least, the outside view offered by the board at an early stage may counterbalance the optimism of the executives driving the deal or the partiality of numerous experts pushing for its completion, resulting in a more "realistic" attitude to the opportunity.

Rérolle and Vermeire (2005) identify a number of useful best practices to assist boards in M&A planning and execution:

1. *Validate the strategic benefits of the transaction.* Every major acquisition must take place within an established strategic framework. Many mistakes are attributable to acquisitions that are justified only after the fact as a "strategic fit." At a minimum, the board should ask how the opportunity came about—whether it is something

the company's management has been working on for some time, whether it concerns a business activity or market with which the company is familiar, and whether it represents geographical or other diversification.

2. Also, rarely can an acquisition be justified solely on the grounds of the savings it will generate because they are often illusionary. It must either meet a need that has been clearly defined up front and which the company cannot meet using its own resources, or it must enhance the company's competitive position. In order to create value, the acquisition must make it possible to build a genuine competitive advantage or to decisively prolong an existing competitive advantage. The directors' role is to test the solidity of this premise.

3. *Verify that the price paid is reasonable.* Ultimately, analyzing an opportunity culminates in a valuation. Such a valuation should reflect a realistic assessment of (a) the intrinsic value of the target in accordance with a number of different scenarios, (b) the value of expected synergies (and the cost of implementing them), (c) the positive and negative impacts of the transaction on the value of the purchaser's company (e.g., management will have to devote considerable time to integrating the target, which may have an adverse impact on the purchaser's business activities), and (d) the price that management offers to pay and the terms and conditions of payment.

4. Furthermore, when a proposed acquisition is of particular significance in light of the company's size and when there is a possibility of a conflict of interest or a challenge by the minority shareholders concerning the price paid, it is advisable to have a fairness opinion drawn up by an independent expert.[14]

5. *Ensure that a comprehensive due diligence process has been carried out.* Due diligence is of critical importance as it enables the purchaser to verify the integrity of the seller's financial statements, representations, and warranties, and to identify potential problems.

6. The due diligence must be based on broad (but relevant) objectives concerning the integration of the target. All too often, due diligence is mainly based on legal and accounting criteria, whereas the company needs to identify all the areas of major risk and, in particular, current and future operating risks, or others that may constitute

229 of an obstacle to effective integration.

an obstacle to effective integration. A comprehensive due diligence process covers items, such as an analysis of the target's competitive advantages and their durability, the identification of key people (in particular those that the company may rely on for the purposes of integration), and the measurement of the stability of the most significant customer relations and the long-term prospects of formal or informal alliances.

7. *Approve a specific integration plan.* Experience has shown that integrating the target is the most complex part of the M&A process. In spite of a broad consensus on this point, this difficulty remains largely underestimated. The board can play an important role in alleviating this major problem by asking management to provide it with an integration plan prior to concluding the transaction. In particular, this plan needs to include (a) a timetable for the integration program, (b) an identification of the main initiatives undertaken by management to recover a significant portion of the control premium paid, (c) an assessment of the human resources and expertise to be earmarked for the integration process, and (d) a detailed business plan showing all the costs and benefits associated with integration.

8. During mergers and acquisitions, boards tend to focus on the strategic, financial, and governance aspects of a transaction. They often neglect one of the greatest sources of value in many M&A transactions: the talent of the management team in the target company. Exercising due diligence about talent is as important as paying close attention to the balance sheet, cash flow, and expected synergies of a deal. By asking management a series of questions about human capital in a merger or acquisition, boards can contribute to a smoother transition to a single company, a better merging of cultures, the loss of fewer "A" players, and a stronger talent bench for the merged company—all of which should ultimately create more value from the deal.

9. *Organize the board's work so that it is able to assist management upstream.* The board's contribution will be even more useful if it is able to contribute to management's thought process as early as possible in the analytical and decision-making process. If M&A is a cornerstone of the company's strategy, creating a special committee may be

a useful way to deal with issues of efficiency, confidentiality, and the constraints inherent in a long and uncertain negotiating process.[15]

## Monitoring Strategy Implementation: Choosing Metrics[16]

A key determinant of greater board effectiveness in the area of strategy is the set of metrics the board selects to monitor a company's performance and health. The goal should be to identify a manageable number of metrics that strike a balance among different areas of the business and are directly linked to value-creating activities. In addition to the standard financial metrics, key indicators should cover operations (the quality and consistency of key value-creating processes), organizational issues (the company's depth of talent and ability to motivate and retain employees), the state of the company's product markets and its position within them (including the quality of customer relationships), and the nature of relationships with external parties, such as suppliers, regulators, and nongovernmental organizations (NGOs).

In selecting an appropriate set of metrics, it is useful to distinguish between value creation in the short, medium, and long-term. Short-term health metrics show how a company achieved its recent results and therefore indicate its likely performance over the next 1 to 3 years. A consumer products company, for example, must know whether it increased its profits by raising prices or by launching a new marketing campaign that increased its market share. An auto manufacturer must know whether it met its profit targets only by encouraging dealers to increase their inventories. A retailer might want to examine its revenue growth per store and in new stores or its revenue per square foot compared with that of competitors.

Another set of metrics should highlight a company's prospects for maintaining and improving its rate of growth and returns on capital over the next 1 to 5 years. (The time frame ought to be longer for industries, such as pharmaceuticals, that have long product cycles and must obviously focus on the number of profitable new products in the pipeline.) Other medium-term metrics should be monitored as well—for example, metrics comparing a company's product launches with those of competitors (perhaps the amount of time needed to reach peak sales). For an online retailer, customer satisfaction and brand strength might be the most important drivers of medium-term health.

For the longer term, boards should develop metrics assessing the company's ability to sustain earnings from current activities and to identify and exploit new areas where it can grow. They must monitor any threats—new technologies, new customer preferences, new ways of serving customers—to their current businesses. And to ensure that they have enough growth opportunities to create value when those businesses inevitably mature, they must monitor the number of new initiatives under way (as well as estimate the size of the relevant product markets) and develop metrics that track the initiatives' progress.

Ultimately, it is people who make strategies work, so a good set of metrics should also show how well a business retains key employees and the true depth of its management talent. Again, what is important varies by industry. Pharmaceutical companies, for example, need scientific innovators but relatively few managers. Companies expanding overseas need people who can work in new countries and negotiate with governments.

## Creating a Strategy Focused Board[17]

Fostering a strategic mindset on the board is difficult and takes time. It requires rethinking its composition, how it approaches its responsibilities, and the way it interacts with management to help develop a strategic vision, although that must originate with the CEO. Progressive CEOs, for their part, must be able to articulate a clear strategy and have the personal confidence to build board teams that include experts who may be far more skilled in certain industry and operational areas than the CEOs themselves are.[18]

Rather than immediately seeking a deeper involvement in the strategy development process, it may be useful to ask boards to first seek a more effective balance between short- and long-term considerations in their oversight. As part of first step, they should identify and agree on a core set of metrics reflecting a balance that is tailored to the specifics of a company's industry, maturity, culture, and current situation. In turn, management should be asked to draw up a set of long-term strategy options that the board can test and challenge. Management then can develop a detailed plan for the board's final approval.

Ideally, this process unfolds over several board meetings and allows board members to probe specific strategic issues—does the company really have the ability to execute in a particular area, for example, and has it analyzed different options to enter the markets it wants to compete in? Finally, the board can play an important role in monitoring the progress of the plan and any changes in risk it involves. While the board can be selective in its focus on details, management must deal with all aspects of the strategic plan. Once accepted, the strategy can be expected to evolve over time, and therefore will require an ongoing dialog between the board and management.

# Notes

## Chapter 1

1. C.A. Bartlett and S. Ghoshal. 2002. "Building Competitive Advantage Through People," *Sloan Management Review* 43, no. 2, pp. 34–41.
2. C.K. Prahalad and G. Hamel. May–June, 1990. "The Core Competence of the Corporation," *Harvard Business Review* 68, no. 3, pp. 79–91.
3. C.A. Bartlett and S. Ghoshal, 2002, p. 35.
4. D.J. Teece. 2010. "Business Models, Business Strategy and Innovation," *Long Range Planning* 43, pp. 172–94.
5. M.E. Porter. November–December, 1996. "What Is Strategy?" *Harvard Business Review* 74, no. 6, pp. 61–78.
6. Amazon - Relentless.com, *The Economist*, Print edition, June 21, 2014.
7. These ideas are based on T.A. Luehrman. September–October, 1998. "Strategy as a Portfolio of Real Options," *Harvard Business Review* 76, pp. 89–99.
8. H. Mintzberg. 1985. "Of Strategies, Deliberate and Emergent," *Strategic Management Journal* 6, no. 3, pp. 257–72.
9. R.E. Freeman. 1984. *Strategic Management: A Stakeholder Approach* (Boston, MA: Pittman), p. 9.
10. G. Hamel and C.K. Prahalad. May–June, 1989. "Strategic Intent," *Harvard Business Review* 67, pp. 63–76.
11. J. Kotter. 1990. *A Force for Change* (New York: Free Press), p. 47.
12. G. Hamel and C.K. Prahalad, 1989.

## Chapter 2

1. A.D. Chandler. March–April, 1990. "The Enduring Logic of Industrial Success," *Harvard Business Review* 90, pp. 130–40.
2. P. Calthrop. November, 2001. "Define the Core: Strategy as Choice," *Management Ideas in Action, Bain International.*
3. G.S. Day. July–August, 2004. "Which Way Should You Grow?," *Harvard Business Review*, pp. 24–26.
4. J.A. Pearce II and J.W. Harvey. February, 1990. "Concentrated Growth Strategies," *Academy of Management Executive* 4, pp. 61–68.
5. R.P. Rumelt. 1974. *Strategy, Structure, and Economic Performance (Cambridge, MA: Harvard University Press).*

6. M.E. Porter. May–June 1987. "From Competitive Advantage to Corporate Strategy," *Harvard Business Review, p. 46.*

7. J.R. Harbison and P. Pekar, Jr. 1993. *A Practical Guide to Alliances: Leapfrogging the Learning Curve (Los Angeles, CA: Booz Allen & Hamilton).*

8. J.W. Bennett et al. 2000. "The Organization vs. The Strategy: Solving the Alignment Paradox," *Strategy + Business, Fourth Quarter.*

9. C. Bartlett and S. Goshal. November, 1994. "Changing the Role of Top Management: From Strategy to Purpose," *Harvard Business Review, p. 79.*

10. It is, of course, no coincidence that during this same period the resource-based view of strategic thinking overtook the industrial economics perspective. See Chapter 1.

11. G. Neilson, D. Kletter, and J. Jones. 2003. "Treating the Troubled Corporation," *Strategy + Business, First Quarter.*

12. J.P. Kotter. 1988. *The Leadership Factor (New York: The Free Press), p. 12.*

13. K. Rebello and E.I. Schwartz. April 19, 1999. "Microsoft: Bill Gates's Baby Is on Top of the World. Can It Stay There?," *BusinessWeek.*

14. L. Soupata. 2001. "Managing Culture for Competitive Advantage at United Parcel Service," *Journal of Organizational Excellence 20, no. 3, pp. 19–26.*

15. J.R. Ross. Spring, 2000. "Does Corporate Culture Contribute to Performance?" *American International College Journal of Business, pp. 4–9.*

16. See, e.g., T. Copeland, T. Koller, and J. Murrin. 1995. *Valuation: Measuring and Managing the Value of Companies (New York: John Wiley & Sons).*

17. R.S. Kaplan and D.P. Norton. January–February, 1996. "Using the Balanced Scorecard as a Strategic Management System," *Harvard Business Review, pp. 75–85; and R.S. Kaplan and D.P. Norton. January–February, 1992.*

18. R. Kaplan and D.P. Norton. May–June, 2001. "Building a Strategy Focused Organization," *Ivey Business Journal, pp. 12–17.*

19. R. Kaplan and D.P. Norton. September, 2001. "Leading Change with the Balanced Scorecard," *Financial Executive, pp. 64–66.*

# Chapter 3

1. P. Ghemawat. March–April, 2007. "Why the World Isn't Flat," *Foreign Policy, no. 159, pp. 54–60.*

2. K. Moore and A. Rugman. Fall, 2005. "Globalization Is about Regionalization," *McGill International Review 6, no. 1;* see also K. Moore and A. Rugman. Summer, 2005. "The Myth of Global Business," *European Business Forum.*

3. The Toyota, Wal-Mart, and Coca-Cola examples are taken from P. Ghemawat. 2007. *Redefining Global Strategy: Crossing Borders in a World Where Differences Still Matter* (Harvard Business School Press), chap. 1.

4.  P. Ghemawat. September, 2001. "Distance Still Matters: The Hard Reality of Global Expansion," *Harvard Business Review*, pp. 16–26.

5.  This framework was first developed in G.S. Yip. 1992. *Total Global Strategy: Managing for Worldwide Competitive Advantage* (New Jersey: Prentice Hall), chaps. 1 and 2.

6.  H.L. Sirkin, J.W. Hemerling, and A.K. Bhattacharya. 2008. *Globality: Competing with Everyone from Everywhere for Everything* (New York, NY: Business Plus).

7.  A.K. Gupta, V. Govindarajan, and H. Wang. 2008. *The Quest for Global Dominance*, 2nd edition (San Francisco, CA: Jossey-Bass), p. 28.

8.  This section draws on S. Behrendt and P. Khanna. 2004. "Risky Business: Geopolitics and the Global Corporation," *Strategy & Business*, 32, no.2.

9.  P. Anton, R. Silberglitt, and J. Schneider. 2001. *The Global Technology Revolution: Bio/Nano/Materials Trends and Their Synergy with Information Technology by 2015* (RAND Corporation Monograph), 86pp.

10.  Y. Bakos and E. Brynjolfsson. 2000. "Bundling and Competition on the Internet," *Marketing Science* at the University of Florida 19, no. 1, pp. 37–52.

11.  J. Manyika et al. May, 2011. *Big Data: The Next Frontier for Innovation, Competition, and Productivity* (New York: McKinsey Global Institute), p. 2.

12.  Ibid., p. 91.

13.  S. Rochlin. 2006. "The New Laws for Business Success," *Corporate Citizen* (A Publication by the Center for Corporate Citizenship, Carroll School of Management, Boston College).

14.  T. Struyk. 2010. "For Companies, Green Is the New Black," *Investopedia* (A Forbes Digital Company).

15.  G. Unruh and R. Ettenson. June, 2010. "Growing Green," *Harvard Business Review*, pp. 94–100.

16.  Xerox Corporation. July, 2012. "Smarter Ways to Green: How to Make Sustainability Succeed in Your Business," *Xerox White Paper*.

17.  H. Courtney, J. Kirkland, and P. Viguerie. November/December, 1997. "Strategy under Uncertainty," *Harvard Business Review*, pp. 66–79.

18.  This description is based on P.J.H. Schoemaker and C.A.J.M. van de Heijden. 1992. "Integrating Scenarios into Strategic Planning at Royal Dutch/Shell," *Planning Review* 20, pp. 41–46.

# Chapter 4

1.  B. Buescher and P. Viguerie. June, 2014. How US Healthcare Companies Can Thrive Amid Disruption. McKinsey & Company. http://www.mckinsey.com/Insights/Health_systems_and_services/How_US_healthcare_companies_can_thrive_amid_disruption?cid=other-eml-alt-mip-mck-oth-1406&p=1

2. M.E. Porter. 1980. *Competitive Strategy* (New York, Free Press).
3. A.S. Grove. 1996. *Only the Paranoid Survive* (New York, Doubleday).
4. M.E. Porter. March, 2001. "Strategy and the Internet," *Harvard Business Review 79 (3)*, pp. 63–78.
5. This section is based on A.M. McGahan. October, 2004. "How Industries Change," *Harvard Business Review 82 (10)*, pp. 87–94.
6. J.N. Sheth and R.S. Sisodia. 2002. *The Rule of Three: Surviving and Thriving in Competitive Markets* (New York: Free Press).
7. *Ibid.*, p. 200.
8. *Ibid.*
9. M. Zanini. November, 2008. "Using 'Power Curves' to Assess Industry Dynamics," *McKinsey Quarterly 1, p. 1.*
10. C.K. Prahalad. 1995. "Weak Signals Versus Strong Paradigms," *Journal of Marketing Research* 32, pp. iii–ix.

# Chapter 5

1. J. Manyika et al. 2011. *Big Data: The Next Frontier for Innovation, Competition and Productivity* (McKinsey Global Institute), pp. 1–143. http://www.mckinsey.com/insights/business_technology/big_data_the_next_frontier_for_innovation.
2. McKinsey & Company. 2013. "Big Data Analytics and the Future of Marketing and Sales," *Forbes.* http://www.forbes.com/sites/mckinsey/2013/07/22/big-data-analytics-and-the-future-of-marketing-sales/.
3. Manyika et al. 2011. *Big Data.* http://www.mckinsey.com/insights/business_technology/big_data_the_next_frontier_for_innovation.
4. J. Brodkin. 2012. "Bandwidth Explosion: As Internet Use Soars, Can Bottlenecks Be Averted?" *Ars Technica.* http://arstechnica.com/business/2012/05/bandwidth-explosion-as-internet-use-soars-can-bottlenecks-be-averted/.
5. V.A. Rice. 1996. "Why EVA Works for Varity," *Chief Executive* 110, pp. 40–44.
6. S. Tully. 1999. "The EVA Advantage," *Fortune* 139, no. 6, p. 210; J.B. White. April 10, 1997. "Value-Based Pay Systems Are Gaining Popularity," *The Wall Street Journal*, p. B8; J.L. Dodd and J. Johns. 1999. "EVA Reconsidered," *Business and Economic Review* 45, no. 3, pp. 13–18.
7. J. Byrne, A. Reinhardt, and R.D. Hof. October 4, 1999. "The Search for the Young and Gifted: Why Talent Counts," *BusinessWeek 3649, pp108–116.*
8. J.A. Pearce II. 2006. "How Companies Can Preserve Market Dominance after Patents Expire," *Long Range Planning* 39, no. 1, pp. 71–87.

9. M. Lindner. March 25, 2008. "The 10 Biggest Blunders Ever in Business," *Forbes.* http://www.msnbc.msn.com/id/23677510/.

10. J.S. Brown and P. Duguid. 2000. "Balancing Act: How to Capture Knowledge Without Killing It," *Harvard Business Review* 78, pp. 73–80.

11. R. Cross and L. Baird. 2000. "Technology Is Not Enough: Improving Performance by Building Organizational Memory," *Sloan Management Review* 41, pp. 69–78.

12. D. Haigh. October 6, 2008. "Brand Values on the Line," *Brand Strategy,* pp. 52–53.

13. M. Banutu-Gomez et al. 2009. "International Branding Effectiveness: The Global Image of Nestlé's Brand Name and Employee Perceptions of Strategies and Brands," *Journal of Global Business Issues* 3, no. 2, pp. 17–24.

14. J.K. Johansson and I.A. Ronkainen. 2005. "The Esteem of Global Brands," *Journal of Brand Management* 12, no. 5, pp. 339–354.

15. G.R. Foxall and V.K. James. 2003. "The Behavioral Ecology of Brand Choice: How and What Do Consumers Maximize?" *Psychology and Marketing* 20, no. 9, pp. 811–836.

16. P. Itthiopassagul, P. Patterson, and B. Piyathasanan. 2009. "An Emerging South-East Asian Brand: MK Restaurants," *Australasian Marketing Journal* 17, no. 3, pp. 175–181.

17. J. Jannarone. February 6, 2010. "Wal-Mart Spices Up Private Label," *Wall Street Journal, B.16.*

18. C.K. Prahalad and G. Hamel. May–June, 1990. "The Core Competence of the Corporation," *Harvard Business Review,* pp. 79–93.

19. Accenture 2009 Global Consumer Satisfaction Survey. http://www.accenture.com/SiteCollectionDocuments/PDF/Accenture_2009_Global_Consumer_Satisfaction_Report.pdf.

20. M. Meyers and M. Cheung. 2008. "Sharing Global Supply Chain Knowledge," *MIT Sloan Management Review* 49, no. 4, pp. 67–73.

21. C.C. Poirier, F.J. Quinn, and M.L. Swink. 2009. "Progress Despite the Downturn," *Supply Chain Management Review 13.7,* pp. 26–33.

22. K. Butner. 2010. "The Smarter Supply Chain of the Future," *Strategy & Leadership* 38, no. 1, pp. 22–31.

23. M. Hopkins. 2010. "Your Next Supply Chain," *MIT Sloan Management Review* 51, no. 2, pp. 17–24.

24. D. Blanchard. 2009. "Moving Ahead by Mastering the Reverse Supply Chain," *Industry Week* 258, no. 6, pp. 58–59.

25. J.A. Pearce II and S.C. Michael. 2006. "Strategies to Prevent Economic Recession from Causing Business Failure," *Business Horizons* 49, no. 3, pp. 201–209.

26. P. Strebel. 1994. "Choosing the Right Change Path," *California Management Review* 36, p. 30.

27.  R.H. Waterman Jr., T.J. Peters, and J.R. Phillips. June, 1980. "Structure Is Not Organization," *Business Horizons*, pp. 14–26.

28.  J.A. Pearce II. 2009. "The Profit-Making Allure of Product Reconstruction," *MIT-Sloan Management Review* 50, no. 3, pp. 59–65.

29.  J.A. Pearce II. October 20, 2008. "In With the Old: Reconstructed Products Offer a Promising Market for Many Companies," *The Wall Street Journal*, p. R8.

30.  R. Kauffeld, A. Malholtra, and S. Higgins. December 21, 2009. "Green Is a Strategy," *Strategy-Business.com.* http://www.strategy-business.com/article/00013?pg=all.

31.  With the rise of green marketing claims, there are instances of deliberate miscommunication in advertising. Known as "greenwashing," it is the act of misleading consumers regarding the company's environmental practices or the environmental benefits of the product. For example, Mobil Chemical added a small amount of starch to their bags and claimed that the bags were biodegradable. A court case against Mobile forced it to withdraw the claims.

# Chapter 6

1.  R. Ribeiro. 2012. "What Industries Will Technology Have Disrupted by 2025?" *BizTech.* http://www.biztechmagazine.com/article/2012/08/what-industries-will-technology-have-disrupted-2025

2.  A.M. McGahan and M.E. Porter. 1997. "How Much Does Industry Matter, Really?" *Strategic Management Journal* 18, pp. 15–30.

3.  A.J. Slywotzky, D.J. Morrison, and B. Andelman. 1997. *The Profit Zone; How Strategic Business Design Will Lead You to Tomorrow's Profits* (New York: Times Books).

4.  J.E. Urbany and J.H. Davis. 2007. "Strategic Insight in Three Circles," *Harvard Business Review* 85, no. 11, pp. 28–30.

5.  J. Webb and C. Gile. 2001. "Reversing the Value Chain," *The Journal of Business Strategy* 22, no. 2, pp. 13–17.

6.  A. Camuffo, P. Romano and A. Vinelli, 2001, "Back to the Future: Benetton Transforms Its Global Network," *Sloan Management Review* 43, pp. 46–52.

7.  O. Gadiesh and J.L. Gilbert. 1998. "Profit Pools: A Fresh Look at Strategy," *Harvard Business Review* 76, no. 3, pp. 139–47.

8.  D. Champion. 2001. "Mastering the Value Chain," *Harvard Business Review* 79, no. 6, pp. 109–15.

9.  F. Budde et al. 2000. "The Chemistry of Knowledge," *The McKinsey Quarterly* 4, pp. 98–107.

10. R.B. Robinson, Jr. and J.A. Pearce II. 1988. "Planned Patterns of Strategic Behavior and Their Relationship to Business-Unit Performance," *Strategic Management Journal* 9, no. 1, pp. 43–60; A.I. Murray. 1988. "A Contingency View of Porter's Generic Strategies," *Academy of Management Review* 13, no. 3, pp. 390–400.

11. C.W.L. Hill. 1988. "Differentiation versus Low Cost or Differentiation and Low Cost: A Contingency Framework," *Academy of Management Review* 13, no. 3, pp. 401–12.

12. M. Treacy and F. Wiersema. January–February, 1993. "Customer Intimacy and Other Value Disciplines," *Harvard Business Review*, pp. 84–93.

13. A.J. Slywotzki et al., 1997.

# Chapter 7

1. B. Buescher and P. Viguerie. 2014. *How US Healthcare Companies Can Thrive Amid Disruption* (McKinsey & Co). Accessed November 13, 2014 at http://www.mckinsey.com/insights/health_systems_and_services/how_us_healthcare_companies_can_thrive_amid_disruption

2. *Ibid.*

3. M.E. Porter. 1980. *Competitive Strategy: Techniques for Analyzing Industries and Competitors* (New York: Free Press), Chapters 11 and 12.

4. J.E. Bleeke. September–October, 1990. "Strategic Choices for Newly Opened Markets," *Harvard Business Review* 68, no. 5, pp. 158-165.

5. R.A. D'Aveni. 1999. "Strategic Supremacy through Disruption and Dominance," *Sloan Management Review* 40, no. 3, pp. 127–35.

6. W.I. Huyett and S.P. Viguerie. 2005. "Extreme Competition," *McKinsey Quarterly* 1, pp 47–57.

7. E. Kim, D. Nam, and J.L. Stimpert. 2004. "Testing the Applicability of Porter's Generic Strategies in the Digital Age: A Study of Korean Cyber Malls," *Journal of Business Strategies* 21, no. 1, pp. 19–45.

8. C. Grosso, J. McPherson, and C. Shi. 2005. "Retailing: What's Working Online," *McKinsey Quarterly* 3, pp. 18–20.

9. R.T. Grenci and C.A. Watts. 2007. "Maximizing Customer Value via Mass Customized E-consumer Services," *Business Horizons* 50, no. 2, pp. 123.

10. M. Koand, and N. Roztocki. 2009. "Investigating the Impact of Firm Strategy-Click-and-Brick, Brick-and-Mortar, and Pure-Click-on Financial Performance," *Journal of Information Technology Theory and Application* 10, no. 2, pp. 4–17.

11. F. Bernstein, J. Song, and X. Zheng. 2008. "'Bricks-and-Mortar' vs. 'Click-and-Mortar': An Equilibrium Analysis," *European Journal of Operational Research* 187, no. 3, p. 671.

12. T. Randall, S. Netessine, and N. Rudi. 2006. "An Empirical Examination of the Decision to Invest in Fulfillment Capabilities: A Study of Internet Retailers," *Management Science* 52, no. 4, pp. 567–80.

13. J.A. Pearce II. 2002. "Speed Merchants," *Organizational Dynamics* 30, no. 3, pp. 1–16.

14. M. Vella. March 14, 2008. "How Hulu's Design Gets It Right," *Business Week*. (Online). Accessed November 13, 2014 at http://search.proquest.com/docview/217404001?accountid=14853

15. J.C. Linder, S. Jarvenpaa, and T. H. Davenport. 2003. "Toward an Innovation Sourcing Strategy," *MIT Sloan Management Review* 44, no. 4, p. 43.

16. P. Engardio and B. Einhorn. March 20, 2005. "Outsourcing Innovation," *Business Week* (Online). Accessed November 13, 2014 at http://www.businessweek.com/magazine/content/05_12/b3925601.htm

17. C.A. de Kluyver. "Innovation: The Strategic Thrust of the Nineties," *A Cresap Insight*, July 1988.

18. C.M. Christensen and M. Raynor. 1997. *The Innovator's Dilemma: When New Technologies Cause Great Firms to Fail* (Boston, MA: Harvard Business School Press).

19. C.M. Christensen and M. Raynor. 2003. *The Innovator's Solution: Creating and Sustaining Successful Growth* (Boston, MA: Harvard Business School Press).

20. D. Dodd and K. Favaro. 2006. "Managing the Right Tension," Harvard Business Review 84, no. 12, pp. 62–74.

21. R. Varadarajan. 2009. "Fortune at the Bottom of the Innovation Pyramid: The Strategic Logic of Incremental Innovations," *Business Horizons* 52, pp. 21–9.

22. V. Bhatia and G. Carey. 2007. "Patenting for Profits," *MIT Sloan Management Review* 48, no. 4, pp. 15–16.

23. *Ibid.*

24. D. Laurie, Y. Doz, and C. Scheer. 2006. "Creating New Growth Platforms," *Harvard Business Review* 84, pp. 80–90.

25. Proctor and Gamble Annual Report, 2009. Accessed November 13, 2014 at http://www.pg.com/annualreport2009/_downloads/PG_2009_Annual-Report.pdf

26. O. Alexy, P. Criscuolo, and A. Salter. 2009. "Does IP Strategy Have to Cripple Open Innovation?" *MIT Sloan Management Review* 51, no. 1, pp. 71–7.

27. H. Chesbrough and A. Garman. 2009. "How Open Innovation Can Help You Cope in Lean Times," *Harvard Business Review* 87, no. 12, pp. 68–76.

28. J.D. Bate. 2010. "How to Explore for Innovation on Your Organization's Strategic Frontier," *Strategy and Leadership* 38, no. 1, pp. 32–6.

29. N. Radjou. 2005. "Networked Innovation Drives Profits," *Industrial Management* 47, no. 1, pp. 14–21.

30. R. Stringer. 2000. "How to Manage Radical Innovation," *California Management Review* 42, no. 4, pp. 70–88.

31. M. Amram. 2003. "Magnetic Intellectual Property: Accelerating Revenues from Innovation," *Journal of Business Strategy* 24, no. 3, pp. 24–30.

32. P. Koudal and G.C. Coleman. 2005. "Coordinating Operations to Enhance Innovation in the Global Corporation," *Strategy & Leadership* 33, no. 4, pp. 20–32.

33. G. Stevens and J. Burley. 2003. "Piloting the Rocket of Radical Innovation," *Research Technology Management* 46, no. 2, pp. 16–25.

34. S. Ogawa and F.P. Piller. 2006. "Reducing the Risks of New Product Development," *MIT Sloan Management Review* 47, no. 2, pp. 65–71.

35. T. Vesey. 1991. "Speed-To-Market Distinguishes the New Competitors," *Research Technology Management* 34, no. 6, pp. 33–8.

36. C.B. Dobni. 2006. "The Innovation Blueprint," *Business Horizons* 49, no. 4, pp. 329–39.

37. M. Sawhney, R.C. Wolcott, and I. Arroniz. 2006. "The 12 Different Ways for Companies to Innovate," *MIT Sloan Management Review* 47, no. 3, pp. 75–81.

38. T. Shervani and P.C. Zerillo. 1997. "The Albatross of Product Innovation," *Business Horizons* 40, no. 1, pp. 57–62.

39. H.W. Chesbrough. 2007. "Why Companies Should Have Open Business Models," *MIT Sloan Management Review* 40, no. 2, pp. 22–8.

40. R.D. Ireland and J.W. Webb. 2007. "Strategic Entrepreneurship: Creating Competitive Advantage through Streams of Innovation," *Business Horizons* 50, no. 1, 49–59.

41. M. O'Leary-Collins. 2005. "A Powerful Business Model for Capturing Innovation," *Management Services* 49, no. 2, pp. 37–9.

42. P. Koudal and G.C. Coleman. 2005. "Coordinating Operations to Enhance Innovation in the Global Corporation," *Strategy & Leadership* 33, no. 4, pp. 20–32.

43. S. Ogawa and F.P. Piller. 2006. "Reducing the Risks of New Product Development," *MIT Sloan Management Review* 47, no. 2, pp. 65–71.

# Chapter 8

1. H. Paul. March/April, 2000. "Creating a Mindset," *Thunderbird International Business Review* 42, no. 2, pp. 187–200.

2. Ibid.

3. C.K. Prahalad and K. Lieberthal. 1998. "The End of Corporate Imperialism," *Harvard Business Review* 76. pp. 109-117.

4. This section draws substantially on M. Aboy. 2009. "The Organization of Modern MNEs is More Complicated Than the Old Models of Global, Multidomestic, and Transnational," *International Business Strategy—Social Science Research Network*, pp. 1–5.

5. See, e.g., C.A. Bartlett and S. Ghoshal. 1987. "Managing Across Borders: New Organizational Responses," *International Executive* 29, no. 3, pp. 10–13; C.A. Bartlett and S. Ghoshal. 1987. "Managing across Borders: New Strategic Requirements," *Sloan Management Review* 28, no. 4, pp. 7–17; C.A. Bartlett and S. Ghoshal. 1988. "Organizing for Worldwide Effectiveness: The Transnational Solution," *California Management Review* 31, no. 1, p. 54; C.A. Bartlett and S. Ghoshal. 1992. "What Is a Global Manager?" *Harvard Business Review* 70, no. 5, pp. 124–132; C.A. Bartlett and S. Ghoshal. 2000. "Going Global," *Harvard Business Review* 78, no. 2, pp. 132–142.

6. Bartlett and Ghoshal. 1987. *International Executive*, pp. 10–13; Bartlett and Ghoshal. 1987. *Sloan Management Review*, pp. 7–17.

7. See, e.g., G.S. Yip. 1981. "Market Selection and Direction: Role of Product Portfolio Planning" (Boston. MA: Harvard Business School); G.S. Yip. 1982. "Diversification Entry: Internal Development versus Acquisition," *Strategic Management Journal* 3, no. 4, pp. 331–345; G.S. Yip. 1982. "Gateways to ENTRY," *Harvard Business Review* 60, no. 5, pp. 85–92; G.S. Yip. 1989. "Global Strategy a World of Nations?" *Sloan Management Review* 31, no. 1, pp. 29–41; G.S. Yip. 1991. "A Performance Comparison of Continental and National Businesses in Europe," *International Marketing Review* 8, no. 2, p. 31; G.S. Yip. 1991. "Strategies in Global Industries: How U.S. Businesses Compete," *Journal of International Business Studies* 22, no. 4, pp. 749–753; G.S. Yip. 1994. "Industry Drivers of Global Strategy and Organization," *International Executive* 36, no. 5, pp. 529–556; G.S. Yip. 1996. "Global Strategy as a Factor in Japanese Success," *International Executive* 38, no. 1, pp. 145–167; G.S. Yip. 1997. "Patterns and Determinants of Global Marketing," *Journal of Marketing Management* 13, no. 1–3, pp. 153–164; G.S. Yip et al. 2000. "The Role of the Internationalization Process in the Performance of Newly Internationalizing Firms," *Journal of International Marketing* 8, no. 3, pp. 10–35; G.S. Yip et al. 1997. "Effects of Nationality on Global Strategy," *Management International Review* 37, no. 4,

pp. 365–385; G.S. Yip et al. 1988. "How to Take Your Company to the Global Market," *Columbia Journal of World Business* 23, no. 4, pp. 37–48; G.S. Yip and T.L. Madsen. 1996. "Global Account Management: The New Frontier in Relationship Marketing," *International Marketing Review* 13, no. 3, pp. 24; G.S. Yip et al. 1998. "The Use and Performance Effect of Global Account Management: An Empirical Analysis Using Structural Equations Modeling."(Stanford, CA: Stanford Graduate School of Business), Working Paper No. 1481

8.  K. Ohmae. 2006. "Growing in a Global Garden," *Leadership Excellence* 23, no. 9, pp. 14–15.

9.  Aboy. 2009. *International Business Strategy*, pp. 1–5.

# Chapter 9

1.  P. Ghemawat. September, 2001. "Distance Still Matters: The Hard Reality of Global Expansion," *Harvard Business Review*, pp. 3–11.

2.  T. Khanna, K.G. Palepu, and J. Sinha. 2005. "Strategies That Fit Emerging Markets," *Harvard Business Review* 83, No. 6, pp. 63–76.

3.  D. Arnold. 2004. *The Mirage of Global Markets* (FT: Prentice Hall), p. 34.

4.  For a more detailed discussion, see G.J. Tellis, P.N. Golder, and C.M. Christensen. 2001. *Will and Vision: How Latecomers Grow to Dominate Markets* (NY: McGraw Hill), p. 86.

5.  S.D. Eppinger and A.R. Chitkara. Summer, 2006. "The New Practice of Global Product Development," *MIT Sloan Management Review* 47, no. 4, pp. 22–30.

6.  J. Santos, Y. Doz, and P. Williamson. Summer, 2004. "Is Your Innovation Process Global?", *MIT Sloan Management Review* 45, no. 4; p. 31.

7.  *Ibid.*

8.  Special Report on Outsourcing, *Business Week*, January 2006.

9.  C.A. Raiborn, J.B. Butler, and M.F. Massoud. 2009. *Business Horizons*, 52. pp. 347-356

# Chapter 10

1.  This Chapter is based on C.A. de Kluyver, A Primer On Corporate Governance, Business Expert Press, 2012, chapter 7.

2.  Bart, C. (2004). The governance role of the board in corporate strategy: An initial progress report. International Journal of Business Governance and Ethics, 1(2/3), 111–125.

3.  Lorsch, J. (1995, January–February). Empowering the board. Harvard Business Review, 73(1), 107–117.
4.  Felton, R., & Fritz, P. (2005). The view from the boardroom: Value and performance [Special issue]. McKinsey Quarterly, 48–61.
5.  de Kluyver, C.A and J. Pearce II (2009) STRATEGY: A VIEW FROM THE TOP, (New Jersey: Prentice Hall) Fourth Edition, Chapter 1.
6.  Bart, C. (2004). The governance role of the board in corporate strategy: An initial progress report. International Journal of Business Governance and Ethics, 1(2/3), 111–125.
7.  Carey, D. C., & Patsalos-Fox, M. (2006). Shaping strategy from the board-room. McKinsey Quarterly, 3, 90–94.
8.  Korn/Ferry International. (2007). 33rd annual board of directors study. Los Angeles: Author.
9.  Nadler, D. (2004). What's the board's role in strategy development? Engaging the board in corporate strategy. Strategy and Leadership, 32(5), 25–33.
10.  Ibid.
11.  Ibid.
12.  Ibid.
13.  Ibid.
14.  This section is based on de Kluyver and Pearce (2009), op. cit., Chapter. 9; and Rérolle, J.-F., & Vermeire, T. (2005, April 29). M&A best practices for boards of directors. From Houlihan, Lokey, Howard, & Zukin, Corporate Board Member Magazine, M&A /Capital Markets.
15.  Usually, such opinions are prepared by the company's financial advisers or other consultants hired by management (who naturally hope to gain repeat business). The board must ensure that this expert appraisal is carried out in a truly independent manner. The board must therefore verify the independence and skills of the expert(s), and, when the report is submitted, it must ensure that the work was carried out properly, in accordance with the professional standards in force. This assumes that at least one member of the board has adequate, relevant experience or that the board is assisted by another expert to help it in this task of supervision.
16.  Rérolle and Vermeire,(April 29, 2005), op. cit.
17.  This section is based on "What directors know about their companies: A McKinsey Survey" (March, 2006).
18.  This section is based on Nadler (2004), op. cit.

# Index

## OTHER TITLES IN THE STRATEGIC MANAGEMENT COLLECTION

John A. Pearce II, Villanova University, Editor

# Announcing the Business Expert Press Digital Library

*Concise e-books business students need for classroom and research*

This book can also be purchased in an e-book collection by your library as

- a one-time purchase,
- that is owned forever,
- allows for simultaneous readers,
- has no restrictions on printing, and
- can be downloaded as PDFs from within the library community.

Our digital library collections are a great solution to beat the rising cost of textbooks. E-books can be loaded into their course management systems or onto students' e-book readers. The **Business Expert Press** digital libraries are very affordable, with no obligation to buy in future years. For more information, please visit **www.businessexpertpress.com/librarians**. To set up a trial in the United States, please email **sales@businessexpertpress.com**.

www.ingramcontent.com/pod-product-compliance
Lightning Source LLC
Chambersburg PA
CBHW050456190326
41458CB00005B/1306